Harvard Studies in Cultural Anthropology, 6

General Editors
David Maybury-Lewis
Stanley J. Tambiah
Evon A. Vogt, Jr.
Nur Yalman

The Harvard Studies in Cultural Anthropology is founded in the belief that answers to general questions about the human condition may be discovered through the intensive study of other cultures. The series will publish books that elucidate and interpret cultural systems in order to contribute to comparative understanding.

Harvard Studies in Cultural Anthropology

Dialectical Societies: The Gê and Bororo of Central Brazil
David Maybury-Lewis, editor

The Flow of Life: Essays on Eastern Indonesia
James J. Fox, editor

Iran: From Religious Dispute to Revolution
Michael M. J. Fischer

Nature and Society in Central Brazil:
The Suya Indians of Mato Grosso
Anthony Seeger

Concepts of Person: Kinship, Caste, and Marriage in India
Ákos Östör, Lina Fruzzetti, and Steve Barnett, editors

A Divided World: Apinayé Social Structure
Roberto Da Matta

A DIVIDED WORLD
Apinayé Social Structure

Roberto Da Matta

Translated by Alan Campbell

HARVARD UNIVERSITY PRESS
Cambridge, Massachusetts
and London, England
1982

Library of Congress Cataloging in Publication Data

Matta, Roberto da.
  A divided world.
  (Harvard studies in cultural anthropology; 6)
  Translation of: Um mundo dividido.
  Bibliography: p.
  Includes index.
  1. Apinagé Indians—Social life and customs. 2. Indians of South
America—Brazil—Social life and customs. 3. Tapuya Indians—
Social life and customs. I. Title. II. Series.
F2520.1.A65M3713   306'.8997   82-1100
ISBN 0-674-21288-6   AACR2

To Celeste

Preface

*T*HIS BOOK WAS WRITTEN with two different reading publics in mind: my professors and colleagues at Harvard, and Brazilian students and specialists. This necessarily created certain problems, problems that are frequently encountered by scholars who live, as I do, outside the dominant and central world that speaks English or French (with which we have more than a simple political relationship, since our ties with it are also intellectual and affective). Although the "peripheral" universe where we reside and work is fundamental for our creativity at all levels, it is composed of a public preoccupied with other problems and dilemmas, speaking and thinking about the world through idioms and categories other than English and French ones. Thus, my quandary at the time I began this book was how best to reach these two disparate realms.

When one writes, one should be thinking of a given reader; but I had two clearly separate readerships with whom I wished to communicate. On the one hand, I addressed my professors and colleagues at Harvard and the Harvard Central Brazil Research Project, which I joined as a researcher. On the other, there was a potential Brazilian public, far more diffuse and difficult to bring into focus, but always present, or rather omnipresent, in my consciousness as a writer. At that time, in the early 1970s, this public was composed of students who needed to be trained in the sociological tradition of an anthropology whose roots were in France and England and of colleagues who—with the exception of those at the Museu Nacional—were largely uninterested in the problems that I discussed. The dominant tendency of the anthropology produced in Brazil was then still culturalogical and evolutionary. Few ethnologists seriously considered the possibility of systematic fieldwork and the monographic study of a tribal society from its own perspective in order to comprehend its system of categories. It was exactly at the time I was writing the first version of this book, at the start of the 1970s, that this situation began to change, thanks to the efforts of Roberto Cardoso de Oliveira at the Museu Nacional and David Maybury-Lewis, director of the Harvard Central Brazil Research Project. It was, therefore, this happy association of researchers that made it possible to create and establish, in the Graduate Program in Social Anthropology at the Museu Nacional, a new area of research and theory in the social sciences.

When I thought of my first public, I could write freely about the method of controlled comparison applied to the sociological studies of the Gê societies, about the theory of personal names and its development in social anthropology, and about the hypotheses developed to explain systems of social organization based on moieties, with "dual organization," as occurred among the Apinayé and the Gê in general. Finally, I could discuss the Crow-Omaha kinship system, whose discovery among the Gê caused me and my colleagues at Harvard to embark upon delirious delights of formal logic. Each of us had the secret intention of discovering the "key" to these complex forms of social relationships, and also to all those aspects of the symbolism, the mythology, the political system, the ritual order, and the diverse ceremonial practices of the Gê that Claude Lévi-Strauss had demonstrated to be the obligatory object of any work devoted to the interpretation of South American tribal societies.

As I thought and wrote about these themes, I had in mind specific readers: David Maybury-Lewis, who taught me the principal secrets of the analysis of social organization and kinship, and my colleagues of the Harvard Central Brazil Research Project, Julio Cesar Melatti, Terence Turner, Joan Bamberger, Jean Carter Lave, and Jon Christopher Crocker. Roberto Cardoso de Oliveira, Luiz de Castro Faria, and my colleague Roque de Barros Laraia, who closely followed the work of the Harvard Central Brazil Research Project, also participated in this intellectual exchange. I enjoyed a special and valuable dialogue with each of these persons. All of them were important for this book and receive, for all that they gave me, my enduring gratitude.

My Brazilian reading public, however, had interests that were much more normative than empirical. When I thought of my Brazilian reader, I saw a diffuse form, a kind of ghost, which demanded explanations for the theories and methods that I tried to use, as well as questioned their utility for Brazilian Indian problems. In response to this, my tendency was often to write an overexplanatory text, offering minute explanations or extensive citations. My problem was to write not only for those who knew about anthropological theory but also for a public that needed to know more about the perspective that I was adopting. In the end, I imitated the famous pianist who, in addition to playing the sonatas, often had to carry the piano onstage and tune it, as well as sell the tickets and seat the audience.

My divisive experience in the writing of this book was so marked that at least two critics sensed and criticized it. When this book was published in Brazil, as *Um Mundo Dividido* (Editora Vozes, 1976), Peter Rivière, of Oxford, in a review published in *Man* ([1978] 13:146–147), criticized some things that the book indeed does to excess. At the same time, Alcida Ramos, in a review published in *Anuário Antropológico* ([1977] 1:263–281), attacked the book for what it does not do. Thus, one critic disapproved of that which I did in my excessive regard for my Brazilian reader—and the other, what I did not do, thinking of my reader as supposedly well versed in social anthropology. I am well aware that this book is not without errors, but I feel it necessary to point out the various levels at which it was written since they may affect the judgment of the work.

In this book I try to describe the way of life of the Apinayé, a small tribal society belonging to the Gê language family in Central Brazil. I take as a starting point the Apinayé's system of ideas about their social relations and institutions, my object being to analyze their culture or ideology. The group of dominant concepts that serves to summarize the social situations and events of these Indians defines their lives as filled with meaning and dignity. My ethnography cannot be compared with that which, after the Harvard Central Brazil Research Project, was developed in the descriptions of the tribal societies of lowland South America, by researchers in Brazil, the United States, and England. But if my ethnography is occasionally wanting, I am very clear in my attempt to relate the Apinayé's ideology to certain aspects of their social practice, especially with respect to their family life. Thus, if this book has any merit, I believe it lies in the way I was able to call attention to the relationship of certain behavior associated with the family, birth, procreation, and etiquette within the houses to ideas about proper names and their transmission and to the ceremonial life of the group. In the process, I compare these relationships with those in other Gê societies as well as draw some more general comparisons. Finally, I try to characterize the so-called Apinayé and Gê dualism, showing that it has nothing to do with direct restricted exchange, as Lévi-Strauss and other analysts of this material in the 1950s and 1960s supposed, since among the Gê there is no marriage with the cross-cousin. The dualism here is not the classic distinction between wife-givers ("kinsmen," us) and wife-receivers ("affines," them), but the distinction between persons who are related through substantive links (by blood, sweat, smells, and bodily emissions in general) and persons related through ceremonial links (names, ornaments, diet, activity restrictions, and so forth). The social universe of the Apinayé is constructed on the basis of two basic and obligatory types of relationship: substantive relations that are affirmed in private life, in the house and in the nuclear family, and ceremonial ties that are publicly affirmed in the patio of the village and among the village members.

As I wrote this book, I received generous financial assistance from the following agencies: the Divisão de Antropologia of the Museu Nacional, the Conselho de Pesquisas of the Universidade Federal do Rio de Janeiro, the Conselho Nacional de Desenvolvimento Científico e Tecnológico (CNPq), the Ford Foundation (Brazil office), the Milton Fund (of Harvard University), and the Peabody Museum, thanks to the generosity of my friend Francesco Pellizzi. Alan Campbell, of Edinburgh, translated this book from its Portuguese original with Calvinist zeal and obsession for detail. I am most grateful to him for his care with this text, which went beyond mere professional duty. David Maybury-Lewis was kind enough to revise the translation; as much as Alan Campbell, he made many suggestions for improving my confused style and corrected some descriptive errors. I gratefully accepted nearly all of the criticisms, and yet, formalism aside, I must insist that everything of error that remains is my responsibility.

I must, at last, thank all of the Apinayé. They welcomed me into their villages, adopted me into their families, and gave me the warmth of their friendship and the benefit of their generosity. Among them, I like to think I made some good friends, who in 1978 welcomed my entire family as long-lost relatives. My debt to them is more tragic: for who was I, after all, but the most recent representative of the society that devoured everything they possessed and are?

Roberto Da Matta

Contents

A Divided World

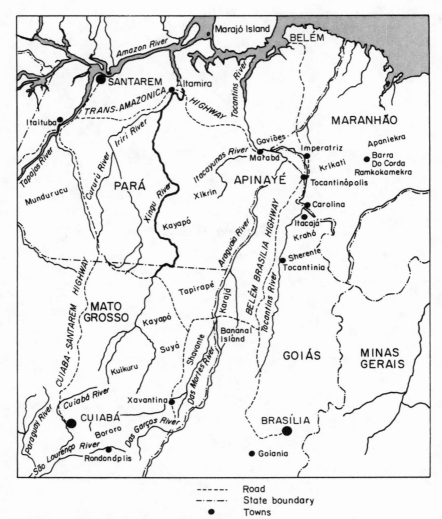

Map 1. *Location of Central Brazilian tribes.*

Introduction

The Problem

The Apinayé Indians are the most famous tribe of all the Gê-speaking peoples in Brazil. The Shavante, the Kayapó, and the Gaviões have been immortalized because of their fierce resistance to the pioneering expansion of Brazilian society.[1] Stories of their clashes with hunters and nut collectors and of their attacks on the camps of road builders are well known. But the fame of the Apinayé is of a quite different kind: their reputation was established by anthropologists and by social anthropology.

Most of the Gê tribes are described in Brazilian history in terms of unfavorable stereotypes. The Shavante, the Gaviões, and the Kayapó were for long notorious in the popular imagination, although they remained academically unknown until the 1960s. The Apinayé found a reasonably secure place in Brazilian society and consequently are to this day little known in the country. Their notoriety is in the academic world.

Indian tribes often become associated with the person who discovered them or who made them famous. Curt Unkel Nimuendajú, a German from Jena born at the end of the nineteenth century, is the person most closely associated with the Gê groups of Central Brazil.[2] It is a commonplace among Americanists that while Curt Nimuendajú made the Gê famous, these tribes in turn established his reputation, principally because of all the Gê tribes the Apinayé stood out as an anomalous group, presenting peculiarities that could not be reconciled with what was known of the other groups. It was Nimuendajú and the "Apinayé anomaly" that first directed the attention of the anthropological world to the indigenous groups of Central Brazil. What, then, caused so much interest in the Gê tribes and what was the nature of the "Apinayé anomaly"?

Briefly, what was striking about the Gê was that they had been found

1

in the immense savannas and scrublands of Central Brazil, without ham-
mocks, with poorly developed agriculture, and with no knowledge of ce-
ramics, but with a social organization that was, to say the least, sophisticated. Their social organization (especially in the case of the Northern
Gê) revealed an intricate profusion of men's groups together with complicated ceremonies in which the fundamental ordering principle was dualism, that is, in which order was created by placing elements in complementary opposition.

Nimuendajú's accounts describe in detail the ceremonial groups, the
men's societies, the emphasis on the "real" and symbolic separation of
the sexes, and the stereotyped behavior—all of which convinced him that
among the Timbira he had found a society that operated like some kind
of clockwork mechanism. For Robert H. Lowie, a colleague of Nimuendajú's and also a German by birth, the Timbira offered the ethnographic
support he needed to refute the exaggerated claims of the evolutionists
and diffusionists, both of whom were prepared to ignore the diversity of
sociological principles in favor of a dubious historical unity.

Lowie focused immediately on a number of specific ethnographic
problems, confirming, for instance, that Timbira relationship terminologies ignored the generation principle and were of a type found also
among the Hopi and Crow, which he had studied in the United States
(Lowie 1935, 1956). One of Lowie's preoccupations, especially toward the
end of his career, was to produce an adequate sociological explanation of
Timbira dualism, of its complex ceremonial style and its family and kinship systems (Lowie and Nimuendajú 1937, 1939; Lowie 1940, 1943,
1959). It was toward the end of the 1930s, when Nimuendajú and Lowie
began to publish material on the Gê-Timbira based on Nimuendajú's
fieldwork, that the "Apinayé anomaly" first became well known.

The Eastern Timbira material proved easier to interpret than the
Apinayé. The Eastern Timbira, represented at that time by the Ramkokamekra-Canela, had an elaborate system of ceremonial groups, various
pairs of moieties with different rules of incorporation, and a Crow-
Omaha relationship terminology.[3] But in spite of these complexities the
evidence appeared to make sense. According to Nimuendajú's description (1946) they had exogamous matrilineal moieties in which women
owned gardens and houses and had considerable prestige within the community. Thus the Timbira were a "normal" case according to the theories
then current which associated lineages with Crow-Omaha terminologies.
At that time, in 1940, the problem of how a society could combine a
Crow-Omaha terminology with a system of direct exchange (as appeared
to be the case with the Ramkokamekra-Canela) had not been dealt with,
and was not until Rodney Needham's work during the 1950s (Needham
1960, 1964; Keesing n.d.). It was therefore possible to arrange the Timbira material into a superficial order.

Making sense of the Apinayé system was far more difficult. Here, although the social organization was also dominated by the dualism characteristic of the other groups, there appeared to be a prescriptive marriage system involving four marriage groups and a curious method of incorporating new members into these groups (Nimuendajú 1939). While the Eastern Timbira apparently had two exogamous matrilineal moieties, the Apinayé had four marriage classes and a rule of parallel descent, that is, sons were incorporated into their father's group and daughters into their mother's (Maybury-Lewis 1960a).

These marriage classes were not the only peculiarity of the Apinayé. The matter was further complicated by Nimuendajú's publication of a list of relationship terms that revealed two paradoxical aspects: (1) the terms were by and large the same as those of the Timbira and Kayapó, but (2) the marriage system was quite different from the Timbira pattern and did not show an obvious correspondence with a Crow-Omaha pattern or indeed with any other.

The relationship terminology, however, was given little attention. The Apinayé remained a focus of interest in the anthropological literature principally because of their marriage system (the so-called four *kiyê*, Nimuendajú 1939:29), no doubt because it is easier to make sense of one isolated aspect of a social system than to try to interpret that particular aspect in terms of the entire system. Murdock, for example, saw the *kiyê* as sections resembling the Australian ones (1949:332), but had he attempted to take account of all aspects of the Apinayé system, he would certainly have had to modify his interpretation and might have produced more profitable insights into Nimuendajú's material. During the 1940s the only anthropologists who came close to this type of analysis were Kroeber, Henry, and Lévi-Strauss (Maybury-Lewis 1960), but even they did not see the *kiyê* as part of a wider system of rules. The first proper analysis of Nimuendajú's material was Maybury-Lewis's article published in 1960, in which are defined the fundamental problems approached in this book.

The principal difficulty appears when one tries to understand how the system of four marriage classes that exchange women is related to the dualism of the Apinayé social system. In his article Maybury-Lewis suggested that the *kiyê* are probably a secondary institution, that they do not regulate marriage, and that, given the evidence as presented by Nimuendajú, there are difficulties regarding certain equations in the Apinayé relationship terminology. The article shows clearly that particular institutions must be examined in relation to other institutions and that this procedure allows new problems to be formulated. The article begins by suggesting a solution to the problem of the relationship between the marriage classes and the descent principle and ends by presenting the problem, taken up at length in Chapter 4, of how a relationship terminology that ignores the principle of generational distinction operates within a system of dual organization.

The general features that distinguish the Gê from other South American groups are their "technological poverty" and their formidable social organization. Among the Gê themselves, the Apinayé stand out as an anomaly because of their marriage system, which appears similar to Australian section systems.[4] One of the objects of this book is to show how the Apinayé can be seen in the context of the Gê in general and the Northern Gê in particular. In attempting to simplify and explain the Apinayé anomaly I offer various suggestions and hypotheses regarding the other Gê groups. The main suggestion is that these societies to a greater or lesser extent apply Machiavelli's maxim "divide and rule" as a basic principle of their social organization. By dividing individual and group loyalties and by following the principle that a relationship that is basic in one domain may never affect basic relationships in other domains, the Gê managed to develop a special kind of social system and produce an extremely viable, though not original, method of resolving the internal differences between individuals and groups.[5]

Facts and Theories: Conditions of the Inquiry

There is a sense in which the goal of any scientific inquiry is to add to our knowledge by resolving anomalies and discovering principles of order that make sense of a set of facts previously seen as incongruous, extraordinary, or out of place. Such is the spirit in which this study was carried out. Having explained the principal problems of the inquiry, I believe it is also appropriate to indicate something of the conditions in which the field study was carried out. I agree with Maybury-Lewis's suggestion that a description of fieldwork conditions can reveal something of the personality of the field-worker, but I do not share his opinion that fieldwork should be viewed dispassionately such that "it would come to be realized that there are difficult field situations and less difficult ones, just as there are difficult languages and less difficult ones" (Maybury-Lewis 1967:xx). It is a reasonable view, but I think it reflects a far too simple approach to the extremely complicated problem of the relationship between the subject and the object of investigation. It is a characteristic of anthropological fieldwork that the researcher becomes profoundly involved with his object of study, which is not, in this case, an impersonal document or a cold set of statistics, but a group of people: that bewildering confusion of individuals and social relationships that the researcher initially confronts. Beginning with this hazy complexity the anthropologist tries to see some sort of coherence that will throw light on his hypotheses and theories. Hence in social anthropology the researcher creates his own documents and facts, and often invents his own research techniques. As Rodney Needham suggested, the anthropologist's activity is similar to the predicament of a previously blind person who is suddenly given sight and must learn how to use this faculty (Needham 1963).

In reflecting on my own experience in the field, I recall feeling that my intellectual interests were being stifled during the first months of my stay with the Indians. The more I began to take part in the daily life of the village, the more remote I felt from the theoretical problems that had led me there in the first place. In a very real sense, intense participation in village life went along with losing sight of the techniques, models, and diagrams that I had studied in my office in Rio de Janeiro. Consequently, after I left the field, it was extremely difficult to transform this intense, concrete experience into sociological facts. Such mental gymnastics depend not only on the basic objectives of the researcher (which would include what I was and was not prepared to "see"); they also involve those difficulties inherent in expressing through the one-dimensional medium of prose a profound and moving experience.

While living with the Apinayé, I became aware of their life in many ways: through seeing and hearing, through smell, and through watching them express their emotions. The Indians had form and substance. Over time I came to like some of them more than others. I had a house and a bed. I slept, dreamed, and woke up with the sun—or with the rain, when the village seemed strangely quiet. In short, the world of the Apinayé was "here and now," my only reality.

But now, as I am writing, my reality is the world of Rio de Janeiro, and the Apinayé appear distant, veiled by layers of nostalgic memories. My task is to reduce their world to a sequence of chapters that claim to delineate the fundamental principles that order their reality—a reality that now lies before me in the form of a bundle of notes, maps, numbers, and dates. The undertaking seems feasible only when I realize that what I present here of Apinayé life is but a few fragments of their social reality. They are fragments that were collected and rearranged according to the theories I am familiar with, the hypotheses I have learned, and all the suggestions and intuitions that I carried with me when I set out to explore the immense savannas of Central Brazil as far as the north of Goiás. On this journey I took along not only the ethnographer's accouterments but also my fears, my follies, and my hopes. The lens through which the Apinayé experience was filtered is therefore of a special kind, since it reflects the concordance between the people studied and the person who studied them. There is a lighthearted commonplace about ethnography that is in fact quite profound and that indicates both the weakness and the strength of the anthropologist's work: it is said that the ethnographer is always strikingly similar to the people he studies—urbane anthropologists find sophisticated people; timid anthropologists find timid groups; artistic anthropologists find societies of deeply sensitive men and women.

Although it is difficult for me to describe my own case clearly, I do see in this account rather too much order and rather too little of the confusion that besets inquisitive persons, who always find themselves caught between the simple clarity of their rules and the perpetual challenge that the complexity of the world presents to them. This is the dilemma that I would like to explore today were I able to go back to the year 1962, when I saw the Apinayé Indians for the first time.

I visited the Apinayé three times. During the first visit, from 14 September to 8 November 1962, I found the Indians excessively demanding and extremely conscious of their position vis-à-vis local Brazilian society. Had I written a report of this first stage of the study I would have concentrated on that theme and produced an objective account with a great deal of supporting evidence, both qualitative and quantitative. Fortunately, I can now see how such a report would have presented a partial view of Apinayé society, and I can now understand why these aspects initially dominated my attention to such a degree. The two factors that made the Indians appear so self-consciously aware of their contact with Brazilian society were, first, my own personal interests, and, more generally, the chronic neglect suffered by both Indian and non-Indian regional populations. I will explain only the second point.

Communities in the interior of Brazil receive little economic assistance and are left in a condition that can only be described as submarginal. This is but one consequence of their being so cut off from the large urban centers. When my wife and I walked in the streets of Tocantinópolis in 1962, we aroused so much curiosity that it became embarrassing, especially if the local people knew that we were also Brazilians.[6] On many occasions I was referred to as "the fat man," "the strong man," "the white man," or described as being "well-mannered," that is, I was seen as a perfect stereotype of the potential local boss. Indeed, the distance between my wife and me and the local population was so great that it would have been quite unrealistic to hope that we might quickly gain the confidence of Indians and Brazilians and get helpful information on the Apinayé.

The field situation can be seen as a kind of dialectical process. The Indians become informants just as the researcher, originally a complete stranger, becomes the "anthropologist" (that is, a person interested in learning and writing about certain specific matters). In my experience in Central Brazil, it took at least three months for the local population to become convinced that this "white, rich, fat gentleman" who took everything down in a notebook was not a government agent, a spy, or mentally defective.[7] Of sociological interest here is the difficulty that the local people have in understanding that a visitor to the area might want to study Indians. Projecting their own motives onto the visitor, they always see him in a more immediately practical role such as a prospector for gold deposits or diamonds—a flattering role that was once attributed to me in Marabá.

This has its effect on the researcher's relationship with the local people, since they all try to take advantage of the stranger's presence by telling him as much as possible about their own problems. During my first months among the Apinayé (which included my first contacts with the local population as well as with the agent of what was then the Indian Protection Service, the SPI),[8] people told me their complaints, their demands, and their excuses. Unfortunately, I did not make notes of this material in a properly critical way. Instead of trying to scrutinize or clarify the situation in which I found myself, as a potential mediator between Indians (or locals) and government,[9] I simply passed over the incidents without comment or question.

My personal interests clearly intruded into this first period of field-work. There is a turn of phrase used in cinematography that is admirably appropriate to this sort of situation—as a warning to those who believe in the total objectivity of photography, it counsels: "director, guide your eye." Similarly, the anthropologist should be aware that he is not simply directing an inquiry but that he can observe only what he is prepared to look at. In other words, while he can certainly direct his study toward particular aspects of the society, he must in the first place be able to "see" the facts.

When the Apinayé said "everything was different in the old days," "today everything is changed," or more frequently, "we are losing our laws," I tended to accept these statements literally and without question. Not only was I missing the opportunity to look into certain matters in more detail but I was also ignoring the universal capacity of human beings to idealize their past and future. Idealizing the past in this way is an intriguing sociological mechanism that is quite evident in the present situation of the Apinayé. However, to accept this view of the past as an actual account of what happened results in bad anthropology.

Such idealization was not restricted to traditional customs; it occurred as well in the Indians' account of their contact with Brazilians. In 1962 one Indian told me that in the past (referring to the time of Curt Nimuendajú, or "in the time of Curto," as the Apinayé say) the local Brazilians always brought gifts to the Indians. "They did not want to take our lands. They were just neighbors." Such statements clearly contradict all the available historical facts as well as the evidence given at a later date by the same informant.

It is now clear to me that these replies were only a way of diverting my curiosity from certain aspects of their society. The Indians wanted to do this because, like all human beings, they prefer to avoid referring to disagreeable events, conflicts, or other unfortunate incidents. On one occasion, for instance, I asked a member of a faction opposed to the chief whether the Apinayé planted their gardens individually or by collective effort. He replied that formerly the work was done collectively but today, since nobody obeyed the chief, the Indians had to fall back on the only possible alternative and plant individually. Being a neophyte in the field and being quite ignorant of how gardens are prepared, I took the reply as indisputable evidence of social change caused by contact with Brazilian society. Later I discovered that the Apinayé still planted collectively (or rather that their method of agriculture involved a number of different stages, some of which were carried out collectively and others individually) and that the informant was not giving me information on agriculture but was trying to denigrate the chief by casting doubts on his authority. As an important individual in the opposing faction, my informant was behaving appropriately: he had seized the opportunity to talk about village affairs with a stranger who was probably a member of the "government."

Lacking an understanding of the political system and a grasp of the various methods of cultivation, I was led to ask if the informant had described something that could be explained by social change or if it might be a structural problem that would show how the harmony of the work force, the authority of the chief, and factionalism were interrelated. The second hypothesis is in fact correct, but in 1962 I was sufficiently naive to conclude that the situation described by my informant was a clear case of social change. Hence both the Apinayé and I were using social change to justify disagreeable conduct and to rationalize difficulties regarding the nature of the social system. Seeing everything in terms of social change also obscured my faulty understanding of other ethnographic problems. For instance, I did not begin to grasp the nature of the Apinayé kinship system nor the way it is manipulated until my second visit. The following observation, transcribed directly from my field diary, is typical of my first period in the field:

> I must note that the informant appeared unsure about his answers and that his information is inconsistent regarding certain kin terms, especially those for cross-cousins. Regarding these particular terms Grossinho says that sometimes a person is called by a term that indicates a close (and incestuous) relationship, but he adds that this "doesn't mean anything." This clearly shows how the kinship terms are being drained of their original content . . . and indicates that they are gradually losing their meaning. Obviously this is a result of social change.

I did not, of course, understand the nature of the Apinayé kinship system, and I quickly attributed details I could not explain to the effects of contact with Brazilian society and cultural change. Instead of approaching the system in its total complexity, I saw it as anomalous before even beginning to understand it. I must say, by way of defense, that this error is common even among the most eminent anthropologists.[10]

The first period of fieldwork did, however, produce some positive results. These included a detailed census indicating the composition of each domestic group as well as a number of genealogies, lists of ceremonial groups and name-givers, and a certain amount of material on culture contact. After the first visit I knew little of Apinayé social life, but I had learned a great deal about the difficulties of undertaking fieldwork with a Gê group, supplementing my previous experience among the Timbira-Gaviões, whom I had studied in 1961 along with Julio Cezar Melatti.[11] The second period of fieldwork ran from 6 January to 19 March 1966.[12] By this time my theoretical preparation was better, and I had the benefit of several years' familiarity with the Apinayé material. Furthermore, between 1962 and 1966 other members of the Harvard Central Brazil Research Project had begun their work in Brazil, and their preliminary findings had been presented at the Museu Nacional in Rio de Janeiro and at Harvard.

By 1966 I was more aware of some of the problems that I have discussed above, and during my second period of fieldwork I was able to direct my research to the more problematic aspects of Apinayé social organization. As I gathered information on systems of classification, I came to understand better the topics I was investigating. I also increased my Gê vocabulary, although I did not succeed in speaking the language properly. Meanwhile I also obtained a surer grasp of the data on contact.

Between the first and second expeditions, as between the second and the third, I elaborated in preliminary form part of the material collected. As I had realized previously with the Gaviões, it became clear that I was dealing with a society whose rules were extremely flexible. Whereas Nimuendajú describes the social rules of the Timbira as constituting an apparently rigid system that allows little possibility for variations, the Gaviões and Apinayé as I knew them made it clear that the situation was quite the opposite (Da Matta 1967c).

Arriving at this conclusion was extremely difficult and required a number of steps. I had to discover, first, that neither the Gaviões nor the Apinayé had exogamous groups (moieties, or *kiyé*); second, that although the evidence suggested a Crow-Omaha relationship terminology, this was not associated with either matri- or patrilineages; third, that the moieties reported by Nimuendajú were ceremonial groups and had little to do with everyday life; and last, that the kinship system caused difficulties not only for the anthropologist trying to understand Gê relationship categories but also for the Indians themselves. Fortunately, these discoveries were consistent with the findings of my other colleagues, Julio Cezar Melatti, Terence Turner, and Jean Lave, who had worked with the Krahó, Kayapó, and Krĩkati, respectively (Melatti 1967, 1970, 1978, 1979;

Terence Turner 1^66, 1979; Lave 1967, 1979).[13] The important conclusion was that contact did not explain the variations that took place, especially in the political sphere of Apinayé society. Furthermore, it became clear that the principal problem of the study was to find a way of understanding the interrelationships between the theory of the system and how it was in fact practiced. This would first require an explanation of the theoretical anomalies mentioned earlier.

In 1961 when I was with the Gaviões, I made every effort to find exogamous moieties. The attempt was fruitless, however, for there turned out to be no such moieties or even lineages. While studying the Apinayé, I kept looking for the *kiyê* until I saw that the Timbira system would be better explained in terms of a "Polynesian model" rather than an "African model," that is to say, in terms of an open system of rules providing various points of reference that influence an individual's behavior in various ways. These points of reference are represented by specific groups. In certain contexts one of these groups might be dominant, but no group is dominant in all contexts. "African models" represent a system of rules in which an individual does not have such choices because one group (the unilineal descent group) dominates and pervades the whole society (Barnes 1962; Goodenough 1955).

In my view Nimuendajú's material is best seen as an account of the *ceremonial* life of the Apinayé and the Canela. His account is based on what a few trusted informants told him (I discovered in the field that he had three such informants among the Apinayé). But the result of collecting information in this way and of concentrating on this aspect of the society was to produce a comprehensive account of stereotyped actions and rules while ignoring the political aspects of the society and the way the rules are translated into everyday life.

It took approximately eleven months of fieldwork (the second stage ran from 6 December 1966 until 17 April 1967 and the third from July to November 1970) to understand that the Apinayé were not the Indians that I knew through the diagrams of Lévi-Strauss and Nimuendajú. They bend and reshape rules just as we do, and they find themselves constantly compelled to struggle with inconsistencies, and even conflicts, which are a part of their everyday life. I arrived at an understanding of Apinayé society gradually, and not through one of those dramatic breakthroughs that frequently take place during fieldwork. Drama requires, among other ingredients, something of the exotic, and exoticism depends on differences and similarities between individuals and societies. Working with the Apinayé, by contrast, meant living in an environment characterized by the drowsy rhythm of the backwoods.

The Apinayé have lived in permanent contact with Brazilian society since the eighteenth century (Nimuendajú 1939:2ff.), and the few traits that distinguish them from the local Brazilians are disappearing. Indian men still wear their hair long, the older men still have pierced lips and ears, and women leave their breasts bare except when they visit Tocantinópolis. But adults of both sexes speak good Portuguese, and anthropologists, especially if they are Brazilian, usually work in this language, as indeed I did.

During my first period in the field I spent most of the time conducting interviews with Indians in their own houses, and my wife also conducted interviews with some of the women. I found it easy to establish a good relationship with the Apinayé. As soon as they knew that I was there "to do the kind of thing Curt Nimuendajú did," many began to ask if I was "Curto tamtxúa" (Nimuendajú's "grandson" or "nephew")! During the second period the interviews continued, but because I was concentrating on particular themes, they took a more polished form. Many of my data are in the form of transcriptions of my questions and the informants' answers. I found this a useful technique by which to control the conditions under which the data were obtained.

During the third stage of fieldwork, I continued both formal and informal interviews, usually paying for them and conducting them in my own house, which was the only place where certain subjects could be discussed and where an informant could give what he considered confidential information. In this way I collected most of my data on intrigues, witchcraft accusations, quarrels, and the killing of cattle belonging to local farmers. These were extremely delicate matters and divulging them could have made the informant's position in the village very difficult indeed. Most of my data, however, was gathered through interviews and observations at certain times of the day: while eating, bathing, or at night after the evening meal. I witnessed only a few rituals and I saw no funerals or marriage ceremonies.

Life among the Apinayé has nothing of the exoticism so often characteristic of fieldwork. One has to make considerable efforts to collect data, seeking out informants and insisting on appointments for interviews. It is only through interviews that one can discover something of what is going on and get occasional insights into the past. One of the striking differences between my fieldwork with the Gaviões (of the middle Tocantins) and with the Apinayé was that, in the first study, it was quite impossible to miss what was happening in the village. From my hut I could see all the daily activities of the Gaviões and could hardly miss their movements, their decisions, and their crises. But among the Apinayé, I soon realized that I could stay ten years in their villages and learn nothing of their social life, as was indeed the case with those backwoodsmen who visited the villages and also with the personnel on the government Indian post.

The Gaviões had not by that time created the protective barriers that follow cultural contact and ensure that interaction between Brazilians and Indians takes place according to their respective positions established by the dominant Brazilian society. The Gaviões simply treated Brazilians as unwelcome strangers and categorized them according to their own scheme of classification. Having no categories by which to distinguish economic, political, or social superiority, they considered all Brazilians as simply *kupen* ("foreigners," "whites"). But prolonged contact between the Apinayé and the national society had created a system of interethnic relations in which an Apinayé could be submissive when he was dealing with a Brazilian, but emerge as an authoritarian leader when there was an argument about a divorce or a theft in the village. I was therefore dealing with a complicated system through which Apinayé society could present two distinct faces.

Collecting material in these circumstances obviously creates uncertainties for the anthropologist. Many of the facts that he collects in conversation depend on his perception of the social role that has been assumed by his informant. Consequently, checking or verifying material can be done only by comparing interviews with different informants or by contrasting opinions offered by the same informant on different occasions. It therefore becomes especially important to gain the confidence of two or three informants who are capable of understanding clearly what the anthropologist is trying to do. This technique is not the traditional way of collecting ethnographic material, but I would guess that this kind of ethnography will become more common in the future.

To be aware of these different kinds of inquiry is not to disparage any particular kind of ethnography. Indeed, it is clear that various methods are present to some extent in any field situation. But it is necessary to recognize different approaches and to make explicit the difficulties encountered in the field and the nature of the material collected, especially when the study is carried out in conditions different from the classic pattern of anthropological fieldwork à la Malinowski. If working with the Sirionó, the Cubeo, or the Yąnomamö was found difficult with regard to approaching the people, learning the language, or even contending with violence, studying the Apinayé presented difficulties of another kind. By far the greatest, from a methodological point of view, was the distressing struggle to find a way to verify the material. Very often I had to try to verify facts that had not been observed and that might well have been the result of social change.

From a personal point of view the major difficulty was to establish a relationship with the Apinayé that would allow them to express their opinions without taking into account what they assumed I might be thinking. The anthropologist is always seen in a number of different roles and one of mine was considered to be the "rich Brazilian." Particularly with certain informants, I was aware of their tendency to agree simply in order to please, a typical trait of the relationship between employer and worker in Central Brazil. In the early stages of fieldwork I found this perception intruding into nearly all my relationships. Even after I was adopted and named, there was always a distance between my family and the Indians. The mild Apinayé were a complete contrast to the Gaviões, who would ask to be given something in such a haughty, arrogant, and harsh manner that asking was an act of aggression (Da Matta 1963). But whereas the Gaviões were still feared as savage Indians, the Apinayé knew quite well that no one was afraid of them. Hence their way of dealing with a rich white man (anthropologist, missionary, or government official of whatever kind) showed much of the servile humility of the poor backwoodsman.

Whereas among the Gaviões I had to make efforts to maintain a distance between myself and the Indians,[14] among the Apinayé the problem was to reduce the distance and to try to get the Indians to consider me, if not an equal, then at least a less superior person. On innumerable occasions informants treated me as they would a Brazilian and tried to please me. A good example was Velho Estêvão, the man who gave me my name and who introduced me to the history and traditions of the tribe. When I tried to get some information on formal friendship, he did his best to clear up the matter quickly by saying simply that there was no difference between this institution and the Brazilian godparent/godchild relationship. On other occasions he tried to translate Apinayé kinship terms into Portuguese because he felt disappointed with my lack of knowledge of the traditional system and upset about my constant questions on the subject. It was only when I returned for the third time, with my whole family, that I felt that my relationship with him had become more clearly established. This pattern was typical of my relationships with all my informants.

In the two existing Apinayé villages I had eight regular informants whom I consulted at various times and on various pretexts. Of those, I would like to think that I managed to establish a relationship of equality with the chief of São José, with Velho Estêvão, with Kangrô, and with Zê Tapklúd from the village of Mariazinha.

1

The Present Situation
of the Apinayé

THE APINAYÉ live in two villages, São José and Mariazinha, in the municipality of Tocantinópolis in the extreme north of the state of Goiás. Geographically, it is an area of transition between the tropical forest and the cerrado, or savanna, typical of the vast watershed of Central Brazil. The rivers in the area, separated by stretches of savanna, run into either the Tocantins River or the Araguaia. Gallery forests are found along their banks. The Apinayé build their villages on the slightly elevated land between rivers where no large trees have to be felled to clear the ground. On that land is imprinted the mark of their culture, typical of all the Northern Gê: a circular village surrounding a central plaza.

The villages have the advantage of being on slightly elevated ground while still being close to a permanent source of water. Like the other Northern Gê, the Apinayé prefer to build their villages on the open land and to use the gallery forests for agriculture and for hunting. The villages are therefore found on the top of a slope with the gardens running down on one side toward the river through a stretch of felled gallery forest.

As well as the low vegetation of the savannas and the gallery forests along the riverbanks, this part of Goiás is covered with the babassu palm (*Orbignia speciosa*). The ecology of the Apinayé is, therefore, a process of exploiting each of these natural features. From what is known of the Kayapó and especially of the Gaviões (T. Turner 1966; Bamberger 1967; Da Matta 1963), it is probable that on first contact the Apinayé used only the forest and the savanna, where they hunted and practiced slash-and-burn cultivation. The babassu palm was not of much importance at that time. All that the Indians required from this tree were the leaves—which today are still widely used for making mats, house roofing, containers, and children's toys—and the oil extracted from the nuts, used by both men and women as a cosmetic for the hair.

Today they depend less on hunting and more on agriculture and on gathering babassu nuts, which they sell at the Indian posts in their villages. Hunting and agriculture are part of their traditional way of life, but since babassu nuts have a permanent exchange value on the regional market, nut gathering involves the Apinayé in the dynamics of the Brazilian economy. Thus Brazilian national society has a considerable influence on Apinayé ecology, both by limiting and destroying the natural environment in which the tribe has lived for so many centuries and by encouraging the Indians to exploit other resources that the area offers.

Instead of trying to reconstruct how the Apinayé exploited their environment before contact, I shall describe their present ecological situation in terms of the effects of contact and the way they have adapted to living alongside local Brazilian society. Describing how the Indians get the best out of their environment must include an account of how they survived contact and what sort of social adjustments they made in response to it. Taking the notion of the "environment" in a broad sense, this approach to Apinayé ecology allows us to see how the geography and the history of the tribe are related.

The Apinayé entered Brazilian history when settlers began moving into the interior of the northeast region of the country and when the Tocantins River began to be used as a waterway. During the colonial period settlers moved into the interior of the states of Maranhão, Bahia, and Piauí, looking for suitable land for raising cattle to provide a meat supply for the sugar plantations on the coast. Moving through the more arid parts of the *sertão* (as the area is called), they eventually reached the natural pastures in the north of what is now the state of Goiás, where the Apinayé are found. As Melatti indicates (1967:18), the discovery of these pastures was the most crucial factor in the subsequent history of the Northern Gê. The Tocantins, as a natural waterway, was also important in opening up the region, but the river did not become a base for any one specific kind of pioneering expansion. Various pioneering efforts took place along the Tocantins and the Araguaia, making these rivers important connecting routes along the frontier areas and leading to the discovery of a number of tribes. But it was only after 1900, when the exploitation of the natural fruits of the region became more intensive (especially Brazil nuts, *Bertholletia excelsa,* and babassu), that large populations settled along the riverbanks (Laraia and Da Matta 1967:75).

Although Nimuendajú cites various instances of contact between the Apinayé and Brazilians from the end of the eighteenth century onward, he does not indicate why Brazilians were in the area nor that their presence was the result of economic factors. It is noteworthy that all the documented instances of contact between the Apinayé and Brazilians that Nimuendajú refers to (1939:1–8) took place on the Tocantins. The increasing movement along this river resulted from the decline of the gold mines of Goiás, which required that the work force employed there be made use of elsewhere. The decline of the Goiás gold mines led the government to attempt a reorganization of the local economy on a basis of trading (Melatti 1967:15). A number of settlements were established along the Tocantins, and as a result previously unknown Indian groups came to be destroyed or integrated into the local Brazilian communities (Laraia and Da Matta 1967:75).

References to the Apinayé become increasingly detailed from the end of the eighteenth century onward, coinciding with the pioneering development of the Tocantins and the Araguaia. In 1774 Antonio Luiz Tavares reported a skirmish with some Indians while he was traveling from Goiás to Pará through the Apinayé area. In his *Roteiro de Maranhão a Goiás pela Capitania do Piauhi* he does not mention the tribe by name, but Nimuendajú assumes that it was a band of Apinayé. By the end of the eighteenth century a number of violent encounters between Brazilians and Apinayé had occurred, prompting the establishment of military posts at Alcobaça (today Tucuruí) in 1780 and at Arapary in 1791 (Nimuendajú 1939:3). The first detailed information on the tribe, then known as the Pinaré or Pinayé, appeared in 1793. At that time they lived on the banks of the Araguaia; they were in contact with the Karajá; and they had canoes and large manioc plantations, "for which reason [the explorer Villa Real] urged peaceable relations with these people who might be very useful in river transportation" (Nimuendajú 1939:3).

Nimuendajú considers that permanent contact between the Apinayé and the national society began in 1797. In that year the settlement of São João do Araguaia was founded, and it was probably about that same time that the Apinayé reacted violently against the Brazilians, who were encroaching upon their territory and destroying their plantations, with the result that their villages were bombarded by cannon.

In addition to the increasing Brazilian occupation and control of the Tocantins (and the Araguaia), the Apinayé came under pressure from the cattle-raising frontiersmen who were moving westward from their base around the town of Caxias in Maranhão. This expansion resulted in the founding in 1816 of a small settlement, which had a mixed population of Brazilians and Apinayé. This soon became the town known today as Carolina. In 1818 the Apinayé lived in three villages: "they . . . were considered peaceable and clever with their hands and would help travelers passing the rapids" (Nimuendajú 1939:6). In 1823 they were, in some obscure way, involved in a factional struggle between two local political bosses—Antônio Moreira, who looked after the interests of the Indians and who enjoyed the support of the governor of Goiás, and his rival José Maria Belém, who represented the interests of the state of Pará. In 1823 the Apinayé also took part in Brazil's War of Independence, sending a contingent of 250 warriors to join the troops of José Dias de Mattos (Nimuendajú 1939:6).[1]

Thus the Apinayé play an important part in the story of the occupation of Northern Goiás by these two pioneering fronts, one consisting of the cattlemen and the other of those who left the gold mines of Southern Goiás and moved down the Tocantins. The history of the Apinayé probably followed a pattern similar to that of the Gaviões in more recent times. The Gaviões are now found in the tropical forest of Southern Pará, on the right bank of the Tocantins, that is, a considerable distance away from the traditional lands of the Timbira. As Nimuendajú suggests, both tribes probably moved west to escape the encroachment of the cattle ranchers who had cut through the territory of the Timbira and reached the right bank of the Tocantins (Da Matta 1967:143).[2] After crossing the Tocantins the Apinayé settled somewhere in the narrow extremity of what is now Northern Goiás. It is possible that the Apinayé came from the west as part of a group of Kayapó, but given the evidence I think it is reasonable to assume that the movements of the Apinayé were directly caused by the various pioneering groups that entered the area and threatened their territory.

Although Apinayé alliances with local political bosses and participation in the War of Independence obviously contributed to the survival of the tribe, the most important factor was the character of the society that occupied the area. The extreme north of Goiás never became important for any one particular economic activity. The cattle-raising pioneers who began to occupy the area in the eighteenth century were relatively few in number. Their advance was slow and it lost much of its impetus when they reached the Tocantins. The land was taken over in such a way that large pockets were left where the Apinayé could survive without interference. Furthermore, the vegetation of the area was not destroyed.

During the nineteenth century the most important factor in the regional economy was the babassu palm, which was found throughout the traditional lands of the Apinayé. Gathering babassu nuts became the principal activity of the region, although farming and ranching always remained important. Figures published in 1956 by the Brazilian Institute of Geography and Statistics (IBGE) for the municipality of Tocantinópolis indicate 17 million cruzeiros as the value of agricultural produce, 7 million cruzeiros for babassu nuts, and 2 million cruzeiros for babassu oil. The value of livestock was considerable (a figure of 150 million cruzeiros given for cattle alone), but the production of meat and milk was relatively small. The 1956 figure for milk production was 3.6 million cruzeiros.

These figures for agricultural products (especially maize, rice, and manioc), extractive vegetable products (babassu), and livestock products show a balance between the three activities. Unlike the Brazil nut industry in Marabá,[3] babassu products did not dominate the economy of Tocantinópolis. This is attributable to several factors, of which the most important are the following:

1. Babassu nuts are collected throughout the year, whereas Brazil nuts are collected only during the "winter," that is, during the rainy season from October to April.
2. It is easier to collect babassu nuts because the trees are found in the savanna and the gallery forests. The Brazil nut is found on firm ground within the tropical forest, and its extraction depends on a rather costly socioeconomic system known as *barracão*. The system leaves the Brazil nut trade in the hands of a few businessmen who have the necessary capital to mount the extractive operation (Laraia and Da Matta 1967:80; Velho 1972).
3. The babassu industry serves a national market, especially Rio de Janeiro and São Paulo, whereas Brazil nuts are exported to Europe and the United States. The price of babassu nuts is therefore low and stable in comparison with the high, fluctuating prices of Brazil nuts on the international market. The Brazil nut industry therefore attracts migrant workers from the lower Tocantins (who return there after the harvest to prospect for diamonds) and from Northern Goiás and Maranhão. Babassu nuts are an essential product for the national food industry, whereas Brazil nuts are a nonessential luxury product on the international market. Political and military crises involving the Western powers have, on occasion, caused abrupt falls in the price of Brazil nuts when trade in that commodity has been suspended. The babassu industry is not subject to such uncertainties (Valverde 1957).

These factors give the Apinayé area a character quite different from that of Marabá, where the Gaviões are found. Indeed, one can detect a structural relationship here, in that if the desired product has a high value, the pioneering group that exploits it will be more unstable and contact with indigenous groups will be more violent and dangerous. This is certainly borne out in Marabá.

Considering the factors that affect the survival of tribes after contact, I prefer to see the relative value of the products sought by the pioneers as the significant variable rather than to explain the problem in terms of each different kind of pioneering expansion, as Darcy Ribeiro does (Ribeiro 1957:23). Ribeiro distinguishes three kinds of pioneering fronts (pastoral, agricultural, and extractive), which affect the Indians in different ways. Here I wish to show how a difference between the value of the products gathered in a single type of front (the extractive) results in two different kinds of relationships between Brazilians and Indians in the Tocantins area.

During the first twenty years of its existence Marabá appeared to be following the classic economic cycle typical of underdeveloped economies: a single activity offering high rewards attracts an influx of pioneers, who later abandon the region, leaving their towns and settlements as little more than empty reminders of former fame and luxury. Two classic examples of this process are Manaus and Maranhão. By contrast the economy of Tocantinópolis was more diversified and therefore more adaptable. Consequently it remained reasonably stable over the years and attracted settlers rather than adventurers. The town began as a Catholic mission and never had the reputation of a place where one might make a quick fortune.

Marabá began as a "boom town" and has always attracted adventurers. Each time the price of Brazil nuts falls on the international market there is a risk that Marabá might become a ghost town.[4] The inhabitants tend to regard the Indians in the area, the Timbira-Gaviões, as one of the natural obstacles that threaten their social and economic system. Just as floods on the Tocantins, prices on the international market, wars, and political crises all cause fluctuations in profits from the harvest, so the Indians are seen as part of this complex of "natural" forces that no one can quite understand or keep under proper control. The possibility of making large profits from nuts is therefore correlated with an unstable social system.

The preceding argument is well reflected in the following extract from a speech made by the mayor of Marabá in 1953, in which he referred to raids by Gaviões on nut collectors: "The Tocantins region is threatened by economic collapse and this will inevitably take place if the present situation continues. Nut collectors are giving up their work through fear of the Gaviões Indians who are making frequent attacks on them" (*Folha do Norte,* 29 October 1953). The inhabitants of Marabá seem to place the Indian quite outside the boundaries of the human community and think of him as part of the natural world. In Tocantinópolis, by contrast, the local population's view of the Indian is based on a different historical experience. Here, there was nothing of the monolithic political structure that developed in Marabá, where rich owners monopolized business and farming as well as local politics. The babassu industry of Tocantinópolis did not come to dominate other basic activities nor was it organized in such a way that a high investment of capital was necessary to get commercial production under way. As a result the Indian is seen as an ambiguous being, half in and half out of the human community. The Apinayé are regarded in terms of a number of stereotypes corresponding to certain social roles, and even though the stereotypes are mostly unfavorable, they indicate the emergence of a more complex relationship with the Brazilians. The involvement of the Gaviões with the regional society was reduced to one choice: either Indians became nut collectors, paid at lower than the going rate for Brazilians, or they rejected the role and disappeared (Laraia and Da Matta 1967). In contrast, the Apinayé could participate in the regional society in a number of ways although they too were facing a pioneering front based on an extractive industry.

The most palpable and frightening result of such involvement was that both tribes suffered a drastic reduction in population. When I visited the Gaviões in 1961 I discovered that their numbers had been reduced to a point where their extinction seemed almost inevitable. Estimates of the Apinayé population over the years show in detail how they suffered a similar fate. In 1843 Cunha Mattos found four Apinayé villages with the following populations: Bom Jardim, near Carolina, with 1,000 inhabitants; Santo Antônio, about thirty kilometers farther north, with 1,300; another village also called Santo Antônio with 500; and a village on the Araguaia with 1,400. In 1859 Vicente Ferreira Gomes estimated the total Apinayé population to be between 1,800 and 2,000. As Nimuendajú points out this indicates that their population was reduced at least by half within thirty-five years. Coudreau in 1897 found three villages with a total population of 400, and in 1899 Buscalioni estimated that the tribe consisted of 150 persons. Between 1928 and 1937, when Nimuendajú visited the tribe frequently, there were about 160 Apinayé (Nimuendajú 1939:7–8).

The demographic evidence shows that although the occupation of Apinayé territory took place gradually, it nevertheless drastically reduced the population of the tribe in less than a century. But because the area had little economic value for the Brazilians, at least during the first years of contact, the Apinayé were saved from a sudden massive invasion and were given time to recover from the effects of depopulation.

Looking at the available evidence we can see what happened to each Apinayé community in turn (see Map 2). Cocal, found on the Araguaia side of the watershed, had in 1842 1,400 inhabitants (Cunha Mattos in Nimuendajú 1939:7); in 1928, 25 inhabitants and three houses (Nimuendajú 1939:11). In 1937, Nimuendajú remarked, "The three huts still stand, but are rarely inhabited, for their residents mostly frequent neighboring Neo-Brazilian homes" (1939:12). Nimuendajú's unfavorable impressions of this village were confirmed by its survivors, who can still be found today in the village of São José (formerly Bacaba). Nimuendajú noted that there were a few Kayapó living in Cocal who were married to Apinayé women, as well as some mestizos. "The inhabitants [of Cocal] produced an impression of unhealthiness and degeneracy. Old custom had vanished. Every night could be heard dances arranged in the village by Neo-Brazilian neighbors with *guitarre* accompaniment. On the other hand, the natives never missed any 'Christian' celebration in the vicinity" (Nimuendajú 1939:12). The destruction of this community must have

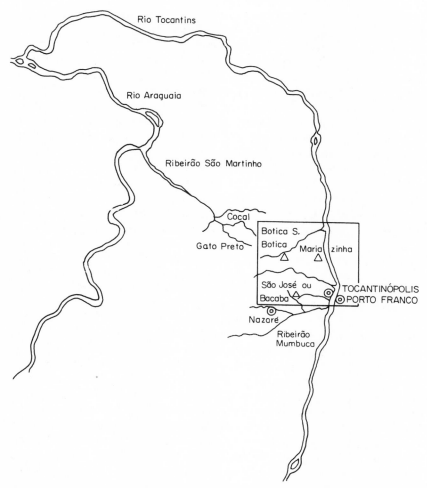

Rio Tocantins

Rio Araguaia

Ribeirão São Martinho

Cocal

Botica S.

Gato Preto | Botica

Maria | zinha

△ △

São José ou

Bacaba △

TOCANTINÓPOLIS

PORTO FRANCO

Nazaré

Ribeirão
Mumbuca

Map 2. *The Apinayé area in 1937 and the location of their four villages. Scale: 1 cm = 6 km.*

begun before 1929, for by this date the village had already lost its lands and found itself surrounded by Brazilians.

My own material on Cocal confirms Nimuendajú's description and also adds to our knowledge of the political system, which is dealt with rather superficially in Nimuendajú's ethnography. A number of informants referred to quarrels between the Apinayé and the Kayapó and also between different Apinayé factions. They explained that it was because of such quarrels that several families left the village.

In 1928 the village of Gato Preto (Botica) had sixty-one inhabitants and seven houses; in 1937 it had eighty inhabitants (Nimuendajú 1939:12). In Nimuendajú's description of this village, there is clear evidence of potential political problems within the community. Nimuendajú reduces them to individual peculiarities, describing the alcoholism of the chief "Pebkób" (Pedro Corredor) as follows: "Unfortunately he is himself addicted to whisky and grows brutal and quarrelsome when under the influence. As a result several Indians have moved to Bacaba and tend in ever-increasing measure not to live united in the aldea, but each in his often remote plantation, the villagers still retaining some land of their own" (Nimuendajú 1939:12).

In spite of this unfortunate state of affairs, the village survived until about 1950, when the inhabitants moved to São José and Mariazinha. A few Indians who were particularly attached to the old village said that they left only because they were explicitly ordered to do so by the official in charge of the Indian post. This official, by the name of Mota, took charge of the post in the early 1950s and wanted all the Apinayé united in one village to make his administrative work easier. Apinayé villages, however, are independent political units. Although isolated individuals can easily be absorbed into a village, it is quite another matter when several entire families arrive from other villages. Part of the difficulty is that social ties in the community receiving them have to be reorganized. Also, the new arrivals often bring illnesses with them. Malicious gossip grows more intense during such a disturbed situation, and witchcraft accusations can often result. One informant said that many of the Botica people got along poorly with those in São José and consequently went off to Mariazinha. An example was given of an Indian named Alexandre who lost all his children through measles and therefore moved to Mariazinha. But even worse than that, my informant went on, was the gossip: "Everything that went wrong was the fault of the Botica people." Because of the gossip, several other families from Botica followed Alexandre to Mariazinha.

Today the Apinayé of Mariazinha still visit the site of Botica when families are traveling in that area looking for food or work on the nearby ranches. In 1967, when I spent two months in Mariazinha, I visited the old village of Botica and found three families camped there. They were living separately, spending their time hunting. The remains of the old village were still visible, and I was able to see quite clearly the original layout of the houses, arranged in the traditional circle.

In 1824 Mariazinha had 1,000 inhabitants (Cunha Mattos, in Nimuendajú 1939:11); in 1928, 14 inhabitants and two houses (Nimuendajú 1939:11); in 1937, 5 inhabitants (ibid.); in 1962, 57 inhabitants and nine houses; and in 1967, 92 inhabitants and sixteen houses. On two occasions this village almost disappeared. The first, about 1928, was mentioned by

Nimuendajú and confirmed by the Apinayé. At this time only two elderly Indians and their families were living there. They and their descendants kept the village in existence until new arrivals appeared from Botica (Gato Preto) to swell the population. The second occasion was in 1962 when a rancher who lived very close to the village threatened the Indians. Chief Zezinho ("Tegatôro") became afraid and decided to move the village. When I visited Mariazinha for a week in 1962 the community had moved to a new site about one kilometer to the west of the present village. Zezinho had previously gone to the village of São José to complain to the official in charge of the Indian post. His excuse for moving his own village was that the original site was unhealthy. It caused illnesses and was full of *me-karon,* a word meaning "spirits of the dead," "images," or "shadows." In fact he was only trying to avoid a confrontation because he did not have the courage to face up to the rancher. The move lasted only a few months until Zezinho was finally persuaded to return to the original site, where the village now stands. A year or so later, in 1963 or 1964, Júlio ("Kongré"), a more vigorous type of person than Zezinho, decided to confront the rancher in person. Júlio's approach was so intimidating that the question of the rancher's claiming the Indians' land by threats seems to have been resolved or at least postponed. It is quite clear that Júlio wanted to be chief, and his firm action, in contrast with Zezinho's weakness, resulted in a considerable change in the status quo. Zezinho's power declined and Júlio Kongré's increased, a situation, incidentally, that is quite normal among the Northern Gê.

In 1844 the village of São José (Bacaba) had 850 inhabitants and twenty-one houses (Castelnau, in Nimuendajú 1939:14); in 1895, 600 inhabitants and thirty to forty houses (Ferreira Gomes, in Nimuendajú 1939:14); in 1928, 50 inhabitants and five houses (ibid.: 14–15); in 1937, 70 inhabitants and seven houses (ibid.); in 1962, 157 inhabitants and twenty houses; and in 1967, 161 inhabitants and twenty houses. Ever since the time of Nimuendajú's visits São José has been the principal Apinayé village. It is the nearest village to the Brazilian towns Tocantinópolis and Nazaré (see Map 2). Since the founding of Tocantinópolis in 1840, São José has played a large part in that town's history. It was also in this village that the Indian post was established in 1944.[5]

The occupation of the area probably went through its most rapid phase during the 1920s when Tocantinópolis was growing and when the extraction of babassu nuts was intensified. During this period ranchers also began to move into the region. São José, then called Bacaba, might have disappeared at this time had it not been for the efforts of a strong chief, José Dias Matúk, who managed to reunite those Indians who had gone to Botica and Krahólândia (Nimuendajú 1939:13ff.). Today the Apinayé are well aware of the importance of the village. They always say that the chief of São José is more important than the chief of Mariazinha, and further, that "if the chief here gives an order, the one there has to obey him." The main reason for the preeminence of São José is that the Indian post is located there. In 1967, for example, the Indians of São José killed two or three head of cattle, but they were not afraid of the local rancher's threats because the official in charge of the post was stationed there in the village.

Even before the SPI (Indian Protection Service) was established in the area, Indians from São José went to Tocantinópolis as spokesmen for Apinayé interests whenever there was trouble. Once, for example, following a serious conflict between the Indians and a rancher over the killing of cattle, Velho Estêvão managed to get Padre Velho to agree to a truce and to explicitly recognize the Indians' right to occupy the area where the village is now located.[6]

The most obvious cause of tension is the stealing or killing of cattle. But the latent cause is population pressure and the constant attempts by the Brazilians to force the Indians off areas of good pasture or good agricultural land, or areas where the babassu palm is found. When the Apinayé speak of the history of their villages, they describe the sequence of events partly in terms of the general history of the region and partly in terms of tribal and village politics. Their accounts always conclude by recalling how villages or families moved as a result of economic pressures or factional disputes. Estêvão, for example, always began his account of the history of São José by describing its relationship with the Brazilian towns, but he would soon turn to a description of events that could be properly understood only in terms of the Apinayé political system.

Although recent demographic data indicate that the population of the Apinayé is increasing, the history of the tribe clearly shows that the general tendency is one of decline. It should be understood that population decline in this context cannot simply be estimated in terms of numbers of people. It must also take into account the decrease in the number of villages as well as the loss of those cultural features that distinguished Indians and non-Indians in the past. Perhaps the most important factor in the history of the tribe has been their proximity to the regional towns. Both Indian villages are about thirty kilometers from Tocantinópolis, and access routes remain excellent throughout the year. Such ease of communication encourages contact between Brazilians and Apinayé and also involves the latter in the babassu industry. Indeed, this industry is the principal way in which the Apinayé are incorporated into the socioeconomic structure of the region.[7]

There are striking differences between the Brazilian system of collecting babassu nuts and that followed by the Apinayé. The two most important are as follows. First, Brazilian babassu nut collectors work in areas owned or leased by someone else, and they must sell their produce to the owner or leaseholder at a lower price than market prices in Tocantinópolis. The Apinayé sell their babassu nuts on the Indian post and have the double advantage of getting a better price and being allowed more flexible credit. Furthermore, they are under no obligation to sell on the post and can, if they want, look for another buyer. Some Indians try to buy the produce of their neighbors and sell it again in town. Their business failures are due more to the enormous debts incurred by their relatives (which are never paid off) than to their incapacity to cope with the astute dealers in town.

Second, the Brazilian babassu nut collector produces as much as he can to fulfill his contract with the "owner" of the land. He is therefore working to satisfy that person's commercial interests. The Indians, in theory at least, occupy their own lands.[8] Furthermore, since their social universe is quite different, their interests only partly coincide with those of the Brazilians. Whereas producing a great deal of babassu nuts enhances a Brazilian's social status, the more time an Indian spends collecting the nuts, the less he can spend on those other activities that would enhance his prestige with regard to Apinayé values.

The Apinayé economy shows a tendency toward multicentricity (see Bohannan 1959, for an explanation of this concept), which, in this case, has been encouraged by the process of contact. In general those activities associated with Brazilian society tend to have a commercial character whereas traditional Apinayé activities are essentially noncommercial, although they can to some extent be translated into monetary terms. The Apinayé view the collection and sale of babassu nuts as an alien activity that does not involve traditional social ties and obligations. It is done individually or by a nuclear family, usually a woman and her smaller children. Hunting and agriculture, however, surround the Apinayé with a whole series of social obligations, for these activities are based on cooperation between domestic groups. But it would be wrong to conclude that babassu production is causing the social values of the tribe to turn more and more toward a kind of individualism. Collecting babassu nuts is becoming firmly associated with the values of Brazilian society in such a way that those values are kept separate from traditional economic activities. Hunting and agriculture are always considered the truly worthwhile activities. Consequently there emerges a clear distinction between two kinds of activity: necessary occupations such as collecting and selling babassu nuts which, in moral terms, have strongly unfavorable connotations, and necessary occupations like hunting and agriculture which are clearly superior since they involve strongly approved moral values such as reciprocity. Thus, as I have pointed out elsewhere (Da Matta 1976), this aspect of multicentricity, which seems to appear in all contact situations, can become a quite complex factor.

It is clear why the Indians would never consider turning babassu collecting into a full-scale commercial activity. Given their concerns, such an idea would be quite foreign to them; babassu collecting is simply a convenient way of making money. But this attitude also explains why difficulties arise. Because of their approach to babassu production, the Indians become both integrated with and separated from the regional society. They are integrated because the activity makes them part of the economic structure of the region, but they are separated because they do not pursue the activity on the appropriate scale nor with the appropriate motivation. Unlike the backwoodsmen, the Indians refuse to measure their success only by the amount of babassu nuts they collect. Consequently they are regarded as obstacles to the economic development of the area since they occupy lands that would be useful both for babassu production and for cattle ranching.

By 1967 the Indians' attitude toward babassu collecting had provoked obvious tensions both with the SPI official on the post and with Brazilian babassu producers. This was particularly clear in Mariazinha, which lies in a valuable babassu area. The SPI official, himself a local Brazilian, could not understand why the Apinayé did not organize their production in such a way that they would be part of "civilization" (that is, the Brazilian regional society). The Indians, on the other hand, did not understand his commercial point of view and complained that the "government" was not looking after their interests adequately. The misunderstanding was made more acute because the official was not simply a buyer of Apinayé produce. His position also made him the political and legal mediator between the Indians and the local Brazilians. In his capacity as a buyer of babassu nuts, the official was operating like a capitalist employer, intent on profits and on establishing good relationships in town with the babassu merchants and the business community in general. But in his capacity as a mediator and as a representative of the official protection agency, his function was exactly the opposite. His role here was to defend the Indians and argue their case whenever there was a conflict of interest between Indians and Brazilians. A contradictory position like this is not just a peculiarity of the Apinayé situation in the 1960s. It is a dilemma typical of a certain kind of role that brings together two different hierarchical arrangements and that places the individual between the conflicting interests of two societies. In this case the SPI official had to extricate himself from an intolerable situation without the benefit of outside support and without the guidance of any clear professional ethic. The easiest solution was simply to take the side of the local babassu producers and the businessmen.

There is an ambiguity in the behavior of those in charge of Indian posts that probably results from a certain sense of insecurity. The root of the problem is that they have to decide between the Brazilian community to which they belong, where they have a certain prestige, social connections, and vested interests, and the tribal community to which their commitments are at best tenuous. In the Apinayé example the SPI official obviously saw Tocantinópolis as the center of his own culture. His connections with the town supported his social identity and prevented his being engulfed socially and psychologically by the tribal society. The Indian village, by contrast, was where he was obliged to carry on his work surrounded by people who were, to him, scarcely human and who, according to his social values, had no prestige whatsoever. Hence whenever there was trouble between Indians and Brazilians he faced a serious conflict of loyalties that was impossible to resolve without damaging his relationship with both parties.

These difficulties were exacerbated because the official found himself in the absurd situation of being "in charge" of a tribal group that had no formally demarcated lands of their own nor any legal or political recognition in the area. In other words, he had been put in charge of something that did not officially exist. Given this absurd state of affairs, his recourse was to try to establish a position for himself in the regional power structure, which regarded the Apinayé as something to be removed or eliminated. Unlike anthropologists, missionaries, and itinerant doctors, who can all be involved in situations like this, the official in charge of the Indian post is not guided by a powerful professional ethic. Paradoxically, it is he more than anyone who requires such a code of conduct, as Marshal Rondon, founder of the SPI, so clearly understood. The Apinayé example shows that the only way to resolve that confusion of roles is to revive Rondon's professional ethical precepts.

The sociological principles underlying the process of contact between Brazilian society and the Apinayé are no different from those operating in other tribal situations. Roberto Cardoso de Oliveira has shown that contact is basically a process where "two populations are dialectically united by diametrically opposed interests" (1964:128). This dialectic appears clearly in my analysis of the factors that mediate between the Apinayé and the national society: babassu production, the ideology of that production, and the role of the government Indian protection agency.

The structural features of intercultural contact result from the fact that different societies are confined within a geographical area such that contact is inevitable. In other words, the structural components are cultural distance and physical proximity. The ambiguity of the situation is therefore obvious. While proximity produces social forces that tend to unite the two populations, the first component, social or cultural distance, produces exactly the opposite effect. I have shown in the Apinayé case how babassu production and convenient access between Indian villages and the nearby towns tend to unite the two populations. But the cultural differences between Indians and Brazilians maintain their separateness.

The opposing tendencies produce a conflict that has to be resolved. One possible solution would require groups to accept both their differences and their proximity to one another. The result would be some sort of federation in which each society has an equal place in the system. This is what takes place in those so-called areas of intertribal acculturation, the best example in Brazil being the upper Xingu. When only two populations are involved, another possible solution is the classic example of dual organizations as described by Rivers. This type of solution emphasizes that the societies that are in contact are symmetrical and equal. The relationship between them is one of complementarity (Lévi-Strauss 1969:chap. 6, and 1963:chap. 8).

A third solution is to maintain physical proximity while safeguarding cultural distance by means of a hierarchical relationship between the two societies. Here the dominant society, seeing itself as superior, does not accept or tolerate cultural differences but simply ignores them. This is what happens in Central Brazil, particularly in those contact situations I have studied.

In structural terms, economic exploitation and racist ideologies are parallel factors in those situations in which there is a "space" between social groups and in which one of those groups can turn cultural differences into a hierarchical relationship. And it is precisely this kind of situation that offers ideal conditions for the entrepreneur because, as Barth has pointed out: "The big potentialities for profit lie where the disparity of evaluation between two or more kinds of goods are [sic] greatest, and where this disparity has been maintained because there are no bridging transactions" (Barth 1966:18).

In any specific case it is difficult to predict whether the solution initially adopted will be that of symmetry (where differences are accepted) or asymmetry (where differences are structured in a hierarchical system). But it seems that the SPI/FUNAI pacification teams who first make contact with the Indians try to achieve the first kind of solution. They try to respect the integrity of the Indian culture and in so doing give the Indians a more humane impression of the white man. Nevertheless, their approach appears to be a function of their fragility. The teams are always small in number, and they are really no more than mediators between the pioneering groups and the Indian groups that have to be "pacified," or, in a more revealing usage, "civilized." Many Indian groups come to complain about the period following "pacification," when their relationship with the pioneering group has become settled and the pacification team's respect for Indian culture has given way to the firm domination of Brazilian society. The Apinayé, with their usual acumen, say that "initially the *kupén* [foreigners] gave away everything just so that Indians would get used to having things. After that they began to charge for them." This insight betrays the philanthropic pretense of the pacification effort and reveals those involved in their true role as mediators of the socioeconomic structures of Brazilian society.

In the Gaviões case, in which the pioneering front was based on Brazil nuts, it seems that an asymmetrical solution was adopted, the Indian and his society being regarded as inferior to the Brazilian (Laraia and Da Matta 1967). In the Apinayé case it appears that although a similar ideology might have existed in the past, it is not nearly so rampant today. There is possibly a correlation between the value of the product sought by the pioneers and the solution adopted to resolve the problems of contact, although an equally plausible explanation is that one solution alternates with another as relations between the two societies develop.

This last point is well brought out in the relationship of the Apinayé with Tocantinópolis, on the one hand, and with the rural society, on the other. The Apinayé word *kupén* is a generic term that covers all strangers. They speak of American *kupén,* Brazilian *kupén,* black and white *kupén,* and especially *"kupén* who like Indians and *kupén* who do not." They say that Brazilians living in the town emphatically do not like Indians. Those who live in rural areas may or may not feel the same way. In keeping with this view they rarely refer to Brazilians from Tocantinópolis by name but refer to them in an impersonal way as "people of the city" or "of the street." On the other hand, those who live in the country, whether they like Indians or not, are always referred to by name.

The Brazilians who maintain social contact with the Indians live in settlements surrounding the Apinayé village—São Domingos, Raiz, Prata, and so on.[9] Contact takes various forms, from casual exchanges and barter to occasional visits. They invite one another to celebrations. Godparent relationships can be established between Indians and non-Indians. Sometimes there are quarrels between individuals of the different societies. And nowadays, an important point of contact between the two populations is football games. Although only the younger people are directly involved in playing the game, the event also brings together the older members of both societies.[10]

Brazilians who live in the vicinity of the village are known to the Indians by name. Many have a godparent relationship with the Apinayé. Some are constant visitors who may even go hunting with the Indians.[11] Their wives and children are known as persons with good and bad qualities, which makes it difficult for the Indians to make judgments about them, inasmuch as that might reflect on the social relationship in which they are already involved.

In Tocantinópolis with its population of five thousand there are only a dozen or so people whom the Apinayé regard as friendly toward them. One of my informants described them as the people who like to talk with Indians and who always offer a cup of coffee or a similar small gift. The Indians see the town as a corporate social unit and, indeed, there is certainly a close sense of community among the inhabitants. Both local Brazilians and Indians see the town and the Indian village as contrasting social entities that are capable of concerted action against each other. The Brazilian rural settlements are quite different in that only a vague sense of community exists among the scattered and isolated population.

An Apinayé who visits the city is always afraid of being attacked verbally or even physically. In fact, the behavior of townspeople toward Indians appears close to what Radcliffe-Brown (1952) called "joking relationships" (in contrast to "contractual relationships"). Similarly, when I was working among the Gaviões I noticed that Indians and Brazilians not only exchanged open or covert insults but even pushed each other playfully or pretended to fight. Radcliffe-Brown explained "joking" behavior as a solution to a situation that is initially contradictory. It is an institutionalized pattern of behavior that maintains both social solidarity and respect in situations in which these are mutually exclusive, as, for instance, in those situations of contact that are described here.

In the case of the Gaviões, Indians and Brazilians adopted joking behavior both in the village and in the town of Itupiranga in an attempt to overcome the contradictions resulting from contact by emphasizing an ideal symmetry between the two populations. The Gaviões (a word meaning "hawks" in Portuguese) have always had a peculiar place in the minds of the local Brazilians and are feared as murderers, savages, and veritable birds of prey, as their name suggests (Da Matta 1963). Among the Apinayé, on the other hand, joking behavior was adopted only, and rarely, toward Brazilians who lived near the village, while in Tocantinópolis the Indians showed great "respect" for Brazilians and were reluctant to take the initiative in talking to them. Such "respect" (shown also toward the SPI official, the doctor, the missionaries, and to "authority" in general) is a result of their finding themselves in a hierarchical system of positions and is also one way of resolving the contradiction between sociocultural distance and physical proximity. Hence joking relationships and relationships of respect represent two sides of a situation of conjunction. The propriety of one or the other depends on whether the subservient group has a greater or a lesser degree of autonomy within the interethnic system into which it has been drawn.

The way the Apinayé are treated in town also indicates how far Tocantinópolis is from being a properly established city. The Indians constitute a threat to the social system of a community that would like to see itself as an urban center with a status similar to that of cities elsewhere in the country. Contact with the Indians is not a matter of routine as it is in rural areas. The appearance of Indians in town is still considered something exotic that is outside "everyday routine structures" (Weber 1947:363), whereas in the country it is commonplace and very much a part of everyday routine.

When contact becomes commonplace in this way the Indian becomes less of an exotic object and the stereotype that makes him part of the animal world tends to disappear. In 1961 it was clear that the inhabitants of Marabá and Itupiranga considered the Indian little more than a kind of animal capable of some sort of speech. In Tocantinópolis, where contact is now quite commonplace, one can still hear the Apinayé described as dirty, smelly animals, but in the surrounding rural areas where the Indian is a neighbor, a companion, a godparent, and a babassu producer, such an attitude is quite impossible to maintain. The problem here is that ideological inconsistencies tend to appear as contact becomes routine. One notices this on hearing Brazilians say, on the one hand, that Indians have a better community life than the frontiersmen, that they fight less among themselves, and that they are intelligent and inventive, while on the other, that they eat any animal they can catch and are therefore not too far from being animals themselves. In addition, the Apinayé are held to be inveterate cattle thieves.

These contradictory opinions suggest that the frontiersmen's idea of Indians is quite complex, being the result of many overlapping social ties. Although there may be tensions in some areas of life (with regard to economic production, for instance) there are also many areas of mutual understanding. The ideological inconsistencies indicate a greater degree of interaction between Indians and Brazilians, which in turn gives the subordinate population greater scope to manipulate their relationship with the dominant one. This greater degree of freedom is a direct result of their being forced to become more involved with the dominant society.

The Gaviões had only two alternatives: either they could disappear and cease to be an obstacle to the extractive industry, or they could take part in the industry as a special category of worker, badly paid and with no rights. Here the Indians were facing an integrated social system completely dominated by a single extractive industry that was controlled by a few bosses. In this kind of system there are direct links between those who control credit, the owners of lands where the nuts are found, and the employees who collect and transport the product. In the Brazil nut industry workers and owners, capital and labor, production and exportation, and the jungle and the city are all dependent on one another and form a tight, complementary system (Laraia and Da Matta 1967; Velho 1972). There is no room for any social role that cannot fit into the system. Such a tightly controlled system is extremely efficient and is commonly found in regions that have the vigorous pioneering spirit that Vianna Moog (1956) calls *bandeirantismo*. Ideological inconsistencies hardly appear, for contact tends to destroy the tribal group either physically or culturally. It was no accident that the Gaviões were consistently described as frightful murderers during the 1960s. The description justified the violence perpetrated by the frontiersmen during their invasion of Indian lands that were known to be so rich in Brazil nut trees.

When the dominant system lacks such integration and is beset by in-

ternal struggles between competing interests, as was the case in and
around Tocantinópolis, the tribal group is regarded in a number of different ways. These inconsistencies reflect the many different ties that the
frontier community has with the Indians, and they also correspond to internal tensions and contradictions within the frontier community itself. If,
for example, a rancher regards the Indians as an obstacle to his work, the
SPI official will consider them quite blameless, while the missionary will
see them as pagans to be converted. An entrepreneur in the babassu industry might consider the Indians lazy, while the small-time babassu collector might well understand the difficulties of gathering the product. The
frontiersman living close to the Indians might even see them as friends
who share the same fate as himself.

These images vary according to the situation, but they all share a common denominator. They all assume that the Apinayé lack something; that
they need help; that they are ignorant; and above all, that they do not
have a will of their own. But the crucial point is that the various images
contradict one another and produce an ideological inconsistency. When
contact becomes a matter of course, the Indians find themselves in a situation in which they have considerable room to maneuver. The many different representations of the Indian that appear in a situation like this are
a direct result of the way the pioneering front is structured. And, as I argued more fully elsewhere (Da Matta 1976), it is the variety of these representations that explains why certain groups are said to remain "conser-
vative" even when they come under the domination of regional and
national society.

Comparing the Gaviões and Apinayé cases, there appears to be a correlation between the way a pioneering front regards Indians and the
structure and objectives of that front. The more homogeneous the pioneering front, the more consistent will be its representations of the Indian
and, consequently, the fewer the possibilities open to the Indian group for
establishing their place within that structure. In such cases the most frequent result is that the Indian group dies out, as appears to be happening
to the Gaviões. But the Apinayé have survived, having come into contact
with a pioneering front that was not so homogeneous and that allowed
them greater freedom in which to preserve their traditional values.

This correlation, however, holds only in those parts of the country
where the national society is in direct, permanent contact with Indians.
Darcy Ribeiro (1957) has already shown that Brazilian frontier society is
not at all homogeneous. Even when a particular pioneering front is of a
firmly consistent type, it is always possible that the Indians will come into
contact with other Brazilians, or even foreigners, whose ideas and interests are quite different from those of the rest of the population. The
Gaviões, for example, came into contact with Dominican missionaries,
with anthropologists, and with medical personnel who had all come into

the region from elsewhere. The Indians are quick to see these differences and classify non-Indians into those who "come from nearby" and those who "come from a distance." Those from nearby are always considered unfavorably since they are seen as oppressors, whereas those who come from a distance are "good" (Cardoso de Oliveira 1964:126; Melatti 1967:143). The dialectic of classification involves a much wider set of considerations and includes the interests, relationships, and images of each representative of the national society who comes into contact with Indians. Because those who "come from a distance" are convinced that the Indians are not hostile and are clearly dominated by the national society, they tend to see the Indians as "good," "pure," "innocent," and so on, while those "from nearby," with vested interests in the area, see the tribe as an obstacle to the pursuit of their goals. In other words, for those who come from the outside the Indian is already classified within the national system. Although he is powerless, his moral superiority is indisputable. For those who come from the locality the Indian is not yet clearly classified; being a threat he is both a man and an animal, good and bad, intelligent and stupid, honest and a thief.

The comparison suggests that the Apinayé have been partially absorbed by the regional system because of the kind of pioneering front that they encountered, while the Gaviões came into contact with a system that could not absorb them at all. Although the Apinayé are incorporated into that system at the lowest possible level, there are compensations that alleviate their position. They may be considered semihuman, but they are a united society. They may not have the Brazilian's literacy nor his knowledge of the laws of the land, but they know the forest and its animals. They may not be as well armed as those who come from the town, but they have what some English anthropologists call "the power of the weak," that is, they have a strong sense of solidarity among themselves. Local Brazilians tend to disparage the Apinayé way of life, but, paradoxically, they appreciate that Apinayé society has a cohesion that theirs, although more powerful, does not have. Furthermore, the Apinayé are admired for their medical expertise. Local Brazilians consider their medicines powerful and are beginning to go to the Indians to seek cures for their ailments.

These facts indicate that the Apinayé case is another example of those societies described by I.M. Lewis (1963), Mary Douglas (1966), and Victor Turner (1969), in which mystical power compensates for a lack of secular power. The so-called power of the weak is the ability of a subordinated group to react against the dominating system by finding compensatory mechanisms of some kind. There is no doubt that the Apinayé are finding a place in the dominant social system; the Brazilians are beginning to recognize their intangible strengths, such as the cohesion and vigor of their society, their curing techniques, their knowledge of the jungle, and so on. In fact, it is only through such open recognition and acceptance of the "power of the weak" that Indian groups can be integrated into Brazilian society.

To extend the hypothesis, the Apinayé case suggests that the integration of subordinated groups does not take place directly by way of the political or economic system, but more through an appreciation of their "mystical talents": their powers of curing and cursing, their knowledge of songs and expertise in cooking, and their stoicism in the face of suffering and anguish. Indeed, it appears that these features will be increasingly recognized by the dominant society as the group becomes politically and economically subordinated. When marginalized peoples or other subordinated sections of a society turn to rebellion they always use a mystical idiom of the language of the oppressed to justify their struggle for freedom. The mystical power of the weak suggests a useful line of inquiry into the way that radically different social groups become integrated into a complex whole in which boundaries are blurred. It also indicates a more important question regarding the limitations of secular power and the various mechanisms of compensation that are used to control that power.

It seems that the Apinayé are going to become more and more involved in Brazilian society both physically and economically, but at the same time they will perhaps become more independent and self-sufficient in areas like art and religion, that is, in areas where "the power of the weak" characteristically comes into its own. There are already indications that this is happening: the Indians are becoming well-known curers in the region, and their handicrafts are being marketed in cities throughout Brazil.

The complex relationship between Brazilian society and the Apinayé rests on a number of factors that are directly related to the way in which a specific kind of extractive industry entered and occupied the area over the years. It is also related to the sociology of the urban and rural settlements that brought the industry to the area. But explaining why the process of contact took the course it did in no way excuses the constant injustices to which the Indians were subjected in the past nor those that continue to the present day. There is still a chronic lack of medical assistance and, more seriously, the Indians have been given no land of their own on which they will be able to decide their own future.

The crucial decision facing the Apinayé is whether to adopt the ways of the Brazilian frontiersmen or to maintain their own traditional culture. The following chapters of this book are devoted to a description and analysis of that traditional way of life.

2

Domestic Life

*T*HE APINAYÉ describe their society in terms of their village. Whereas other tribes might consider a lineage, an age set, or a clan to be the principal component of their social lives, the Apinayé always talk of the village community. But what emerges from their descriptions is not the village as I knew it. São José was about two hundred fifty meters long and two hundred meters wide, with twenty houses lined up to form streets (see Figure 1). It was built on a long slope running west; grass grew on all sides; the houses were all of different sizes and had been built in many different ways (eight of mud bricks, the rest of straw); and a stranger would not have noticed anything that could be called a plaza. This was not the village the Indians were describing to me.

Their description was of an ideal village, built in a perfect circle, each house being of the same size. Within such a village they would distinguish three areas: a central patio called *ingó* or *me-ingó* (*me* being a collective prefix) or sometimes *ipôgo* ("center"); the peripheral area where the houses stood called *ikré*; and the clearing immediately beyond the limits of the village, referred to as either *atúk* (*túk* meaning "black") or *ikrékatuli* (*katuli* meaning "behind"). Hence they conceive of the village as a concentric structure (Lévi-Strauss 1963:chap. 8) as can be seen in the diagrams drawn by the Indians themselves (see Figures 2, 3, and 4).

But the reader will note that a diametric division is imposed on the initial concentric pattern (Lévi-Strauss, ibid.). Thus in Figure 4 the informant linked houses that were opposite on the larger circle. This represented possible marriages, considered correct but not prescriptive. In Figure 2 the informant indicated the four most important ceremonial groups: the *Kolti* and *Kolre* moieties and the related groups *Krénotxóine* and *Ipôgnotxóine*.[1]

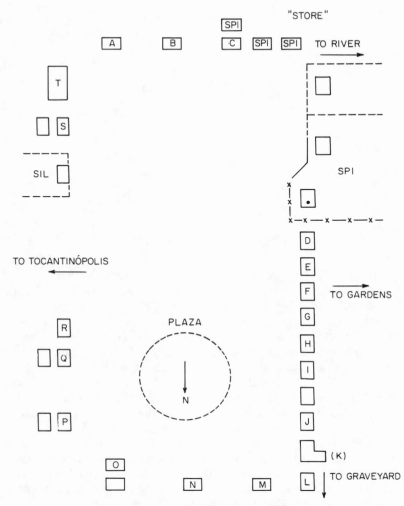

Figure 1. *The village of São José in 1967.*

It is not unusual for the Northern Gê to draw villages in this way.[2] But I should emphasize that these Apinayé drawings are not completely abstract representations of a village. When I asked my informant to draw "the village we are staying in" (São José), including all the details of the surrounding area, the result was Figure 3! It is clear that these drawings of villages are schematic representations of the most important areas of Apinayé society. The diagrams always represent oppositions between center and periphery and between east and west, as can be seen in Figure 3. Both concentric and diametric dualism are represented in the same

Figure 2. *An Apinayé diagram of the society indicating the four most important ceremonial groups.*

diagram, and they are distinguished according to context, that is to say, depending on which part of the diagram one chooses to focus on.[3] In the center of the diagram diametric dualism is dominant, men and women being symmetrically placed within the same circle. But the drawing as a whole is dominated by a concentricity in which as one moves out from the center one moves from culture to nature, that is, from the village through the cleared land toward the forest and the rivers where fish, animals, and other non-Apinayé beings live. Thus the first opposition is in some way resolved by the second. This is even clearer in Figure 5, drawn by the same exceptional informant, which is a representation of the entire universe.

In Figure 5 the pattern is most obviously concentric, but one should not overlook the diametric aspects. The concentric design moves outward as follows: fire, plaza, houses, village, gardens, tamed Indians, water, wild Indians, Brazilians, earth, sky, village of the dead, and finally sun and moon. At the same time there are the following diametric oppositions: man/woman, raw/cooked, women and children/men, water/fire, and sun/moon. It is as if the concentric dualism conceptualizes gradations while the diametric divides the world in a more extreme way.[4]

The Apinayé are justly proud of the form of their villages. Although today they are not built in a circle, their sociological form, so to speak, is circular. Although the houses of Mariazinha are built in straight lines the community operates as if the inhabitants lived within a circle. When they

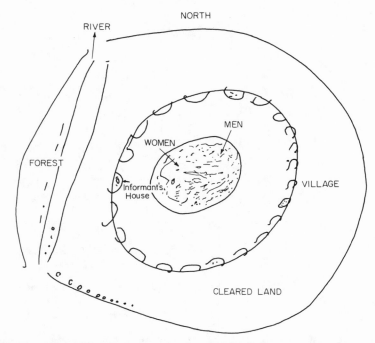

Figure 3. *An Apinayé diagram of the village of São José in 1967. I specifically asked the informant to draw "our village." This representation should be compared with the diagram of the "real village," Figure 1.*

talk of marriages they point to the other side of the village; they say that formal friends (*krã-geti/pá-krã*) live opposite; and when they refer to their own faction they indicate the house next door.

An Apinayé village has what in urban studies is called "legibility": "By this we mean the ease with which its parts can be recognized and can be organized into a coherent pattern" (Lynch 1960:2). The term is extremely appropriate for all the Northern Gê. A "reading" of their villages not only indicates the ecological adjustments they have made to their environment but also reveals their world view. For the Apinayé their village is a diagram that sets out the relations between the categories of their world.

The Apinayé are aware that the form of their villages has certain disadvantages. They point out, for instance, that since the circle of houses has to be maintained, an increase in population means that the houses become overcrowded, making them uncomfortably hot in summer. Solving the problem by building a large village requires another circle of houses outside the first, and it is said that people do not like living in the outer circle. Neither can the circle be maintained if the population falls to

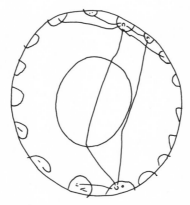

Figure 4. *An Apinayé drawing of a village.*

any considerable extent because a minimum of four or five houses is required for a proper circular pattern.[5]

The Apinayé make an interesting comparison between their own villages and Brazilian settlements. They note that Tocantinópolis and the surrounding settlements consist of lines of houses running alongside a road or a river. Hence they say that it is difficult for an Indian village to accommodate a change in population, whereas the villages of the *kupén* can expand infinitely because another house can simply be built at the end of the line. The Indians see the Brazilian settlement pattern as open and their own as closed.

When the Apinayé describe their own society they first take the village as the main point of reference and then construct a series of oppositions, both diametric and concentric, between social groups and categories. The social world is ordered in this way, and its dynamic consists of a movement between two antithetical dimensions. Understanding Apinayé society requires an explanation of how these dimensions are distinguished and the significance of the movement between them. This chapter is an account of the social groups that constitute one of those basic domains.

Both domains are apparent in the above diagrams. One is the periphery of the village, consisting of the houses and the domestic groups. The other is the central plaza, represented by the two pairs of ceremonial moieties (see Figure 2). These are temporary, nonresidential groups. The first is associated with everyday life, and the second is associated with the ceremonial life of the community.

Social Groups

In the context of everyday life, the two best-defined groups in Apinayé society are the nuclear family (husband, wife, and children), and the ux-

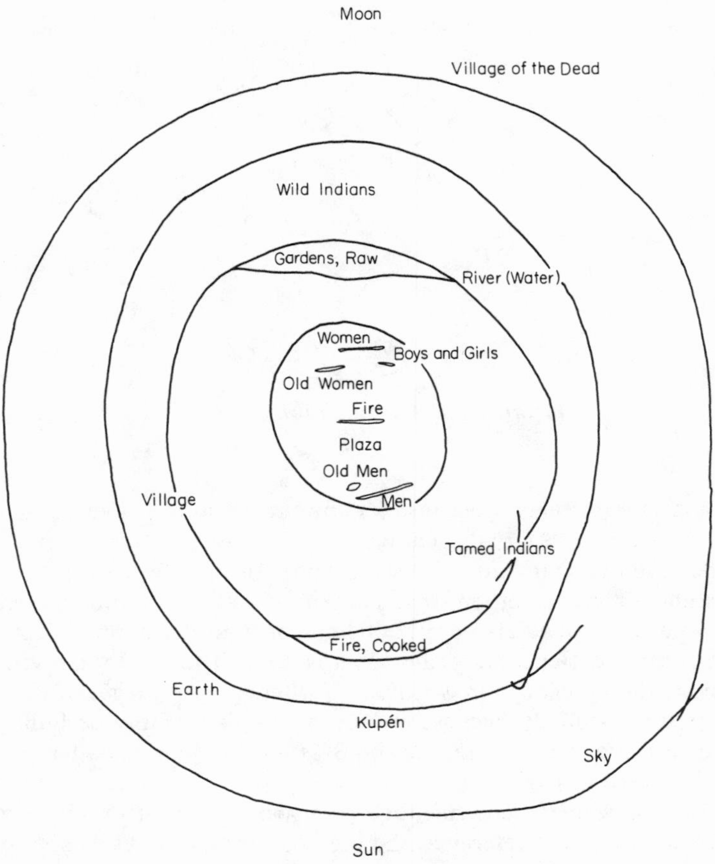

Moon

Village of the Dead

Wild Indians

Gardens, Raw

River (Water)

Women

Boys and Girls

Old Women

Fire

Plaza

Old Men

Men

Village

Tamed Indians

Fire, Cooked

Earth

Kupén

Sky

Sun

Figure 5. *An Apinayé representation of the universe.*

orilocal extended family, which includes a married couple, their daughters, and the husbands and children of their daughters. Extended families are not found in every house, but each house contains at least one nuclear family. Unmarried men and women cannot build a house of their own. Lacking the institution of the Men's House, which in Kayapó society is a permanent residence in the center of the village for unmarried men and boys (T. Turner 1966), Apinayé boys who are to be initiated spend only a short time living with other members of their age set during the actual period of initiation.

In both São José and Mariazinha most of the houses are occupied by extended families.[6] The extended family is based on uxorilocal residence; men leave their natal group and are replaced by their sisters' husbands. It is therefore based on female links between mother and daughter. The nuclear family, by contrast, links father, mother, and children in a symmetric and complementary relationship. It is also the basic unit of production and reproduction, each group having rights over a piece of land that the parents cultivate. Within the nuclear family each person has certain rights and duties regarding sexual and economic matters. Both husband and wife should work for each other's benefit and both should be sexually faithful.

Apinayé gardens are found on the slopes near rivers where gallery forests provide fertile land. Either the man or the woman may choose a site, and the garden is then cleared by the usual slash-and-burn techniques. The whole village takes part in felling, burning, and clearing the large trees, the chief being responsible for organizing the able-bodied men of the village into a work force. Ill will and misunderstandings inevitably result when the whole village has to be involved in a task that benefits only a few people.[7] Fencing, clearing undergrowth (*encoivarar* in the local Brazilian dialect), weeding, and planting are tasks for everyone in the nuclear or extended family. Harvesting is usually done by women. As among the Krīkati (Lave 1967:chap. 3), the gardens are places where people can find some privacy. A married couple or a family might, for instance, go there to eat secretly so that they are not disturbed by other relatives asking for food. Women own the gardens and visit them daily. If divorce occurs the house and garden are left to the woman, and the man goes back to his mother's house or, if she is dead, to the house of a sister. Often a man plants a piece of his garden for his wife's father, for, as the Indians say, "a man likes to pay the man who gave him his *iprom* [wife]."

Planting takes place from November through the end of January, leaving the beginning of the dry season (*angrô*) for clearing land. Burning takes place in the middle of the dry season. Certain products have specific planting times: peanuts and tobacco are planted in October, and potatoes, maize, and manioc in November, December, and January. The Apinayé prefer to build and repair houses during April and May since after that it turns much hotter and there is greater risk of fire. House building requires the help of relatives and involves everyone in the extended family. The dry season is also the time when festivals and marriages take place.

In houses occupied by an extended family, each nuclear family has a sleeping area of its own, which gives them a certain amount of privacy. The Apinayé are sensitive to the difficulties of communal living and say that nuclear families who share a house together must have a private area of their own since they have *piâm* toward one another. This concept can be translated as "respect," "shame," or "social distance."

It is certain shared activities rather than any specific property that defines the extended family as a social group. Usually it is an extended family that is involved in fencing a garden, clearing an area of land, or going on a hunt. Tasks that require collective effort may thus be carried out by a family without their having to seek help outside the group. Even more important is the power of the group in political machinations. If the group is fairly well united and includes a large number of married, able-bodied men, it can give considerable political support to any individual member. The cohesion of a group depends on the relations between the nuclear families who share the same roof. This in turn depends on how domestic authority is organized within each nuclear family. The Apinayé are aware of these problems and say that when many people are living in the same house a great deal depends on the old people, that is, on a man's wife's parents.

In São José the political unity of extended families is quite strong. But even where there are only two nuclear families living together and where the old people have clearly established domestic authority, that may not be enough to guarantee the political cohesion of the group as a whole. Old people, wives' parents, and wives' brothers are usually respected, but there are exceptions, and it may well happen that a young couple leaves to set up their own house next door. Authority within the extended family as a whole is based on consent, there being no rigidly defined set of positions that automatically give power to certain persons. Since each nuclear family has its own garden and produces its own food, it can detach itself from the larger group without too much difficulty. But setting up a separate house may have disadvantages, for living with a large group means that there will always be something to eat.

One of the principal aims of my field study was to look at the nature of prescribed authority within the Apinayé household.[8] I discovered that the extended family had no clearly defined structure of authority and that house leadership depended on a number of factors of which the most important was the age of the husband and the length of time he had been in residence. A young husband joining his affinal household tended to be timid and respectful toward his wife's parents and brothers. But over time, with the arrival of children, the departure of the wife's brothers to other houses, and the aging of the wife's parents, the husband came to occupy a position of authority. This, at any rate, was the usual pattern, but there were exceptional cases in which the wife's parents held supreme authority well into old age and young husbands had sufficient prestige to become household leaders before having any children or grandchildren of their own.

An advantage of such a flexible domestic structure is that the extended family can absorb people of different personalities and different statuses. The major disadvantage, always mentioned by the Apinayé themselves, is that all sorts of injustices can appear in matters like sharing food. Friction can result when a husband complains that his parents are not receiving enough meat, or not receiving a share often enough, or even that they are receiving no meat at all. When an Apinayé brings home meat it has to be distributed among those considered blood relatives (his parents, and in some cases his brothers) to whom he has imperative obligations. But if the extended family is large and the catch is small, there is little chance that the husband's parents and brothers will be given anything. After a time, especially if the man is young and does not have children, his closest relatives will begin to complain that he is forgetting them and being niggardly (being *ontxú*).

A similar source of friction is a husband's complaint that he is not getting enough food from his wife's mother and that the other male members of the household are being lazy, implying that his efforts alone are maintaining the household. In these circumstances (or rather when a man is convinced that this is taking place), he simply visits his mother's house more frequently and begins to take his meals there. His frequent visits are a clear message to the rest of the village that his affines are not treating him well and that he is forced to go back to his mother's house to find something to eat. An incident like this gives rise to a great deal of discussion and gossip.

These difficulties are a consequence of the rule of uxorilocal residence, which results in each man's having two places of residence and two reference groups after marriage. They are thus associated with that critical period when a man moves from his "family of origin" over to his "family of marriage." The problems at this stage of his life are related to the questions of domestic authority, because the extended family is not a clearly defined group with its own clearly defined scope. As a result, a man cannot make an abrupt transition, as happens in many other societies when a husband or wife leaves the household of origin and is promptly incorporated into the affinal household. Among the Apinayé there is a gradual transition that depends very much on the strength of the conjugal as opposed to the filial ties of the person concerned. The former are strengthened at the expense of the latter. However, it should be emphasized that the process is by no means automatic. Since a man marries in the same village in which his parents live, it is easy for him to maintain close connections with his "family of origin" and he may exploit that connection, as the examples in the previous paragraph show.

Although the extended family and nuclear family are closely interrelated the distinction between them is clearly maintained because of the autonomy of the nuclear family. Whereas the extended family is a secondary grouping operating within a diffuse social context, the social context of the nuclear family is clearly defined, having its own space within the house, its own lands, and so on. Hence the two groups are not seen as mutually exclusive such that the nuclear family must inevitably be absorbed into the larger group. Their relationship is rather one of complementarity.

This is reflected in the fact that the Apinayé have no words for "nuclear family" and "extended family." The distinction is rarely made and then only by resort to certain circumlocutions. They do not speak of extended families as potential kinship groups nor of nuclear families as parts of the larger group. When they talk of social units they refer simply to houses. Each house (*ikré* or *nhõr-kwan*) consists of a family (nuclear or extended) that is, in theory at least, a politically independent social unit.

The importance of the house as a social unit and the fact that ownership of houses passes from mother to daughter place a clear emphasis on the maternal line, but in spite of this the Apinayé have no unilineal descent groups. This is because each nuclear family is semi-independent within the extended family. Husbands have authority over wives, although establishing such authority may take some time. Similarly, a woman's father and mother's brother begin to lose their authority over her as her marriage becomes more stable and especially after she has had children. In these circumstances the extended family can remain a united group only through the consent of its adult members. The group will hold together if there is someone capable of influencing everyone, a role that is usually fulfilled by the older people. When an extended family breaks up the Apinayé always say that it is due to the death of an old person, but should the family remain together, it is quite normal for one of the husbands to take over the leadership.

The lack of a clear structure of authority does not mean that there is no code of behavior within the house. Indeed there are elaborate rules of etiquette that apply particularly to the behavior of affines toward one another. This, as one might expect, is the area in which tensions are most likely to appear. Before looking at these rules in detail, we must first consider how the Apinayé conceive of the layout of their houses.

In the diagram of the village (Figure 6) all the houses are shown joined together across the central square. The Apinayé say that all the houses are *apten burog* (equal, the same), in other words, they are represented as having the same social importance. It seems that the drawing shows not the *ikré*, that is, the actual material constructions, but the *nhõr-kwán,* the dwelling places conceived of as the social space that each family has a right to and that is passed down from mother to daughter. Hence a kindred might occupy various *ikré*, but in terms of social space they would have only one *nhõr-kwán* in the village.

The diagram in Figure 6 does not reveal the size of the households, nor does the informant indicate the extended families or the factions formed by groups of houses related by kinship and residence. It is an ideal representation of the village in terms of the social groups that are capable of independent action. Formally, these are equally related to one another, as the pathway to the central plaza indicates. It should also be noted that each house is shown with two doors, one connected to the pathway (*ngó prú*) that leads to the center, the other leading out to the back of the

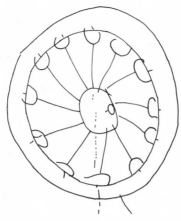

Figure 6. *An Apinayé drawing of a village showing the pathways to the central plaza.*

house. Like the village as a whole, the house is divided into two parts, *ikré kapême* (the front of the house) and *ikré katúd-lé* (the back), the front being associated with the ceremonial and public life of the central plaza and the back with private, everyday life.

The back of the house is where the Indians plant their fruit trees and where the daily exchange of food takes place. Following the example of Brazilians, they have also taken to building latrines there. The back is therefore a marginal area, considered to be on the edges of society, in contrast to the front of the house, which is totally immersed in the social system.

Just inside the front door is an area called *ikré kaprú* (*kaprú* meaning "empty"). This is a public area furnished with some stools where visitors are received, where meetings are held, or where a man might sit to do some household task. The rest of the interior is divided into small rooms, *ikré itôme* (*itôme* meaning "closed"), which are particularly noticeable when the house is made of mud bricks. The term "closed" gives a clear idea of how the nuclear families are cut off from one another. They sleep in these compartments and keep there what they consider to be personal valuables: beads, shotguns, gunpowder, clothes, photographs, mirrors, and so on.

Etiquette

Dividing the house in this way has obvious social implications, and it is not surprising that there is an explicit code of etiquette associated with these divisions. Although the Apinayé are quite clear about the code, they may not follow it to the letter. It is said that one should never enter a room without asking the permission of the man or woman who owns the house. Where a number of nuclear families occupy the same house, a father-in-law is free to enter the public area but should ask leave before going into the son-in-law's room. He must also ask before he takes anything belonging to the son-in-law. When visiting another house one should not ask for anything except water and fire.

A woman should distribute food fairly to everyone in the house and should not keep the best pieces of meat for her own husband. Her daughters' husbands deserve to be served generously since they supply the meat. A woman is always in charge of the distribution of food and is expected to know how much should be given to each relative, although a husband may often make suggestions about the distribution. If he is consistently ignored there may be a quarrel, but this kind of disagreement is most frequent between a man and his wife's mother. In cases where the mother-in-law is in charge of distribution, the rules are quite complex. The daughter's husband goes hunting and hands over what he catches to his wife. She gives the food to her mother, who invites everyone in the house to eat. The men gather and wait to be served by the women. The woman's mother should begin serving by giving a piece of the animal to the man who killed it. Younger men should eat in silence, and a man should not address his father-in-law or his brothers-in-law. Children eat last, after the best parts of the animal have been given to the adults.

Etiquette is particularly important between a man and his wife's parents. The Apinayé say emphatically that a man does not speak to his wife's father (*imbré-geti*), his wife's mother (*papan-gedy*), or to his wife's brother (*imbré*), at least until his position in the household is clearly established. The rule is particularly strict regarding the wife's parents. He can, however, converse with his wife's sister (*papani*). In the early stages of marriage the wife acts as a mediator between her husband and his affines. It is she who crosses the physical and social boundaries that separate nuclear families living in the same house. Furthermore, she is not subject to the same rules regarding her own affines. Since she stays in her natal home after marriage, the physical distance between a woman and her affines is enough in itself and does not have to be hedged about with elaborate rules of behavior.

Bearing in mind that the nuclear family is a potentially independent group, avoidance behavior between affines can be seen as a way of resolving the following problems: (1) the lack of any clearly defined domestic authority within the extended family; (2) the man's slow integration into the household upon marrying, which depends on the establishment of a firm relationship between himself and his wife; and (3) the threat that the husband's arrival poses to both the unity of the sibling group and the link between mother and daughter: a relationship that has a particular importance within the domestic group.

Moving to the house of his affines presents the husband with a difficult situation because he has to contend with opposing social forces. There is, for instance, a certain inconsistency between the situations in (2) and (3). Although his commitment to his wife's household is gradually established, he must nevertheless immediately assume certain responsibilities toward his wife.

Because such contradictions are difficult to resolve, *piâm* is necessary in the relationship between a husband and his wife's parents and his brother-in-law. *Piâm* has various connotations. The Indians sometimes translate it as "respect" or "shame." One often hears: "When a man has no more *piâm* for his wife's parents, the quarrels begin." For the Apinayé it is a sociological axiom that a certain amount of *piâm* is necessary for any relationship to succeed. Respect and shame, or we might say, social distance, is necessary so that the rights and duties of the relationship are observed. But the Apinayé also point out that there are areas of the social system in which *piâm* is not necessary. One informant explained that "between parents and children *piâm* is unnecessary since they were all brought up together." Similarly, after a marriage has become firmly established there is no *piâm* between husband and wife. *Piâm* is therefore a sociological marker indicating the necessary degree of respect that certain relationships require. That is to say, it denotes separation. But at the same time it reveals a disposition on the part of each person to conduct the relationship in a properly reciprocal way. Hence it also indicates conjunction. I may have *piâm* toward my brother-in-law because we are in separate social domains, but I also wish to show that we can live harmoniously together. This is the essence of those behavioral patterns that Radcliffe-Brown called "joking" or "avoidance" situations (Radcliffe-Brown 1952:91).

Whereas Radcliffe-Brown and his followers explained joking relationships in terms of links between individuals, I wish to show here how they relate to different social domains. Avoidance behavior among the Apinayé is a mechanism for controlling certain contradictory tendencies that result from the rule of uxorilocal residence. It is also a way of stressing that certain social fields are more or less independent of one another, though they are nevertheless related.

A nuclear family that is part of a large household is kept separate from the rest of the extended family by these rules of etiquette. From the husband's point of view the separation is maintained by avoidance behavior, which can be interpreted as a way of relieving the tensions that result from his change of residence. By not speaking to his wife's parents and brothers, he strengthens the ties with his wife and children. As the marital bond is reinforced and becomes socially more important, the ties between his wife and her parents and brothers become more tenuous. As this happens the husband is also separating himself from his natal home. The

Apinayé say that brothers are very close before they marry (because they are "of the same blood"—*kâbrô apten burog*), but after marrying they tend to lose this intimacy. From the husband's point of view the separation of the nuclear family and the extended family into distinct domains is expressed in social terms, since by moving to his wife's household his ties with his natal household are physically broken. A woman, by contrast, is always physically separated from her affines. Her husband comes to live with her from another house "on the opposite side of the village." Hence it is much more difficult for a woman to find a way to cooperate with her affines.

Since the nuclear family becomes an independent entity, the continuity of the extended family as a matrilineal unit is destroyed. Without a clear structure of authority, the extended family cannot function as a matrilineal, uxorilocal descent group. Instead of the husband's kin and the wife's kin being divided vertically into matrilineal descent lines that "give" and "receive" men, both groups intermingle and become structurally identified.

Ideologies

The Apinayé regard the nuclear family as a natural group in the sense that it has an actual, physical existence because of the close biological ties between its members. It is particularly distinguished from other social groups because of its profound associations with the formation, composition, and functioning of the human body.

Like us, the Apinayé are well aware that the human body consists of separate organs, each with its own function. Their knowledge does not come from autopsies, as is the case, for instance, among the African Azande (Evans-Pritchard 1937), but from what they know of the bodies of animals that they cut up for food. They know about bone structure, veins, and various organs. In my discussions with them they described the inside of the body as consisting of the following parts: *ontó* (tongue), *amdjôro* (heart), *baga kríti* (lungs), *bá* (liver), *tú* (stomach), *ankré* (probably the pancreas), *kukatíre arína* (kidneys), *ôtxó* (bladder), and *batxó*, which from their description that it has "green water inside it" I took to be the gall bladder. Drawings by a number of informants (the best is reproduced in Figure 7) showed a complicated pattern of connections between those various parts, but the basic structure was simple. The inside of the body was always shown as a line running from the head (containing the tongue) to the genitals, *txôto* (penis) and *grénikô* (scrotum). As to the function of these organs, they say that those higher up (heart, lungs, liver, stomach, and pancreas) require "a lot of water to purify the blood." The genitals need less water. The presence or absence of water is fundamental to the way the Apinayé classify the various organs and to the way they think the body functions. Their account of physiology consists

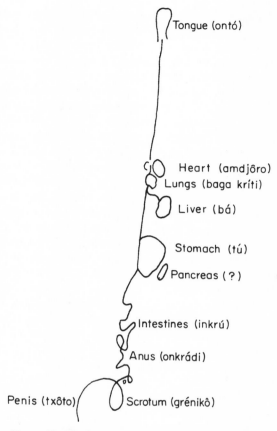

Figure 7. *The human body as drawn by Grossinho.*

of the action of a few basic substances that form and maintain the body and that also account for its extinction. Water (*kó*), blood (*kãbrô*), mother's milk (*kó-kagô*, "white water"), and sperm (*hôko*) are the most important. When they drink water a series of organs transforms it into blood, hence the more water one drinks the more blood one will have. Old people, thin people, and babies, who drink little water, consequently have little blood and dry skin. The same process takes place with food. Meat is always considered in terms of the amount of water and blood that it contains.

In common with the other Gê, Apinayé notions of sex and childbirth are quite accurate in a number of respects. They know that menstruation (*kãbrô*) ceases on pregnancy. They say that the placenta (*kratí*) is "the child's companion" and they bury it immediately. They know of the changes that pregnancy causes in a woman's abdomen and breasts, and that breast milk appears only in pregnancy. Along with these notions, they also say that a woman cannot menstruate until she has had sexual intercourse. Defloration causes a woman to begin menstruating, and it is menstruation that indicates whether a woman is pregnant or not. The important implication here is that a man is necessary to fulfill one of the most basic aspects of a woman's physiology. Without a man's intervention, a woman would lack the basic physiological mechanism that endows her with her distinctive natural characteristics.

Conception and birth result from the mixing of masculine and feminine substances. A man marries a woman who is a virgin and first causes her to menstruate by having sexual intercourse with her. When his sperm mixes with her menstrual blood she becomes pregnant. Thus the child is formed partly by the father and partly by the mother. Some Apinayé say that the father gives the child its bones (which are white, like sperm), as well as its flesh and skin, and the mother gives the child its blood. Others say that the mother gives more in the formation of the child since the quantity of menstrual blood is greater than that of the father's sperm. When menstrual blood and sperm are mixed a potential human being is formed,[9] "potential" because to the Apinayé the conception of a new human being is more than a simply physical matter; it also requires certain social procedures. First, a man and a woman must copulate (*baguni*) constantly. Then they must become a unit distinct from all other social groups.

Constant sexual intercourse is required for the child to grow properly in the mother's womb.[10] If a man dies soon after his wife has become pregnant, it is said that the child will be born weak and will not develop properly. They also say that two or more men can be a child's genitors if they have had intercourse with the mother during her pregnancy. But although they recognize this as a possibility, they attach little importance to it, saying that it is only the "pater" who should properly be the "genitor."

The notion that it is necessary to copulate a great deal to form a child has social implications. Ideally Apinayé marriage is a monogamous union in which a man and a woman form a social and economic unit providing a context in which children will develop into mature adults. Copulating a great deal to form a child not only reflects the idea that a man and a woman should have an exclusive sexual relationship; it also implies that the couple should provide a family context that is devoted to the well-being of the future child. This emphasis on the unity of the nuclear family (which emerges over time as an autonomous unit within the society) is summed up in the notion of *piangrí*. The word seems to be composed of *piâm* (respect, shame) and the suffix *grí*. It has connotations of protection, avoidance, and precaution, and it describes the period of seclusion associated with childbirth.

I have described a pattern of formal behavior that is essentially careful and precautionary and that is appropriate in those relationships requiring respect, shame, or social distance (*piâm*). It is an etiquette that governs one's manner of speaking, gestures, and general behavior as a member of a social group. Relationships between affines require formal behavior of this kind. So also does the relationship between formal friends. Briefly, the relationship between such friends (*krã-geti/pá-krã*) is one of considerable formality and requires the greatest amount of *piâm* from both parties. A man should treat his *krã-geti* (and a woman her *krã-gedy*) with exemplary respect. If, for example, a man is about to kill someone and his *krã-geti* intervenes and advises against it, he should immediately give up his intention. If he gets angry with his formal friend, he may go blind in one eye, or his body may break out in lumps. Among the Apinayé these relationships that are so full of *piâm* have that "mystical influence" that according to Leach is characteristic of relationships of affinity (Leach 1961:9).

Piangrí, the precautionary behavior associated with childbirth, is of a quite different character. In this case the formalized behavior is for the Apinayé a rationalization of biological facts, stressing the unity of the family. The emphasis is not on any mystical link but on the actual biological links between husband, wife, and children. *Piangrí* refers to the period of seclusion during and following the birth of a child, and it has to be considered alongside two other types of ritual seclusion followed by the Apinayé. The first of these is *amnía angrí*, referring to the period of seclusion that a man must observe after he has killed an enemy. *Amnía* is reflexive, and a rough translation of the expression would be: "the safeguards I take on my own behalf." The Apinayé themselves refer to this in Portuguese as "the seclusion of the criminal." The second is *amní kãbrô iangrí*, which describes the period of seclusion observed by a menstruating woman (*kãbrô* meaning "blood"). The seclusion of the killer and of the menstruating woman are both "reflexive" in that the person undertakes the procedure for his or her own benefit. The period of seclusion associated with the birth of a child is a collective undertaking for the benefit of husband, wife, and child. Yet there are important common features in all three rites of seclusion.

The Apinayé consider blood a vital substance essential for all kinds of animal and human life. Blood gives one the capacity to move, and it accounts for qualities like aggression, strength of will, and vigor, hence old people and children have little or nothing of these qualities. They are at extreme points on the continuum of life: old people are approaching death, and children are still very close to nature. The process of growing old is seen as a gradual loss of blood. Blood and water, both vital substances, are volatile and can escape from the body. Under normal circumstances blood escapes gradually, causing the skin to dry up and ultimately resulting in death. When someone suffers a cut, blood escapes

violently and the person can die. I once witnessed a man being treated
who had accidentally cut a vein in his foot with a machete. He lost a lot of
blood, which the Indians kept the dogs away from. Later, when he had
recovered, the man explained: "That day I nearly lost my *me-karon*
[image, shadow, soul]." The "soul" leaves a body that has lost its blood,[11]
although the soul is thought to have a kind of blood of its own. This is a
weak, pale, greenish blood described as *gran-gran,* the term for both
green and yellow, and it is thought of as a "vegetable" blood.[12] The process of aging and of gradually losing one's life is therefore associated with
the idea that one's blood becomes gradually weaker. This suggests that
"blood" and "soul" are equated. A further point is that having a great
deal of blood is considered to make a person heavy. Women are therefore
considered heavy in contrast to the masculine ideal of lightness and
speed. This explains why males undergoing initiation rites are subjected
to a diet and why they are sometimes deliberately cut in order to draw off
some blood (Nimuendajú 1939:72).

The Apinayé say that all three types of seclusion are undertaken because of blood. In the case of seclusion following the killing of an enemy,
blood, the vital substance that has been taken from the dead man, contaminates the killer. Blood is more than simply a liquid. It is thought of as
a fluid with a powerful smell. Being volatile, it contaminates the killer
and introduces into his body more blood (and more soul) than is normal.[13] The soul of the dead man also remains close to the killer and this
can cause madness. For the killer to be restored to normality the social
relationship established with his victim must be broken. During his seclusion the killer eats the flesh of the hairy armadillo (*Euphractus s. fla-
viaramus; aptxête* in Apinayé) mixed with a great deal of pepper. The armadillo then takes revenge by eating the body of the dead man. This gets
rid of the body and its contaminating fluids more quickly. When a man
kills someone else he creates a physical tie between himself and his victim. This is dangerous, and the purpose of the period of seclusion is to effect the separation of the killer from his victim. This type of seclusion involves only the killer.

The reason given for the seclusion of a menstruating woman is that she
is weak because she is losing a lot of blood. She must remain within her
house and must not work. She must not have intercourse. Indeed, anyone
coming near her would become hot (women and blood are both considered hot), weak, and listless. Above all a woman must keep away from the
gardens. Her seeing the gardens would be enough to attract fire ants (also
red, like blood), which would eat all the plants. She should eat only well-
cooked food, such as manioc bread, and should not eat certain kinds of
meat that are considered *onduí* (unpleasant, heavy). This includes paca
(*Coelogenis paca; grá* in Apinayé), which has very soft fur and would
cause the woman's hair to fall out. She should take particular care not to

eat anything that lives in or near water: fish or the land turtle (*Testudo tabulata; kaprán* in Apinayé). Eating these animals would cause a great loss of blood, there being a close relationship between water and blood. When a man marries a woman who is still a virgin, he too must observe the period of seclusion when her first menstruation appears (Nimuendajú 1939:75). Because of the care taken to avoid the excessive loss or evaporation of blood during this period, a woman should not scratch herself with her fingers but should use a small scratching stick (Nimuendajú 1939:75). (The scratching sticks are little used today.) Hence in certain cases the seclusion of a menstruating woman also involves her partner. The link between them is stressed in terms of a physical substance: blood.

It seems apparent that menstruation not only means that a woman loses some of her vital substance but that it also contaminates the man who is responsible for the loss. This would explain why the Apinayé say that a man observes the seclusion "because he owes blood." Furthermore, since a woman is subject to recurrent losses of blood (and therefore of a part of her soul), we can understand why the Apinayé, like the Kayapó, think of menstruation as an illness (*kané*). The Kayapó regard menstruation as normal only if the woman is young and unmarried. Since married women are in a permanent procreative relationship with a man, it is considered abnormal that they menstruate and they should try to avoid doing so by using certain drugs (Bamberger 1965).

The most elaborate type of seclusion is that associated with birth. It involves both husband and wife; it continues after the birth of the child; and it is later reactivated should any member of the family fall ill. The mother observes birth restrictions for two months and the father for four. It is explained that restrictions on the mother are of shorter duration because she has to breast-feed the baby and therefore has to eat "so that the making of the child will be completed." Today the restrictions are not completely adhered to and many young women say that they could not put up with the long seclusion that was required in earlier times. I did, however, see older people observe a two-month seclusion. Traditionally a man would wait for twenty days before bathing in the river and would stay in the house, near his wife, doing only light household tasks. Bathing in the river would send his blood to his head and make all his hair fall out.

The Apinayé explain that the restrictions are principally for the well-being of the child. Here, as in other areas of the social system, the idea of process is fundamental. The child is made gradually and grows gradually after it is born. Hence, as one informant explained, "the seclusion is to safeguard the child's blood, which is still very weak." Newborn babies (*karô-re*), who "cannot see and who do not know anything," have very little blood, and the quantity increases very slowly.[14] While the quantity of blood increases the child goes through a critical transition from nature to society, and the parents must take great care to see that nothing goes wrong. Restrictions have to be followed until the child is about two or three years old (*prin-re*), that is, when it has become strong enough to walk. Walking indicates that its blood and soul are, as the Indians say, "guaranteed." The formation of both body and soul depends on the gradual increase of blood. Hence blood is responsible for the child's physical and social characteristics. The parents, or more precisely the genitors, have the greatest responsibility for the child's development since their association with the child is so complete. Everything associated with them is associated with the child, and it has not yet emerged completely from the natural world. The Apinayé therefore explain food prohibitions in the following way: "The parents do not eat meat because the child has not yet eaten it. The child is very young and only knows its mother's milk. It does not know of meat yet. So its parents do not eat meat either."

There are a number of specific ailments that can result from breaking food prohibitions. If the parents ate armadillo the child would get *coruba,* an inflammation of the skin. Deer meat is full of blood and eating it would result in the child's death, for its blood would increase too quickly. Eating fish causes diarrhea in the child. If the parents ate monkey the child would stay away all night (as monkeys do). Eating seriema (*Microdactylus cristatus; brekê* in Apinayé), a bird that is constantly moving about, produces madness. Eating rats would make the child cry for water at night because rats like water, and so on. There are certain animals that, if eaten by the father, affect mother and child in different ways. If the father eats caititu (a wild pig, *Dicotyles tayassu; amgrô-re* in Apinayé), the child will go mad and die, but the mother will not be affected. If he eats tapir or coati the child will get diarrhea but again no harm will come to the mother. But if the father eats rhea, only the mother will be affected. The father is therefore responsible for the well-being of both the child and the mother. The mother, by contrast, can affect only the child and not the father. The asymmetry probably indicates that the biological tie between mother and child is maintained during the period when she is breast-feeding.

Obligatory restrictions observed by members of a nuclear family to protect one another may be reactivated at any period of a person's life. If a parent falls ill, the children are expected to observe restrictions. Siblings do so for one another, and parents observe restrictions for their children's sake. The symmetry apparent in these relationships is not found among the Shavante nor among the Kayapó, where a child cannot prejudice its father's health (Maybury-Lewis 1967:66; T. Turner 1966:xvii).

The various seclusions and prohibitions that the Apinayé have to observe concern those occasions when a person becomes particularly vulnerable to certain influences. Because a person may be affected by the soul or blood of food, excessive consumption of certain vegetables or animals may provoke illness (cf. Nimuendajú 1939:146). To cure the sickness the patient must be separated from the agent that caused it, and food prohibitions are an obvious way of doing this. Loss of blood, or causing blood to be lost by killing someone, also places a person in a state of liminality. As in other illnesses, a vital substance is lost. The soul, the essence of a person's physical and social being, is located in the blood, hence any loss of blood leaves a person particularly susceptible to illness or even death. In general, these notions express a lack of harmony between the social world of human beings and the natural world of animals and spirits.[15] From a sociological point of view, these ideas are important because they allow distinctions to be drawn between different individuals and different groups by discriminating between social relationships and physical relationships.

Illness is seen as a dangerous conjunction of two *me-karon* within the same body, and curing consists of separating these entities again. A man who has killed another is exposed to a similar danger, and a menstruating woman is also periodically exposed to a dangerous contact with nature that results in the loss of her vital fluids.

In pregnancy and birth the problem is the reverse. The danger to the child is that it might revert to blood and return to the world of nature. The process of rescuing the child from the natural world has two stages. First, a disjunction has to be established between the child and the natural world, hence the food prohibitions on those animals considered *ondui.* Then the child has to be placed in contact with the people who are responsible for its transition between nature and culture. Thus the process of disjunction is followed by a process of conjunction in which parents and their children are brought together.

The process of disjunction effected by the birth restrictions is of the same kind as that effected in the other rites of seclusion. The parents observe food prohibitions and avoid any strenuous activity that might cause them to sweat and lose water from the body. Any contact of this kind with the natural world would cause death or some kind of behavior that could not be socially controlled, as in the case of a sick person adopting the behavior of the animal that has made him ill. The process of conjunction is effected by establishing an identity between the child and his genitors. A structural analysis of Apinayé birth restrictions suggests that this relationship of identity is the crucial principle that explains the sociological importance of the rites.

The reason why the father observes food prohibitions and avoids certain kinds of behavior is not, as Tylor (1889) suggested, because he wishes to call attention to himself and in so doing establish his own line of descent. It is clear that *both* the father and the mother observe the food prohibitions, and they do so because the child has not yet eaten those kinds of food. Hence the so-called couvade cannot be explained as the father imitating the mother, nor as a set of magical beliefs that attempt to combat the high incidence of infant mortality, as Fock (1960:143) would have it. It is certainly the case that the parents to a certain extent "imitate" the child.[16] Yet we know that this explanation is not sufficient, for the precautions followed by the Apinayé when a birth takes place are only one of a series of rites whose purpose is to restore order by separating domains that have been brought into a dangerous conjunction. This is done by drawing attention to group boundaries and to the distinctions between various social fields. Thus, if any member of a nuclear family falls ill, everyone else in the family will observe the same food prohibitions as the sick person. The principles of identification and separation draw attention to the physical ties that hold the nuclear family together.

From a structural point of view the problem of the couvade—like the problem of totemism—disappears. These ethnological puzzles, as Lévi-Strauss (1962) has shown, can be reduced to basic social mechanisms that are used to classify and categorize groups and social relationships.

For the Apinayé, the relationships within the nuclear family are defined by links of physical substance. Human beings are formed by the mixture of the vital fluids of the parents: mother's blood and father's sperm. The family is a veritable factory of social production and reproduction. In cosmological terms one might say that the nuclear family is the domain that transforms natural products (food, blood, sperm) into potential human beings.

Looking at the Apinayé nuclear family in this way allows us to understand the cycle of development through which it passes. It begins with marriage. Since marriage among the Apinayé is not defined in terms of prescriptive categories, wives are simply considered distant, that is, not related to the husband. But since the nuclear family is based on genetic relationships of blood, once the marriage becomes established, the purely social link between spouses is transformed into a biological link. The Apinayé say that a woman has the same blood as her husband because, as they put it, the couple are "plaiting" their vital substances. In an even more poetic turn of phrase they explain that the couple "sleep in the same heat," that is, they sleep intertwined with each other. The social relationship is genuinely transformed into a biological one, because the appearance of children turns the abstract relationship into something that has material existence. The relationships that spread out around the nuclear family may also be considered actual physical ties of blood, but these may not all be considered equally strong. In unilineal descent groups, ties between members tend to be considered all of a kind, but in this case relationships become weaker and more tenuous the further away they are from the nuclear family itself. This is represented in Figure 8. "Culture" and "nature" and the categories of kin and affine are all brought together within the circle representing the nuclear family. It is an area in which

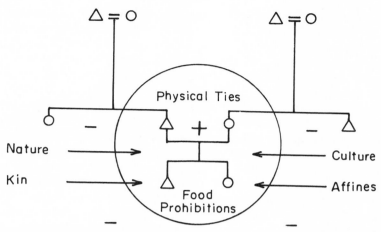

Figure 8. *The Apinayé nuclear family distinguished from surrounding relationships.*

distinctions between those categories dissolve. The plus sign within the circle represents the strong physical ties between its members, and the minus signs indicate the gradual weakening of what the Apinayé regard as blood ties. Eating restrictions are therefore observed only on behalf of other members of the nuclear family. One informant explained the matter in more or less these words:

> The only relatives that, because of their blood, oblige one to observe restrictions are one's father, mother, children, and one's brothers and sisters. One does not observe restrictions on account of a grandchild [who, among the Apinayé and the other Northern Gê, is classified along with opposite sex sibling's children]. When someone is seriously ill, the close family [that is, the nuclear family] has to observe food prohibitions and eat only what the sick person eats. One does not have to do this on behalf of grandchildren and nephews because the blood is far away and weak. One would only observe restrictions for a grandchild or a cousin if its mother had died and if my wife had breast-fed it and brought it up. But if we take in the child after it is weaned we do not have to observe food prohibitions on its behalf.

In his explanation, the informant puts an interesting emphasis on one of the essential aspects of Apinayé ideology, namely the gradation that exists between different social ties. Relationships between members of a nuclear family always have a firm physiological justification, but moving away from this center, relationships become more tenuous as the physiological links grow weaker. This is why imperative duties exist only between parents, children, and siblings. A son or daughter should always help his or her parents, and siblings can call on one another for help in a variety of situations. If a man brings home meat, it should be shared first with parents and then with siblings. More tenuous relationships outside the nuclear family may be given more or less emphasis in appropriate circumstances. Thus, if for some reason the relationship between a man and his grandfather or uncle (both classified as *geti*) becomes socially important, they may wish to emphasize their physical bond of common blood.

There are a number of social factors that interfere with the unity of the nuclear family. The most conspicuous is the rule of uxorilocal residence, which separates brothers from one another and interrupts the intimate social contact they had when they lived in the same house. The same rule separates brothers and sisters, but in this case one can see that the rule that separates them also reflects the basic physiological differences between men and women. They are separated both by the rule of uxorilocal marriage and by the fact that, according to Apinayé physiology, the sister has more blood than the brother and is therefore heavier than he.

The nuclear family is clearly distinguished from the other blood relationships that surround it. The strength of these surrounding ties is a matter of degree and depends on how far a person is reckoned to be from the Ego. This allows considerable room in which to maneuver in classifying people, and manipulating the system is particularly important with respect to those relatives nearest the nuclear family. A person may be able to manipulate the system to his advantage by asking someone to fulfill certain obligations and justifying his request through appeals to ties of blood.

The Apinayé social system is made up of two kinds of relationships: those that are justified in purely physiological terms and that center around the nuclear family, and those that are strictly social or ceremonial, for which the Apinayé do not use any kind of physiological metaphors. Both, of course, concern social relations between people, but only the first kind is described in a biological idiom. Hence the Apinayé world consists of two complementary areas: domestic life and "social" or ceremonial life. The second takes the form of ritual and political obligations. Both are part of everyday life, but it is important to understand that the Apinayé regard them as distinct, separate domains. The ceremonial domain of Apinayé life is a system of relationships established as a counterpart to that built around the nuclear family.

3

Ceremonial Life

*D*OMESTIC LIFE among the Apinayé is organized around certain social groups, namely the nuclear families and the uxorilocal extended families. Family groups form what we might call the *continuum* of everyday life. As the Apinayé become increasingly involved in local Brazilian society, their ceremonial life tends to disappear; hence at the present time social life is becoming more and more centered around these family groups.

The ideology of the family group has a biological infrastructure that can also be seen in terms of a continuum. The continuity consists of blood ties that weaken progressively as they get further away from the nuclear family, the paradigmatic focus of such ties. Thus the idea of a biological continuity between all the members of Apinayé society is rooted in the ideology of the nuclear family. As a result of this network of biological ties, it is difficult to establish the boundaries of kindreds, for, as the Apinayé themselves say: "Blood is dispersed throughout the village."

But in addition to these relationships there are others that the Indians clearly recognize as nonbiological. They are not justified in terms of blood, for they are outside the immediate network of relationships established around the nuclear family. I call these "social" or ceremonial relationships, which is very close to the way the Apinayé themselves describe them. This does not mean that the Indians think of "social" relationships as less important than "biological" ones. Both obviously involve social ties. It is simply a distinction that divides their relationship system into two dimensions,[1] one composed of persons related biologically, where ties are justified in terms of blood, and another composed of persons related by formal or ceremonial ties that are established at birth. Social ties and blood ties are both fundamental ordering principles that give coherence to the system. The logic of proportioning the system rests, as Melatti (1970, 1978) clearly established, in the greater or lesser emphasis given to the biological relationships, which concern reproduction, and the social relationships, which are involved in the ceremonies.

There is a clear contrast between Apinayé daily life and ceremonial life. The public, ceremonial domain is associated with the plaza in the center of the village, and the collective ritual activity is organized by moieties that stand in a balanced relationship of complementary opposition. Hence, whereas daily life is an unbroken continuum of repetitive activities—visits, gossiping, working at home or in the garden, casual conversations, informal exchanges of food—ceremonial life takes place in a context of clearly defined discontinuities. Here individuals and groups are separated from the area of ordinary, everyday life, and relationships are reorganized in terms of another social order. It is in terms of this ceremonial domain that the Indians can best make sense of their own society, for in this realm everything is stereotyped, formal, integrated, and theoretical. It is no accident that when the Apinayé talk of their own society, their descriptions give obvious priority to their ceremonies. Indeed, Nimuendajú's emphasis on ceremonial life in his descriptions of the Canela and the Apinayé (1939, 1946) reveals that he took this domain to be the very *social structure* of both these peoples (Da Matta 1967).

Seen in terms of its ceremonies, the Apinayé system can be understood as a set of discrete social groups and relationships, established by means of well-defined rules. In a domestic context, where relationships are based on a biological continuum, it can be difficult for an individual to say just where his group of relatives ends, but in the ceremonial domain he knows exactly how the groups are composed and discriminated as well as the social relationships associated with each one. The contrastive opposition between the groups is an essential part of their conception as discrete units. Hence, given an individual's name, the Apinayé know exactly which ceremonial group that person belongs to. But it may be much more difficult to say whether or not that person is a relative.

The only way to distinguish one group of relatives from another is to look for certain practical criteria. Residence, for instance, is a prominent factor in deciding membership in a family group. But even when such distinctions are made, it is always possible, at least in theory, to find a relationship between two different domestic groups by taking a "pivotal relative" as a point of reference. Ceremonial groups, by contrast, are practically and conceptually distinct. There are no gradations between them, and they are clearly distinguished by changes of names and of formal friends.

In the following description of the ceremonial groups I pay particular attention to the principles whereby membership is established. My account is based largely on secondhand information, especially with regard to the actual ceremonies, for the ceremonial side of Apinayé life is in a state of decay. Nevertheless, the ceremonial groups persist and the Indians still readily discuss the ways in which these groups are formed. Although the groups are not as active as they once were, all members of Apinayé society belong to them and can point out those persons responsible for their induction into them. The reader should bear in mind that I am describing a set of social rules that still persists even though it does not find expression in practice. In addition, one should remember that the decline of traditional social practices is an interesting fact in itself since it can reveal certain conditions and potentialities inherent in the nature of the social system.

An Outline of the Ceremonial Groups

The Apinayé always refer to the ceremonial groups by their proper names. The general term for these groups is *pikiyê-re* or *pikizê-re*, meaning "part," or "division," but it is unusual to hear someone use the term. The word *kiyê*, which according to Nimuendajú (1939:29ff.) referred to a set of special groups whose function was to regulate marriage, was not understood by my informants. Unlike domestic groups, the ceremonial groups are not immediately apparent in everyday life. Domestic groups can be seen working together in the gardens or in the home, or they may appear in the form of political factions. They are formed and reorganized according to ad hoc relationships between nuclear families and are far more dependent on contingent factors such as residence and frequency of contact, or exchanges of labor and food, than on membership in a specific ceremonial group. I often heard Indians justifying their conduct in terms of kinship relationships, but never in terms of common membership in a ceremonial group. The ceremonial groups are used on a classificatory level to indicate an area where positions and social relationships are reorganized in terms of entities that are by definition both discrete and complementary.

Apinayé ceremonial groups do not regulate marriage and are not the primary basis on which political factions are formed. This is also the case among the other Northern Gê groups, with the exception of the Kayapó, among whom the men's houses are a basic factor in the alignment of factions within the village (T. Turner 1966:chap. 3). But the most singular characteristic of Apinayé ceremonial groups is their total separation from everyday life. Ceremonial groups and domestic groups are like opposite sides of the same coin. They are complementary but do not interconnect and affect each other, as they do among the Kayapó and the Akwẽ-Shavante.

As the Apinayé are becoming more involved in the surrounding economic system, their ceremonial groups are gradually losing their sociological importance, although the Indians still think of their society in terms of these groups (see, for example, Figure 2). Social relationships are being reduced; multiple relations, which formerly produced an equilibrium between the domestic sphere and the ceremonial domain, are progressively giving way to relations derived from residential alignments and from everyday life. Despite this it is still possible to discern that the ceremonial domain is divided into two pairs of groups and that there are two kinds of relationships that determine recruitment into these groups.

Groups and Ceremonial Relationships:
The Problem of Dualism and the *Kolti/Kolre* Moieties

All Apinayé of both sexes belong to either the *Kolti* moiety or the *Kolre* moiety. Membership is handed down along with a person's names. Sometimes, when a person has received two sets of names, he or she can belong to the two groups at the same time. This does not, however, present the individual with a problem of identity or of divided loyalty. Indeed, the Apinayé regard the opportunity to choose one's moiety as an advantage. The decision has to be made only when the festivals take place, for it is only then that the groups become fully active. At that time the individual with double membership, having chosen the group he or she wants to appear with, enjoys all its privileges.

Following Nimuendajú and others, I shall refer to these groups as moieties. The usage is consistent with the way the Indians think of these divisions. The Apinayé, like all other Gê groups, conceive of the universe as a closed totality, wherein all elements are organized two by two in a series of oppositions (see Figure 5, for example). For the Apinayé, ordering the universe consists of creating antitheses between its elements. But in contrast to Christian dualism, the Apinayé do not organize elements in a *relative* manner; that is, they do not explicitly emphasize one unit as prior, preeminent, or more important than its opposite. They try to avoid producing a hierarchy of opposed terms, as happens in the dualism of Catholic theology. In the latter, God and the devil (Good and Evil) are in complementary opposition only when certain aspects of human life need to be interpreted. But since in the Christian tradition God is the supreme creator and the source of everything, and also the final objective of the evolution of man and of the cosmos, it can be said that Christian dualism is *hierarchical, relative, nondialectical,* or, as Lévi-Strauss and Hertz put it, a concentric dualism (Lévi-Strauss 1963:chap. 8; Hertz 1960:96).

Christian dualism is conceived as an integral part of the supreme divinity that created it, yet this dualism in turn creates Lucifer. This paradox produces a set of moral and religious problems. The Manichaean heresies of the Middle Ages can be seen as a radical attempt to confront and interpret the fundamental logical and philosophical problem set by a hierarchical or concentric dualism (Runciman 1960:chap. 7; Weber 1963:44). The reader may recall that in the Manichaean doctrines, Good and Evil are considered parallel, independent creations, it being inconceivable that the source of all Good (God) could also be the source of all Evil.

From a structural perspective Manichaeanism can be seen as a logical solution to a problem of classification. These doctrinal heresies attempted to view the dualism of Good and Evil in an integrated way. And in this sense the problem of Manichaeanism is the perennial problem of all dualism, namely: how to combine two apparently discrete elements, Good and Evil, into an integrated totality.[2]

Apinayé dualism appears similar to Christian or Manichaean dualism depending on one's perspective. Initially it seems relative, like Christian dualism. For the Apinayé, Sun and Moon are the two masculine entities that created order in the universe and in society when they descended to earth, which was then still in chaos. But the Indians always refer to Sun as the principal character. It was he who came to earth and he who usually takes the initiative in the incidents described in the creation myth. It is always Sun who initiates something, which is then immediately upset by Moon. But when one looks at the myth from a more general point of view, it is clear that the existence of Sun is inconceivable without the existence of Moon, in the same way that in Apinayé society it is impossible to have the *Kolti* moiety (associated with and created by Sun) without having the *Kolre* moiety (associated with and created by Moon). Hence from a general point of view Apinayé dualism appears Manichaean. When one looks at the way the elements interact, a tendency toward a hierarchical arrangement is evident: Sun is preeminent, and so, therefore, is the *Kolti* group, which takes precedence in the rituals. But in the hierarchical arrangement one can detect a relationship of polarity and complementary opposition in the relationship of *Kolti* (and Sun) as leaders and *Kolre* (and Moon) as followers:[3]

Sun   Moon
Kolti   *Kolre*
Leader Follower

The purpose of hierarchical ordering is therefore not so much to establish the absolute superiority of one group over the other as simply to establish yet another relationship between two antithetical groups or elements.

The *Kolti* and *Kolre* groups bisect Apinayé society and in this way reduce the diversity of families, of residential groups, and of individuals to a duality that has a complementary form. Since the two groups can exist only as a unit, it is particularly appropriate to refer to them as moieties, a term that emphasizes their relationship of complementary opposition. It is also the most precise way of translating Apinayé notions when they say, for instance, that *Kolti* and *Kolre* are *apten burog* (meaning "identical," "of the same weight," "equal").

The relationship between the moieties is a paradigm of a series of cosmological oppositions. Thus we find the following classic scheme:

Kolti	*Kolre*
sun	moon
day	night
men	women (together with children and old people)
fire	water
summer	winter
right	left
(north)	(south)[4]
east (sunrise)	west (sunset)
savanna	forest
red	black
buriti palm (which has red fruit)	babassu palm (which produces a lot of fruit in winter)
dry season	wet season
"tame" animals	"fierce" animals
tapir	rhea
right	wrong

These oppositions can be extended or contracted. Beginning with any pair one can extend the associations and arrive at all the others. Sun/Moon and *Kolti/Kolre* act as catalyzing elements for more concrete or more abstract pairs of oppositions (Lévi-Strauss 1966:chap. 5). Hence the scheme above moves from oppositions between more concrete elements such as tapirs (*Tapirus americanus*) and rheas (*Rhea americana*),[5] or "tame" and "fierce" animals, to highly abstract ones, like the antithetical ways of behaving that I have loosely translated as right and wrong.

A classificatory system of this kind has two advantages. First, it effects a radical reduction of empirical reality by uniting entities, elements, objects, and human beings in a single formula. It makes it possible to bring some order to the heterogeneity of animal species; to order colors by arranging them along an axis that opposes them with regard to their proximity to red and black; and to arrange the periodicity of the seasons in harmony with other parts of the cosmos. In short, the system integrates the social and the natural order by means of a series of reductions. As Bergson (1935) and Evans-Pritchard (1937) pointed out, such a system endows everything in the natural world with a human significance.

The second advantage, which is primarily sociological, is that these oppositions make it possible to focus on certain aspects of society while ignoring others. The *Kolti/Kolre* division emphasizes a certain number of distinctive features peculiar to those who belong to one or the other group. Whereas in everyday life individuals are separated and united into different groups according to their residential groupings, nuclear families, or political factions, ceremonial life classifies people according to the relationships involved in the transmission of proper names. The social system becomes organized through a dichotomy between individuals and groups that is quite different from that which ordinarily occurs. *Kolti* and *Kolre* realign social relationships according to principles that cut across the entire society, drawing individuals into the more universal dimensions of the system. Victor Turner has pointed out that the Ndembu of Zambia use a similar mechanism whereby "the categorical relationships are ritualized in opposed pairs and in this way a transference is made from struggles between corporate groups to the polarization of social categories" (V. Turner 1968:138–139). Similarly, among the Apinayé the division into *Kolti* and *Kolre* directs social behavior toward more fundamental and universal categories, such as the opposition between sexes, ages, and marital status.

Often the *Kolti* and *Kolre* moieties form the basis for the teams that take part in the well-known log races, found among all the Gê groups of Central Brazil. Nimuendajú writes: "The two opposing teams are recruited from the men and youths of the two moieties. As among the Serente and the Eastern Timbira, the race starts from the place where the logs are manufactured and ends in the plaza" (1939:113–114). The Apinayé also hold other races "that do not create any stir, being merely organized by a handful of men returning to the village from some joint labors" (ibid.:114). In both kinds of races, however, the division into two competing groups stresses the physical act of the race and not its result. Thus one can see the log races as an activity situated between ritual (which produces conjunction) and competitive games (which produce disjunction) (Lévi-Strauss 1966:32). When I asked the Apinayé about the competitive aspect of log races, they said that although there were occasionally discussions about which team had won and which had lost, the ideal was for both teams to arrive together in the village.[6] Whether they would see it as a game or a ritual seems to depend on a variety of circumstances.

The *Kolti/Kolre* division is essential during the two phases of the initiation rites. The moiety division appears as soon as the young initiates (at this time called *pẽb-kaág, kaág* meaning "false" or "synthetic") are separated from their maternal homes. Not only are the log-racing teams formed but features peculiar to each moiety are marked in a number of ways to bring out the contrast between them. The following are some examples of how the contrast is established:

1. When leaders of the initiation rites are chosen, their names are always associated with *Kolti* or *Kolre.*
2. When emblems such as ear and lip plugs and feathered headbands are worn, a *Kolti* man chooses those with red feathers and a *Kolre* man those with black.
3. Each moiety has its peculiar style of dancing and singing, and the *Kolti* moiety always takes precedence in rituals and sports.
4. When the groups take up their special positions in camps to the east of the village, the *pẽb* (young men) of the *Kolti* moiety always take the north (or right) side, and those of the *Kolre,* the south (or left).
5. The *pẽb* are always divided into *Kolti* and *Kolre* when they take part in collective activities. Even the young girls involved in these rituals are attached to one or the other of the groups.

These contrasts divide the initiates into groups that have, temporarily, a corporate character. This is facilitated by the use of emblems, different places of meeting, distinct styles of dancing and singing, and so on. However, the division is never followed through to its final conclusion. The distinction between *Kolti* and *Kolre* produces a complementary opposition and not a total separation. The ritual activities of one moiety complement those of the other; it is as if the Apinayé want to indicate that each group is essential to the performance of the ritual. This is clearly borne out during the initiation rituals. During the second part of the ritual, the initiates are divided into the *Kolti* and *Kolre* moieties and perform a ritual game called *peny-tág,* in which small balls of latex are thrown from one group to the other (Nimuendajú 1939:61ff.). As is made clear both in the ritual itself and in the myth that serves as its text,[7] the purpose of the game is to gain possession of the balls. Passing the balls between the groups therefore shows that both groups share the same ritual objectives.

In a series of articles devoted to understanding rites of passage Victor Turner suggests that these rites direct people's attention toward certain fundamental aspects of their society (V. Turner 1967:chap. 4). In the Apinayé case, the continuous use of the *Kolti/Kolre* dichotomy during the initiation ritual and the disproportionate emphasis placed on emblems, meeting places, and dancing and singing styles peculiar to each group indicate that dualism and complementary opposition are basic principles of Apinayé society.

Domestic and ceremonial life are concerned with different relationships and different groups. The *Kolti* and *Kolre* moieties are as important in the ritual and ideal domain as houses and nuclear families are in the domestic sphere. The initiation ritual takes the initiate out of the maternal household and introduces him into another set of relationships that have greater public importance.

Proper Names and the *Kolti* and *Kolre* Moieties

Each moiety has its own repertoire of proper names. By learning an individual's names, therefore, one can tell to which moiety he belongs. I found it impossible to collect an exhaustive list of names associated with each moiety because after my informants listed about ten names, they would simply say that there were no more. What is known about Apinayé names and name-giving suggests that there is indeed a finite repertoire of names.

Apinayé names are sets of at least four separate words. Many names can be translated. Others have no literal sense, being rather sociological signs that indicate a person's right to perform certain ceremonial roles. A name may also have various forms, for instance, Tamgáaga (a name that gives the bearer the right to a ceremony in which, among other things, wives are exchanged) is recited in five forms when it is transmitted: "Tamgaá-ti, Tamgaága-glú-ti, Tamgaága-rerég-ti, Tamgaá-ga rãtém-ti, Tamgaága-rái-ti" (see this formula in Nimuendajú 1939:24).

The Apinayé distinguish two kinds of names, *ixtí máati,* "great names" (*máati* meaning "large"), and *ixtí kakríte,* "little names." The first are associated with ceremonial roles whereas the second are not. The Kayapó make a similar distinction, and in both societies the relatives of those who are given great names have to organize a ceremony for the recipient (T. Turner 1966:170). But the basic difference between these two systems of name-giving is that Kayapó great names are not associated with the moiety division, nor indeed with any specific ceremonial group. The activities that take place during Kayapó festivals involve the entire local group, and the great names serve only to set apart a small number of people. By contrast, Apinayé great names are always associated with one of the moieties to the extent that some of them, such as Vanmen and Katam, are used as substitutes for the words *Kolti* and *Kolre.* Furthermore, Apinayé great names are associated with specific ceremonial roles.

The following table lists some Apinayé great names and indicates the associated moiety and ceremonial role (Nimuendajú 1939:24ff.).

Kolti	*Kolre*	*Ceremonial role*
Tegatóro	Rãraké	Leaders of the initiation ceremonies
Amdyí	Koko	Girls associated with the *pẽb* in initiation rites
Konduká	Konduprin	Those with the right to demand food for their ceremonies

Pánti   Ngrére   Those whose fathers (pater, not genitor) are
                         obliged to organize a festival that involves
                         the special preparation of a garden. When
                         the maize planted there is ripe, the inhabi-
                         tants of all the surrounding villages are in-
                         vited to the celebration, which is character-
                         ized by extramarital license

Since each name indicates a specific role, it tends to be used as a title.
Consequently there emerge two groups of titles associated in turn with
one or the other of the moieties.

Certain resemblances and differences between the Apinayé system of
names and those of the Kayapó and the Eastern Timbira (the Krahó,
Canela, and Kríkatí) are noteworthy. Like the Kayapó, the Apinayé
make a distinction between "great" and "little" names, but Apinayé great
names refer to the moiety division whereas Kayapó names do not. Both
the Eastern Timbira and the Apinayé have naming groups, but among
the Apinayé these groups are never dissociated from the moieties,
whereas among the Eastern Timbira *groups with common names* are of
special importance since they form a system *parallel* to the moieties (Nimuendajú 1946:77ff.; Melatti 1970, 1979; Lave 1967:chap. 5).

Among the Kayapó a very young child cannot be given a ceremonial
name, for such names are potent and dangerous and can be lethal (T.
Turner 1976:171). The Apinayé (and the Krahó, Canela, and Kríkatí)
have no such mystical beliefs about names and give a set to a child soon
after it is born. This can even be done prior to its birth, and the person
who bestows a name when the mother is still pregnant establishes a special relationship with the child and its parents. This explains why there
are men with women's names, and vice versa (Nimuendajú 1939:22). The
only important prohibition is that the true parents, *pam* and *nã kumrendy*
(that is, the genitors), cannot give their own names to their children. As
the Apinayé themselves explain: "This would not be proper since the parents have already made the body of the child."

Names are transmitted in sets, and the formation of these sets depends
on how many people give their names to a specific child. Hence a particular set of names is derived from other sets, which themselves have no
fixed form. Thus although the repertoire of names is finite and associated
with the *Kolti* and *Kolre* moieties, the transmission and organization of
these names into sets of four, five, or up to eight or nine names allow for
an inexhaustible number of combinations. Combining names in this way
is quite sufficient to indicate a person's individuality, for every man and
woman has a certain set of names that is a reflection of the repertoire of
names available in the village and of the persons who bestowed the

names. The names I collected in the field suggest such various combinations. If each Apinayé had only one name-giver the sets of names would probably acquire a certain rigidity, and it would follow that a person's ceremonial roles would be immediately recognizable. But because it is possible to have more than one name-giver, the sets are always changing and reforming. Thus the sets of names are subject to permutations that greatly increase their capacity to individualize.

The Apinayé are not, of course, walking computers. Ordinarily a person is known by just one of his names, and the others are temporarily held in abeyance. Nowadays ceremonial activity is declining, and the moiety division is seldom formed. As a result many people, especially the young, have difficulty remembering all their names. Sometimes even parents cannot remember all the names of their children. "Ask the person who gave the name," they say to the perplexed anthropologist. Whereas in our society names are associated with our "families" and each discrete family group has its own set of names, among the Apinayé and Timbira, names are the property of the ceremonial moieties. Hence one might say that while our names separate people, theirs unite people and are therefore used as classificatory devices. This becomes especially apparent when the Apinayé abbreviate their names, choosing one name from the set instead of using them all.

When collecting names I noticed that after an Indian had told me his names he would go on to mention both who had given them and in what context each one was used as a term of address. Informants always referred to names used in the home "when I was a youngster," then to those used in initiation rites and in later ceremonies. Thus each name has a use according to the specific area of the system in which the individual is placed.

Transmission of Proper Names

Among the Apinayé, the Kayapó, and the other Timbira, the transmission of names involves a name-giver and a name-receiver (Nimuendajú 1946:77; Melatti 1970, 1979; Lave 1967:chap. 5; T. Turner 1966:171). But the Apinayé system is peculiar in that it involves a third person, the one who seeks out or "arranges" the name-giver. The names always pass from the categories *geti* (or *keti*) to a *tamtxúa* in the case of males and from a *tui* (or *tukatui*, or *tui-re*) to a *tamtxúa* in the case of females. When a man receives the name of a *geti* he begins to address this person as *id-krã-tum* and is called in turn *id-krã-dúw* (Nimuendajú 1939:24). These expressions mean "my old head" (*id* = my, *krã* = head, *tum* = old) and "my young head" (*dúw* = young), symbolizing the sense of common identity and solidarity that is expected to hold between people with the same name. Women do not address one another in this way. Female names and the transmission of rights through women are of little importance in establishing membership of ceremonial groups.

The genealogical specifications of these categories are:

Male side: *geti*   = MB, FZH, MF, FF
             tamtxúa = ZC, CC, WBS, WBD (reciprocal specifications for the above)

Female side: *tui* or *tui-re* = FZ, MBW, MM, FM
             tamtxúa = BC, CC, HZS, HZD (reciprocal specifications for the above)

The Apinayé often say that the MB and FZ are the *geti* and *tui* who must give their names to their *tamtxúa*, since these are considered the ideal categories from which names should be passed on. But an examination of genealogies reveals a considerable variation from this ideal. In thirty cases in which the precise genealogical relationship between name-giver and name-receiver could be verified I discovered that only four of those classed as *geti* were MB's. It is significant that all these cases concerned the transmission of names from older men who already had grandchildren. It is possible that the flexibility that allows a *geti* or a *tui-re* to be chosen outside the ideal position is a result of depopulation and the consequent decay of ceremonial life that followed contact with Brazilian society. But the existence of the "arranger of names" indicates that the structure of the system itself permits flexibility and genealogical variation.

When an Apinayé is asked about those who gave names to a certain child, he always indicates the person who arranged the giving of the names. This is the child's adoptive father or adoptive mother, *pam* or *nã kaág*, which the Indians translate as "foster parent" using the Portuguese term *de criação*. It is this peculiarity that explains why Nimuendajú's description of Apinayé naming makes the system appear quite different from the pattern found among other Northern Gê groups (Nimuendajú 1939:22). And indeed, during my first period of fieldwork I made the same mistake, noting the adoptive parents as the child's name-givers. What appeared, of course, was a very odd system, for all father's brothers, actual, adoptive, putative, or classificatory, were name-givers, and the corresponding anomaly appeared on the female side. During my second period in the field I managed to correct the error, and I discovered that in terms of category (as opposed to genealogy)[8] the Apinayé system was not structurally different from the other Northern Gê, given that names always pass from a *geti* to a male *tamtxúa* or from a *tui* or *tui-re* to a female *tamtxúa*.

The Apinayé naming system does differ from that of the Eastern Timbira and the Kayapó in a number of ways, however. First, among the Apinayé the link established between name-giver and name-receiver is not a direct one, as it is among the Eastern Timbira, because an intermediary is involved in passing on the names. The child is first adopted, and it is the adoptive parent who has to find the name-giver.

Second, as with the Eastern Timbira, Apinayé names confer rights to certain ceremonies, but this does not result in the formation of special ceremonial groups separate from the moieties.[9]

Third, the role of the "adoptive parent" among the Apinayé is similar to that of the "adoptive father" among the Kayapó. The "adoptive father" is important during initiation rites, when the child is introduced into the Men's House (T. Turner 1966:145). But the difference is that Apinayé naming incorporates a child into a *moiety;* the institution of the Men's House is not found in Apinayé society.

Finally, Kayapó names have only minor significance in their social system, naming being little more than an appendix to the initiation rites (T. Turner 1966:169). Among the Apinayé (and the Eastern Timbira), naming is of primary importance in classifying individuals and incorporating them into the moieties, and the distinction between the moieties is essential in the rites of passage.

All three societies have in common a prescriptive rule for the transmission of names. Among the Apinayé, names are transmitted prescriptively from a *geti* (or *tui*) to a *tamtxúa*. Although there are statistical variations in the genealogical position of the name-giver, the category remains the same and does not allow for choice.

This is an important point, for it shows how certain differences between the relationship terminologies of Northern Gê groups are variations that result from the application of a single set of rules. That is to say, although the transmission of names is structurally the same, in the sense that all these societies follow the same rules, the actual results can vary considerably. For example, there may be variations in the genealogical positions within the category that can transmit names; in the emphasis given to names as instruments of classification; and in the importance of certain social groups. Such variations produce different terminological results in each case. The same rule can have different sociological results, in the same way that a grammatical code or rule can generate different sentences. Consequently these apparently diverse relationship terminologies can be interpreted in terms of the same set of rules or cultural code. Although Lévi-Strauss (1963:chap. 7) has already established that the Gê groups make use of the same institutional repertoire, we have to follow the example of transformational linguistics in order to explain the specific differences between the groups.

The examples shown in Figures 9–13 illustrate the process of Apinayé naming and show how it reflects fundamental aspects of the relationship system.

The genealogical connection in Figure 9 between Santana's mother

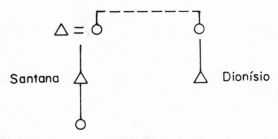

Figure 9. *Santana's daughter.*

and Dionísio's mother is obscure, but informants stated firmly that they are *itõ-ti* (sisters). Consequently, Dionísio is the putative brother of Santana: his *kaág* ("false") brother, as the Apinayé say. When Santana's wife was pregnant, Dionísio offered to arrange names for the future child and declared Santana's mother the child's *tui-re* and name-giver. Thus, though Dionísio may have chosen the name, the name-giver is a *tui-re*.

One of Cândido's mother's sisters decided to adopt his son before it had been named (see Figure 10). Although this woman was a *tui-re* of the child, the relationship was redefined as foster mother/foster child as soon as the parents agreed to the adoption. The woman therefore became Cândido's sister. She declared her own sister (Cândido's mother) the child's name-giver. Naming in this case involved redefining a relationship in such a way that a link was established across generations. A further peculiarity of this case is the transmission of names from a woman to a man.

Kãgrô and Alcides are putative brothers (see Figure 11). Alcides asked Pedro Viado, a *pam-kaág* ("false" or foster father), to give names to the child.

Sebastião suggested that his father, who is also Miguel's father, be the name-giver (see Figure 12). This man named his grandchild, Miguel's son. This case illustrates how names can be passed down within a group

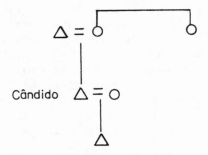

Figure 10. *Cândido's son.*

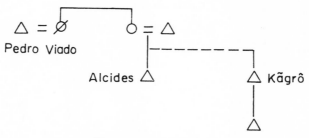

Figure 11. *Kãgrô's son.*

of relatives who form part of the same residential group. The practice is quite common today among the Apinayé and the Timbira.

The case shown in Figure 13 is interesting because the precise genealogical connections are known. Permino and Cândido redefined their cross-relationship as a parallel one, becoming brothers to each other. The genealogical connection justified the alteration, but a more compelling reason was their wish to establish a firmer relationship, Permino being part of a very strong faction and Cândido belonging to an opposed group. Cândido therefore adopted Permino's son and asked his own father's brother to be the name-giver. It is factors like these that produce genealogical redefinitions.

Names and Social Relationships

A "foster" relationship between an adult and an adopted child (that is, between the arranger of names and the name-receiver) is not simply a matter of formality. It is expected to be cordial, like a parent/child relationship, and it also involves a number of obligations. It is said that the *kaág* parent may have to "finish bringing up" the child if its true parents die and if there are no other close relatives to do so. A decision of this kind seldom presents difficulties since ideally the adoptive parent is a sibling of one of the child's real parents (as occurred in the case of Miguel's son). The adoptive parent pays and receives indemnities in the event of adultery, or in the event of divorce when the girl is still a virgin. In cases of theft or murder he has to see to satisfying the stipulated payment, by

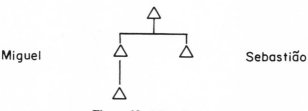

Figure 12. *Miguel's son.*

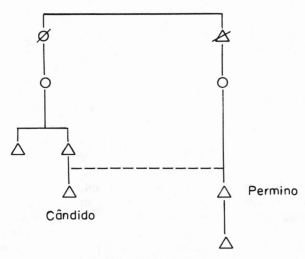

Figure 13. *Permino's son.*

either giving the goods himself or arranging payment from all the of-fender's relatives. He is expected to make up the adornments required for certain ceremonies, especially those that concern formal friends (*krã-geti/pá-krã*). The Apinayé also insist that adoptive parents should inter-vene when their children are involved in a quarrel. In this way the dispute is resolved calmly. One informant said that when the true parents become involved, "the matter always ends in a fight." An adoptive parent is, then, an actual mediator between the domestic area (typified by the child/true parent relationship) and the public area. The relationship established be-tween adoptive parent and child shifts the emphasis from blood and bio-logical paternity to social paternity. The difference between the adoptive parent and the *geti* (*krã-tum/tui*), that is, the actual name-giver who con-fers the rights of incorporation into ceremonial groups, is that the former acts, as it were, in the wings, having a much more important part to play in juridical matters than in ceremonial matters. His relationship with his "child" is not as formal as that between name-giver and named person.[10]

The relationship between name-giver and name-receiver is much more ritualized. Even today, when the social system is losing many of its dis-tinctive traits, the "joking" aspect of these relationships is still obvious. A *geti* will often make fun of a young *tamtxúa* by referring to the boy's lovers, making a point of mentioning women who are either married or very old. The boy reacts with embarrassed laughter. Radcliffe-Brown (1952:chaps. 4 and 5) has shown that joking relationships of this kind are characteristically associated with certain contradictions inherent in the relationship. The basic contradiction in this case is evident in the light of the following two points. First, between name-giver and name-receiver there is a strong ritual relationship. Since both have the same name they fulfill the same ceremonial roles and belong to the same moiety. Names therefore establish a social continuity: they become substitutes for the physical person and they continue to exist when their bearers are dead. Some Apinayé are explicitly aware of this aspect of name-giving and emphasize that passing on one's names to a number of young people is some sort of guarantee of one's social survival.

Second, between name-giver and name-receiver there is also a certain social distance, often simply because they live in different houses and because their residential groups have divergent interests in the business of the village. But the most important reason is that they invariably fall into alternate generations, or into a structurally equivalent position, the adoptive parent being Ego's parent's opposite sex sibling.

The fact that the instructors at initiation ceremonies also bear the title of *geti* (*krã-tum*) is further evidence of the formal character of these relationships and of the mediating role of the *geti* (*krã-tum*). During these rites the group becomes symbolically divided into *krã-tum/krã-duw* (*tamtxúa*). This is an important point, for it reveals a fundamental difference between the systems of the Apinayé and the Kayapó. The principal role assumed by the Apinayé *krã-tum* during these rituals is carried out by an *adoptive father* among the Kayapó. Thus while the two groups of men that form temporarily during Apinayé rites symbolize the name-giver/name-receiver relationship, the corresponding group distinction in Kayapó rites symbolizes the father/son relationship, suggesting that there are important differences between the roles of the adoptive parent among the Apinayé and the Kayapó (T. Turner 1966:chap. 4, part 3).

There are two noteworthy Apinayé ceremonies that give ritual expression to the relationships I have been discussing. One, which emphasizes the adoptive parent/child relationship, is a rite designed to treat a child suffering from accidental soul loss. During this ceremony, soon after the soul has been restored to the child's body by the *vaiangá* (medicine man), an old woman who is a *tui-re* of the child takes a long rod and goes around beating the adoptive parents who, because of their carelessness, are said to be responsible for the loss of the child's soul. Another ceremony, emphasizing the *geti/tamtxúa* relationship, takes place when a child is stung by a hornet. If the child is stung and cries incessantly, one of his *geti* goes off to destroy the hornet's nest. The task is usually done by the child's name-giver, or the *geti* who feels most identified with the child, and in payment he receives food or beads from the child's adoptive parents. An informant explained that the *geti* carries out the task "so that he can be like [*apten burog*] the child."

The most important aspects of the naming system can be summarized as follows: first, a child is not incorporated directly into the *Kolti* and *Kolre* moieties. The involvement of adoptive parents as well as name-

givers means that there is a great deal of choice and variability in the relationships that can be established. Second, the adoption of the child symbolizes a change of its parents. The initial attention given to blood relationships within the nuclear family (seen in the birth restrictions and food
prohibitions) is here shifted to the sociological aspects of parenthood
when parents' siblings become adoptive parents and arrangers of names.
The emphasis is finally transferred to a person in a marginal category
outside the nuclear family, namely the *geti* or *tui-re* who actually gives the
child's names. Naming is therefore a process that gradually leads the
child out of the nuclear family into a wider social world.

Figure 14 is a visual representation of the important relationships that
a person enters into as he moves toward maturity. It distinguishes three
areas:

I: The domestic area of the nuclear family, where social relationships
are expressed in biological terms. This area mediates between nature and
culture; between what is outside and inside Apinayé society. Here the
body of the child is formed and guarded for a time by the rites of seclusion.

II: The area of Ego's foster parents, the "arrangers of names." This is
the first stage in the broadening of Ego's social ties. In contrast with the
third area, relationships here are not particularly formalized. This sphere
is essentially juridical and political, halfway between the domestic sphere
and the public or ritual sphere. Disputes, for instance, are resolved within
this area. It should be noted that whether Ego is male or female, there is
no terminological distinction between parents and parents' same sex sib-

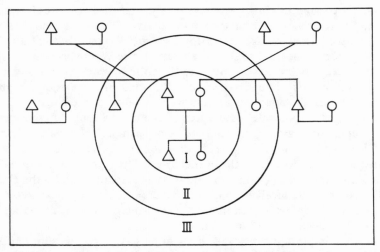

Figure 14. *The important relationships a person enters into as he moves toward maturity.*

lings. Hence a basic element in the structure of Apinayé relationship terms is the feature: "same sex as my father or same sex as my mother."

III: The area of Ego's name-givers. Whereas areas I and II contain his *pam* and *nã*, area III is represented by his *geti* and *tui*. Here we can see that in the Apinayé system the contrast between the sexes is structurally equivalent to the contrast between generations since parents' opposite sex siblings are identified with grandparents. What these have in common is that they are all Ego's real or potential name-givers. Area III constitutes the actual limits of Ego's relatives. Relationships established here mediate between Ego and the rest of the village, an area composed of nonrelatives and potential enemies.

Relationships become more formalized as one moves from area I to III and approaches the effective limits of the group of relatives. The movement is from blood relationships in the first area toward the social or ceremonial relationships of the third.

Comparative Aspects of Naming

Apinayé names are transmitted in sets, which are formed by combining names taken from other sets, and all sets of names are associated with the *Kolti* and *Kolre* moieties. Although the repertoire of names may be finite, the possibilities of combining them are immense. This is one solution to the fundamental problem of all naming systems which, as Lévi-Strauss has suggested, fall between two extreme types: "At one extreme, the name is an identifying mark which, by the application of a rule, establishes that the individual who *is named* is a member of a preordained class (a social group in a system of groups, a status by birth in a system of statuses). At the other extreme, the name is a free creation on the part of the individual who *gives the name* and expresses a transitory and subjective state of his own by means of the person he names" (Lévi-Strauss 1966:181). The logical problem is therefore whether names are to individuate or classify. We might see the Apinayé solution as an attempt to *individuate by classifying,* that is, each person would have a set of names that accords him various roles in a social context, but the set is also a unique and personal combination that is never repeated. Although this is a plausible explanation, there are two objections to it. First, it would obviously be difficult to remember all the names in a set. Second, naming would work like that only when a person has two or more name-givers. Although this does happen, I do not think that it is the general rule.

The solution that the Apinayé seem to adopt (and perhaps also the other Northern Gê) is to call the individual by only one name while disregarding the rest. This is the solution adopted by the Krĩkatí (Lave 1967:156), and it is also the one we choose in our society. Take the example of a family with the surname Jones, and three members, Peter, James, and John. Different contexts decide whether the first name or the surname is appropriate. Within the family only the first names are used since it would be a source of confusion to use the surname as a form of address. The surname is "forgotten." Perhaps John Jones is known as "Johnnie" at home to distinguish him from a grandfather called John, but in the office he would be known as Jones if he were the only person there with that surname. The full form "John Jones" is used only in formal situations, for example, when he receives a degree or is fined in a court of law.

The Apinayé also distinguish between their different names. They say that some are formal and are used only as forms of address when the person is fulfilling a ceremonial role. Although the name used in the home may well be a kind of nickname, I am inclined to see it as a sign that indicates a *context* where a person is *to some extent classified* as belonging to a ceremonial group. Names such as *Kapran gri* (small turtle), *Kambôta* (night), *Bokrãi, Xukaxuro* (woodpecker), *Pêb grire,* and so on, are said by some to be household names, meaning that a child is called by that one name until the time comes when he is finally given all the names of the appropriate series. While the single name is being used on an everyday basis, the others remain in the background to be used later in the appropriate ceremonial context.

My suggestion that names are used to indicate a context might well be the solution adopted by those groups in which names are obviously classificatory devices, as in the Timbira case. Paradoxically, the solution indicates a weakness in Lévi-Strauss's speculations on proper names (Lévi-Strauss 1966:chap. 6). A society might well use names as a classificatory device, but this does not exclude the possibility that the system also provides nicknames or household names and that it is these that are used to individuate. If one approaches the problem in this way, the question then becomes not to what degree names are used as classificatory devices, but how much a given naming system can reveal of the social structure of the society that uses it. In my view the first problem is indeed important— and Lévi-Strauss's approach is certainly authoritative—but it is a question better left to philosophers. From a sociological point of view, as the Apinayé example shows, the opposition between classification and individualization is not central to the question of social structure.

Lévi-Strauss approaches the problem of names and social structure on a very general level, concluding that social systems can be divided into those in which names emphasize social position and those in which they emphasize social relationships. I think the most helpful approach to these problems comes from Ward Goodenough (1965). Goodenough begins by contrasting the use of proper names in two Oceanic societies that he studied, Truk and Lakalai. On Truk the number of names is the same as the number of individuals. Kinship terms are not used as forms of address, not even by children addressing their parents. All are addressed by their proper names. "Every individual in Truk has a distinctive personal name that he shares with no one else, living or dead, and he expects to be addressed by that name and in no other way by everyone on almost all occasions" (Goodenough 1965:267). Clearly, then, Truk names individuate.

On Lakalai exactly the opposite takes place. Individuals have more than two names: almost everyone shares a name with another person; and names do not distinguish sex or age. Kinship terms are frequently substituted as forms of address. Furthermore, everyone has various kinds of names. Initially a person is given a name, "what may be called a primary name (*la-isa-la sessele*, 'his true or proper name')." Goodenough explains that "he may also have a secondary name (*la-tohilovula*) and a defecation name (*la-tohilovula-la-tatahe*)" (1965:267–268). Names have complex rules of transmission. Some, for example, have to be passed on to the first child regardless of sex, resulting in what Goodenough calls a cycle of names (1965:268–269). There are also prohibitions that limit the free use of names. For example, if a man has a son with the same name as his father-in-law, he will not address his son in this way but will use a nickname or secondary name. Lakalai names, like those of the Timbira, are *classificatory or relational mechanisms.*

Besides dealing with the logical functions of names on an abstract level, Goodenough also looks at their relation to social structure. He explains that on Truk, names are used individually since there are other institutions (corporate unilineal descent groups) that undertake the social classification of individuals. Indeed there is little possibility for individual choice on Truk since the matrilineages are a powerful focus of reference for any person's actions (1965:272). He concludes: "In the light of these considerations, I infer that Truk's naming and address customs compensate in another way for the suppression of individuality in Truk's social system. A person's name emphasizes his uniqueness as a person, and whenever anyone addresses him, his individuality is acknowledged" (1965:273).

On Lakalai it is quite the opposite. Choice is greater since there are no classificatory institutions. Lineages are "undeveloped," leadership being based on seniority and not on a person's position in a lineage system (1965:273–274). Positions in the social system have to be won, and there is ample scope for choice and for different possibilities of social and political alignments. Goodenough concludes: "Naming customs and modes of address in Lakalai function to offset competition by serving as continual reminders that people are, after all, part of a social order, inextricably tied to others by obligations deriving from birth and contract" (1965:274–275).

If I interpret this correctly, Goodenough's argument is that in these social systems, names, as classificatory institutions, are in complementary distribution with other kinds of institutions that classify and give order to social relationships. Where a lineage system (or some other institution) is the basic classificatory principle, names are mechanisms that individuate, and where lineages do not carry out such functions, names classify.

I believe this interpretation helps us understand naming systems among the Gê groups and draws our attention to similarities and contrasts between the various systems. It is clear that among the Eastern Timbira and the Apinayé names function in the same way as on Lakalai. In these societies names are important instruments of classification, for there are no other institutions with comparable classificatory power. There are no lineages among the Timbira, and social behavior is determined only by individual choice.

Whereas Apinayé and Eastern Timbira names are associated with ceremonial groups, Kayapó and Shavante names are not. In the latter cases names are a secondary institution, used not to classify but to indicate the limits of paternal authority. This is brought out clearly in the Shavante naming ceremony, which "establishes formally that the MB, who has now moved out of his ZS's household, has rights *in personam* over the boy" (Maybury-Lewis 1967:232). Name-giving therefore expresses a relationship of filiation. Since Shavante social life is organized in terms of patrilineages, the most important affinal relationship in any residential group is that between the father and the mother's brother, that is, between brothers-in-law. Names are a function of this affinal relationship between lineages, establishing a formal, secondary connection between a man and his wife's brother. These are individuals of different lineages who are in a sensitive position with respect to one another.

Shavante naming emphasizes individual relationships. It is not a technique for classifying individuals into social groups since that is done by the system of lineages and clans. Naming fulfills a complementary function by giving formal recognition to the named person's relationship to two lineages: his father's and his mother's brother's.

Although Kayapó naming has a more important classificatory function, the institution is embedded in a similar type of structure. The father/child relationship is extremely important in Kayapó society both in itself and because it constitutes the symbolic basis of political groups. The center of political life is the Men's House, to which a child is introduced by an *adoptive* father. Hence political groups are formed on the basis of symbolic father/child relationships, which gives these groups the appearance of lineages. One could say that the Kayapó Men's House consists of *symbolic patrilineages* that affect the entire political and social life of the village. Names, therefore, function in the same way as they do among the Shavante.

Among both the Shavante and the Kayapó, when the MB names his ZS he also gives him various adornments. This emphasizes the personal nature of the relationship and suggests that names are not being used to establish relationships between groups but to indicate the specific points of contact between kin and affines. In both societies names are not transmitted at birth but only after the child attains a certain age (T. Turner 1966:167ff.). As we saw there is a "mystical" aspect to Kayapó names that they themselves explicitly recognize. If we remember Leach's point that a "mystical aspect" of this kind is characteristic of the ambiguous nature of affinal relationships (Leach 1961:19), we can then see how Kayapó and Shavante names are really expressions of the relationships between husband (father), wife's brother (mother's brother), and son (sister's son). They carry a mystical connotation because they symbolize affinal relationships and not incorporation into a social category. This perhaps explains why Shavante names change when their bearer's status changes. They seem to emphasize a personal and individual status rather than the status automatically conferred by virtue of the individual's membership in a certain clan or patrilineage (Maybury-Lewis 1967:235).

There are some interesting variations among the Gê groups in the way names are related to men's groups. First, where age-classes and men's groups, based on institutions like the Men's House and patrilineages, are important as classificatory devices, names tend to individualize. A possible solution to the problem of Shavante naming is to see it as a catalyst that helps establish an individual's status. It operates in a system in which the number of individual choices is limited by the lineages, which tend to have an effect on all aspects of social life. As a result, as Maybury-Lewis observed (1967:235), names are constantly changing since each movement within the social structure corresponds to a new name.

Second, the Kayapó case appears similar in that names become links between people and between "symbolic lineages." The names remind members of the tribe of other relations beyond those established in the Men's House. Among the Apinayé and the Eastern Timbira, names have an inverse function: because there are no lineages or Men's Houses, they become the basic instruments of social classification. Among the Shavante and the Kayapó the relation between parent (real or symbolic) and child appears to transcend the domestic group and is projected onto the social system. It is by means of such relations that a youth is incorporated into the political and ceremonial system of the society. By contrast, the relationship with the MB (and other genealogically equivalent positions) is a personal link. Among the Timbira the same formula is inverted. The MB is essentially a public figure, passing on his "social persona" to his ZC (Melatti 1970, 1979), whereas the parent/child relationship is of a private kind. The Apinayé case seems to be a synthesis of these two positions, but it must be emphasized that here the adoptive parent acts as an arranger of names, and as a result the public and ceremonial symbolism appears to be much closer to that of the other Timbira.

Finally, we saw that the application of the same rule to different social

contexts can produce entirely different results. Rules of naming throughout the Gê groups are the same, but there are variations and possibilities
of choice that are extremely important when one wants to determine all
the results produced by the rules. These different results are transformations of one another and are the products of the same rules being applied
in the context of each society. Thus, among the Shavante, the genealogical position and category that is given a distinct position in the system of
terminology is the MB. But among the other Northern Gê, although there
is a certain emphasis on the MB, transmission of names is prescribed
through a category that covers a large number of genealogical positions
on both paternal and maternal sides. Because there is a choice of name-
giver in these systems, there is also a choice of either separating these
maternal and paternal "lines" or uniting them. The possibility of choosing alternatives is an integral part of the system of naming by definition,
and makes it quite different from the Shavante system. There are, therefore, different ways of realigning social relationships in each of these societies. The Shavante emphasis on a particular genealogical position indicates that in their society lineages are both the best defined groups and
the most effective political groups. Hence transmission of names among
the Shavante is done according to a genealogical connection that also
permeates the lineage systems and the political system.

The transmission of names in Apinayé society affects the way relationship terminology is used. This is a function of Apinayé names being instruments of social classification, which is not the case among the Shavante and the Kayapó. Thus, although the Gê groups have basically the
same rules of naming, the systems that result are quite different.[11]

The *Ipôgnotxóine/Krénotxóine* Moieties

The Apinayé have a second pair of moieties called *Ipôgnotxóine*
(meaning "people of the center," or "of the village square") and
Krénotxóine ("people of the periphery," or "of the houses"). Every Apinayé belongs to one of these. Membership is established through formal
friends (*krã-geti/pá-krã*) by a process of filiation that is structurally similar to the one outlined in the above discussion. Their names indicate an
opposition in that one is considered nearer the center of the village than
the other, that is, *Ipôgnotxóine* is associated with the area that is most
public and social.

Whereas the *Kolti/Kolre* moieties have a social character in that they
appear as ceremonial groups in initiation ceremonies and log races, the
Ipôgnotxóine/Krénotxóine moieties are more conceptual in nature. They
are not as clearly distinguished as *Kolti* and *Kolre,* and the groups they
refer to are seldom formed. During my fieldwork the *Ipôgnotxóine* moiety
was formed only once, during a ritual that acts out the myth of the
kupen-ndíya (Nimuendajú 1939:177). The theme of the myth is that the

women are angry because their lover, the caiman, has been killed by the men. The women then decide to build a village exclusively for themselves. During the ritual, which I saw in 1962, some people belonging to *Ipôgnotxóine* gathered into a group and ran through the village visiting each house. They pointed shotguns at the spectators and made comic gestures, provoking considerable laughter, for much of their behavior mimicked sexual intercourse. Arriving at each house in turn, they would pretend to shoot into the spectators at those who belonged to the same moiety. These people in turn would jump around, to everyone's amusement. My informant, Velho Estêvão, said that I must keep quiet since I belonged to the other moiety, *Krénotxóine,* and therefore my behavior should be serious and restrained.

Nimuendajú seldom refers to these moieties as corporate groups. He mentions a ceremony related to the initiation rites (1939:30) in which he saw exactly the same behavior as I did in the *kupen-ndíya* ritual. He also mentions a symbolic sweeping of the radial paths of the village during the first phase of initiation (*pēb kaág*) (1939:36, 51). Today the Apinayé talk much more readily about *Kolti* and *Kolre* than about this second pair of moieties. When they do discuss them, they always describe them in terms of the distinctive behavior associated with each one: people belonging to *Ipôgnotxóine* are "liars"; they are indiscreet, impulsive, and comic, whereas people of *Krénotxóine* are serious, discreet, restrained, and controlled. People of *Krénotxóine* should not trust those of *Ipôgnotxóine* nor take part in their pranks. To do so would be to run the risk of being beaten and immediately expelled from the group.

In my view the opposition between these groups is of a residual nature. The *Ipôgnotxóine* moiety always appears in the center during ceremonies because of the distinctive behavior associated with it, while the members of *Krénotxóine,* as one might expect of "people of the houses," are spectators watching the other moiety's pranks.

One should also note that the dualism underlying the *Kolti/Kolre* distinction is diametric, emphasizing the symmetry and complementarity of the two groups, while the duality of *Ipôgnotxóine/Krénotxóine* is concentric, emphasizing asymmetry and hierarchy, as follows:

Ipôgnotxóine = irregularity, unpredictability
Krénotxóine = regularity, predictability

The first is explicitly associated with the moon and the second with the sun. Curiously, the Apinayé always say that *Ipôgnotxóine* is more important. They justify this by reference to the myth of Sun and Moon, in which an exchange of roles took place. Sun, who should have been *Ipôgnotxóine* (center, regularity, man, red, day, and so forth), changed sides with Moon, who changed from a role associated with irregularity, woman, night, and so on, to the opposite. A possible explanation of this exchange is that *Ipôgnotxóine* is obviously more dynamic than *Krénotxóine.* The movement associated with the action and irregularity of the first suggests a superior role similar to the role of Moon in the corresponding cycle of myths (Nimuendajú 1939:133, 158). Hence, like the people of *Ipôgnotxóine,* Moon is always playing pranks and wanting to do the opposite of what Sun wants to do, a role similar to that of man in the face of nature, or the way man applies and manipulates social rules.[12]

We can say, then, that *Kolti/Kolre* is a relationship of perfect symmetry whereas *Ipôgnotxóine/Krénotxóine* indicates a hierarchy, or more precisely, a complementary opposition that is arranged hierarchically, the center being superior to the periphery. Hence *Ipôgnotxóine* has the more conspicuous role in ceremonies.

Ipôgnotxóine/Krénotxóine and the Problem of the Four *Kiyê*

In his monograph of the Apinayé, Nimuendajú mentioned four marriage groups called *kiyê,* which exchanged women according to a prescriptive rule (Nimuendajú 1939:29–36). This suggested a marriage system similar to those found in Australia. My field research revealed that there were actually only two groups, *Ipôgnotxóine* and *Krénotxóine.* This is in fact confirmed if we examine Nimuendajú's evidence. We can explain his error by showing how the four *kiyê* can be reduced to a pair of moieties.

EVIDENCE FROM NAMES AND DECORATIONS

The moieties *Ipôgnotxóine* and *Krénotxóine* are the names of two of the four *kiyê* that Nimuendajú mentions. The two other *kiyê* are *Krã-ô-mbédy* ("beautiful hair") and *Kré'kára* ("eaves of the house"). A man of one *kiyê* supposedly marries a woman from one of the other three according to the following rules: an *Ipôgnotxóine* man marries a *Krénotxóine* woman; a *Krénotxóine* man a *Krã-ô-mbédy* woman; a *Krã-ô-mbédy* man a *Kré'kára* woman; and a *Kré'kára* man an *Ipôgnotxóine* woman. Hence the marriage circle is closed (Nimuendajú 1939:30ff.; Maybury-Lewis 1960a).

A peculiarity is immediately evident, however. While *Ipôgnotxóine* and *Krénotxóine* refer etymologically to actual groups of people, the other two names refer to the adornments that members of the supposed groups are said to wear. According to Nimuendajú, "Krã-ô-mbédy means 'beautiful (mbédy) hair (ô) of the head (krã).' This refers to the decoration of the members' hair with pulverized snail-shells. The hair topping the hair-furrow circling the head is first made sticky by rubbing almecega rosin into it, then this powder is sprinkled on it" (1939:30). He goes on: "Kré'kára means 'eaves'; possibly here, too, there is reference to a typical kiyê decoration, viz., a cord with short pendent arára feathers tied to the furrow, these little feathers being compared to the pendent thatch of the roof" (1939:30).

There are two obvious difficulties here: first, neither the etymology of the names nor an explanation of their possible associations indicates that they refer to groups of people, as the first pair of moieties clearly does; and second, the decorations that the words are held to refer to have nothing particularly distinctive about them. Indeed, the second decoration (*Kré'kára*), as Nimuendajú states, refers to a "typical kiyê decoration" that is still in use today. Furthermore, we know that body painting is the distinctive mark of ceremonial groups not just among the Apinayé (*Kolti* is associated with black body paint and *Kolre* with red) but among all the Gê peoples. Of the four so-called "kiyê" only *Ipôgnotxóine* and *Krénotxóine* are said to have their own distinctive styles of body painting and decoration. Thus according to Nimuendajú, "the ikrényõčwúdn are painted all over and wear a short arára wing feather in the wrappings of each forearm; while the ipôgnyõčwúdn paint themselves with stripes or only on one side of the body and wear long arára tail feathers in the forearm wrappings" (1939:30). I was told of the *Ipôgnotxóine* and *Krénotxóine* moieties during my own fieldwork, and to this day the Apinayé can illustrate the designs associated with each one. I heard no mention of the other two groups.

EVIDENCE FROM APINAYÉ SYMBOLISM

We have seen that both *Kolti/Kolre* and *Ipôgnotxóine/Krénotxóine* are based on a symbolic dualism, either symmetric or hierarchical, which is found throughout the Gê peoples. The institution associated with the second pair of moieties is that of formal friends, which pairs off men of different age-classes in a relationship of senior and junior. Here I simply wish to emphasize that *Ipôgnotxóine* and *Krénotxóine* are clearly related to oppositions such as center/periphery; plaza/house; painted over part of body only/painted over whole body; long arára feathers/short arára feathers; irregularity/regularity. There is no evidence that the other two groups mentioned by Nimuendajú have such associations and nothing to suggest that they can be related in terms of oppositions.

Furthermore, the decorations associated with *Krã-ô-mbédy* and *Kré'kára* are also associated with "head" and "house," the first referring to hair decorations and the second "being compared with the pendent thatch of the roof" (Nimuendajú 1939:30). The association "head" = "center" or "plaza," and "house" = "periphery" is one that I found on innumerable occasions, and even in Nimuendajú's account there is evidence of it if we remember the various social relations in which the term *krã* (head) is important. The term appears both in the name-giver/name-receiver relationship and in the terms used between formal friends, where *krā-geti* and *pá-krā* most probably mean "older head" and "my head" respectively. These relationships are all marked by a formal, ceremonial content, and they are always associated with the center of the village. There appears therefore to be a direct relationship between the first two names and the second, thus:

> *Ipôgnotxóine*   *Krénotxóine*
> *Krā-ô-mbédy*   *Kré'kára*

A number of Apinayé who still know something of the ceremonial groups confirmed this association, saying that the second pair of names referred to the decorations used by *Ipôgnotxóine* and *Krénotxóine*.

ETHNOGRAPHIC EVIDENCE

My own field material revealed that in a census of the entire population, not one Apinayé informant said that he or she belonged to one of the second pair of groups. They mentioned only *Ipôgnotxóine* and *Krénotxóine*. Furthermore, genealogies that cover the whole society reveal that marriages do not follow any pattern that would fit regular exchanges among the so-called *kiyê*. A superficial examination of the genealogies is enough to show that we are dealing with a bilateral group in which marriage is in no way prescriptive. I used to ask the Apinayé, somewhat provocatively: "Isn't it a good thing to know that you can only marry a woman from such and such a moiety?" And they consistently responded with some vehemence: "No, we always choose our wives." There is nothing in the way they think about their marriage rules to indicate a prescriptive marriage system, nor is there any statistical evidence to suggest a pattern of preference.

Nimuendajú's statement that there were four marriage classes still needs to be explained. One probable reason for the error was that he took the names of decorations as names of groups. But this does not explain why he says that the four groups appear as corporate units during the initiation ceremonies (Nimuendajú 1939:30, 36, 52). Let us look at these references in detail.

> When the ipôgnyôčwúdn appear in a body at a festival . . . they affect a behavior strongly suggestive of the Canella Clown society. That is, they indulge in all sorts of nonsense, partly of ribald character, lie and steal, but without anyone's resenting it. (1939:30)

> It is in fact during the Pebkaág initiation that the kiyê organization is most clearly noticeable, partly through the antics of the ipôgynôčwúdn [*sic*], partly by the differences in decoration and separate appearance of the several kiyê when the radial paths are symbolically swept. For this ceremony the villagers, segregated by kiyê, take up positions at the edge of the plaza, but their places there are not fixed, members of each kiyê standing before

the opening of the radial path they intend to sweep. So far as I know, this is the only occasion on which the participants are divided according to kiyê affiliation. (1939:36)

On page fifty-two, he describes another appearance of the *Ipôgnotxóine kiyê*. It is significant that although certain roles are ascribed to members of the other three *kiyê*, there are no descriptions of their appearance in a group.

I was extremely fortunate to find a manuscript of Nimuendajú's in the Department of Anthropology of the Museu Nacional in Rio de Janeiro that included his field notes on the Apinayé. In examining these notes, written in German, I discovered that there are a number of discrepancies in the order of events in the ceremonies as well as in the way various people participated. In addition, there are only a few genealogies, and there is one unsuccessful attempt to work out a genealogy according to *kiyê* affiliation. And finally, an important passage runs as follows: "Ikrenyčwúdn, Ipôgnyŏčwúdn, Krãkára, and Krã-ô-mbédy refer only to kinds of decorations used." There follows a short description of the decorations, which appears in a more detailed form in the book. Nimuendajú then goes on: "[These forms of decoration] are handed down to a person by the godfather who has brought him up." Later he writes: "Kramgeti—godfathers of Pepkahak, arranged according to the body painting of each group, sweep the paths of their godchildren [*sic*], pa-krãm." And between the lines of the notebook is written: "kiyê = faction?"

These notes, which concern the *pēb-kaág* ceremony, show that Nimuendajú was not quite sure at this point just what kind of groups the *kiyê* were. But since he did note (as I later did) a direct relationship between the decorations and names of the groups, it is probable that there were indeed only two groups with their own distinctive decorations. But the most important point is that incorporation into these groups is not passed on from father to son and mother to daughter as Nimuendajú states, but from *krã-geti* to *pá-krã*. Perhaps Nimuendajú misunderstood the Apinayé translation of *krã-geti* as "godfather" and took it to mean "father." In any case the Apinayé nowadays do not understand the word *kiyê*, though they recognize the other terms in Nimuendajú's discussion. It is clear, therefore, that we are dealing here with an error in the ethnography. Whatever the explanation of Nimuendajú's error, the best way to exorcise the "Apinayé anomaly" is to understand the mode of incorporation into the moieties and the role of formal friends.

Formal Friendship

Apinayé of both sexes are incorporated into the *Ipôgnotxóine* or *Krénotxóine* moieties through a formal friend known as *krã-geti* if a man or *krã-gedy* if a woman. The reciprocal term is *pá-krã*. As with proper names a person can have more than one formal friend and belong to both moieties at the same time. And as with double membership in the *Kolti/Kolre* moieties, this is considered an advantage since it allows a person to choose which moiety he wants to belong to in participating in any specific ceremony. My impression was that the Apinayé think favorably of trying to give an individual as many choices as possible, thereby giving him greater room in which to maneuver. Nevertheless, there are those in both villages who are considered exclusively *Ipôgnotxóine* or *Krénotxóine,* showing that even in cases of double membership an individual can always choose to define himself as belonging exclusively to one group. In São José, for example, there is a woman by the name of Maria Barbosa who is famous for her association with *Ipôgnotxóine.* It is said that her unconventional behavior was the principal reason for her choice of this moiety. The same happened in the case of Zezinho Tapklúd of Mariazinha. But the chief of São José belongs to both groups and makes a point of mentioning how he can choose which one he belongs to.

Formal friends who pass on rights of membership to the moieties are chosen by adoptive parents (*pam* and *nã kaág*) after a child learns to walk, although the ceremony of incorporation does not take place until the child is about ten years old. It is at this ceremony that the child is painted in the manner of the appropriate moiety.[13] The *krã-geti* should be a son of the adoptive father's *krã-geti,* and a *krã-gedy* a daughter or the adoptive mother's *krã-gedy.* Hence the rules of incorporation into these moieties establish a formal continuity between a man and his *pá-krã* and his son and son's *pá-krã.* There must be at least two lines, one consisting of a man and his son, who pass on rights of membership to another line, which also consists of a man and his son. The two lines are linked by formal friendship such that one is always the *krã-geti* and the other the *pá-krã.* Hence father/son and mother/daughter relationships stand out very clearly in "lines" which, formally, are *parallel.* But it should be emphasized that these relationships are between *adoptive* parents and children and that the "lines" are not corporate groups. Although the moiety may appear in an attenuated form on certain ceremonial occasions, the only grouping that appears is that which links two persons who find themselves in different lines, as Figure 15 illustrates.

Here the broken lines represent the adoptive parent/child relationship. On the right is a "line" of *krã-geti* and on the left a "line" of *pá-krã.* The first in both "lines" belongs to *Ipôgnotxóine* and the second to *Krénotxóine.* It should now be clear why I am using the term "line" with a certain suspicion. The diagram shows that incorporation into the moieties emphasizes the relationship of formal friendship but cuts through the relationship between adoptive parent and child. These ceremonial groups put aside the second relationship in favor of the first.

Young children do not receive formal friends because, as it is said,

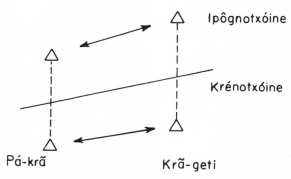

Figure 15. *The* Ipôgnotxóine *and* Krénotxóine *moieties and the* krã-geti/pá-krã *relationship.*

"They are not old enough to understand the importance of the relationship." Once a person receives a *krã-geti* he will refer to that person only by the appropriate term. Also, a *pá-krã* calls children of his *krã-geti*, *mebó-re* or *mebó-krá-re* (*mebó* meaning "thing" or "animal," *krá-re* meaning "son"). This is a reciprocal form of address. The daughter of one's *krã-geti* is addressed as *iprõ-ti* (*iprõ* meaning "wife" and *ti* being an augmentative). The term does not indicate any marriage prescription (as I initially thought) but distinguishes this category from that of a wife. *Iprõ* is indeed "wife," but *iprõ-ti* when applied to a young girl suggests not that the man who addresses her in this way will marry her but that he will rape her. When I called young girls in São José by this term they always became afraid or began to cry. Another reciprocal form of address between a *pá-krã* and the children of his *krã-geti* is *ikamde-re* (meaning "assassin" or "criminal," *kandê* meaning "he who kills"). Informants explain that having these different forms of address is a way of maintaining a clear distinction between *pá-krã* and *krã-geti*. But establishing these relationships produces redefinitions within the system of genealogies and social ties in the same way that naming does.

The Apinayé translate *krã-geti* and *pá-krã* using the Portuguese words for "godparent" and "godchild." They notice that in local Brazilian society, as in their own, people related in this way must treat each other with respect and must avoid certain topics of conversation, especially anything to do with sex. In Apinayé society the relationship is clearly one of avoidance, in which one person can speak to the other only on certain specific occasions. They must not look each other in the eye nor argue together. A *pá-krã* has to obey his *krã-geti* and do whatever is required to please him. If a *krã-geti* and a *pá-krã* find themselves on the same path, it is the latter who has to get out of the way. Sexual relations and marriage between a man and a woman related by these categories is strictly prohibited. The ideal that they should not be closely related, however, certainly works against the ceremonial behavior required of the relationship. When an Apinayé talks of his *krã-geti* he always points to the other side of the village (see Figure 16). As in the Brazilian godparent institution a *krã-geti* is always at least ten years older than his *pá-krã*. The age difference further emphasizes the respect and avoidance that the relationship involves. As in the case of the Brazilian godparent/godchild relationship, the Apinayé institution concerns the transmission of rights to the child from a person outside the immediate circle of the nuclear family. This is done at a ceremony in which the *krã-geti* gives adornments that identify him with the child and is given a pie made of manioc and meat in return. In the words of one of my informants: "When I have an *i-krã* for whom I arranged names, I go and ask one of the sons of my *krã-geti* to make adornments for the child. As soon as the adornments are ready, the relatives and I make a meat pie that I give to the son of my *krã-geti*, who then becomes the *krã-geti* of my son."

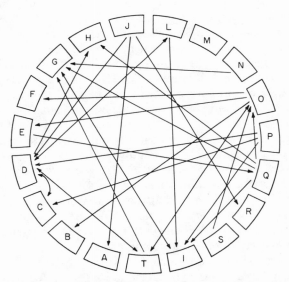

Figure 16. *Relationships of formal friendship* (krã-geti/pá-krã) *in the village of São José, 1967. The diagram does not represent the entire web of relationships, but it does show how these tend to cut across the village diametrically and link houses on opposite sides of the circle. There are only a few cases of neighboring houses being linked in this way* (C *and* D, Q *and* O). *The lettering corresponds to that in Figure 1. The diagram is circular to give a clearer impression of the pattern of relationships. Arrows running in one direction indicate a* krã-geti *to* pá-krã *relationship. Arrows running in both directions indicate reciprocal relationships between houses where another member of a* pá-krã's *household becomes* krã-geti *to a child in the other house. The position of group* I *reflects the fact that in 1967–68 this group left faction III and joined faction I* (see Chapter 5).

The true parents do not take part in the ceremony but leave it in the hands of the adoptive parents. Exchanging adornments for meat pies is an expression of how rights pass from the domestic area to a juridical one (the adoptive parents) and finally to a public area on the edges of the bilateral system of relatives (the formal friends). The meat pie given by those who represent the child is something associated with physical maintenance; food is always associated with the home and with women; hence giving the pie shows how the child is related to the private domain of society. Also, the pie is made of manioc and meat, the white of the manioc and the red of the meat suggesting the physical formation of the child's body by sperm and blood. The meat pie therefore symbolizes both what is essential in the domestic area and the association of man and woman, in which the man contributes meat and the woman manioc. The adornments that are exchanged for the meat pie symbolize the public and ceremonial side since they are not connected with blood ties and are made up only on formal occasions. In one sense the ceremony symbolizes an exchange of physical energy for experience and sociability. It is this exchange that marks the initiation rites and the associated myth of "Kenkutá and Akréti" (Nimuendajú 1939:170ff.), in which two young brothers, with their grandfather's help, channel their physical energy into social experience and thereby are able to kill the huge falcon that has destroyed their village. What is exchanged between *krã-geti* and *pá-krã* is therefore symbolically consistent with the social position of each "friend" within the society as a whole.

Formal friendship is associated with a series of obligations that involve both the *krã-geti* and the *pá-krã*. First, during the initiation rites the *krã-geti* make an elaborate set of decorative articles for their *pá-krã* consisting of three pieces (Nimuendajú 1939:48ff.).

Second, the *krã-geti* cut the children's hair. This symbolizes the child's entry into an area in which his physical appearance must be controlled and made to conform to certain social rules. Hair-cutting denotes the group's control over the individual (Leach 1958). At puberty the *pá-krã* receive adornments as befits the occasion. Young men receive their second decorative outfit during the initiation rites. Young women are given adornments after they marry, an occasion that usually coincides with their first menstruation. Among the Apinayé a girl's first menstruation means that she has had sexual relations. She therefore has two alternatives: either she chooses a husband and marries (by publicly declaring one of her lovers, who is then urged to marry her) or she becomes a promiscuous woman, *me-kuprú* ("woman of the plaza" or "public woman"). This is done by means of a ritual in which the girl's *krã-geti* makes new adornments for her and escorts her into the plaza, where she is formally presented to the village. After a few days the girl receives gifts from all the men who have had sexual relations with her. Two men, who do not have to be relatives, are appointed guardians to protect her. They are called the *krã-tum* of the *me-kuprú*. In São José in 1969 there were at least three *me-kuprú*. The ritual by which a woman takes on this role is the equivalent of the men's receiving adornments from their *krã-geti* on being initiated. In both cases they are changing their position in society and entering the public area of the community where their behavior must conform to the rules of the system.

Third, in the case of death the *krã-geti* or *pá-krã* is responsible for decorating and interring the corpse. Close relatives of the dead person, members of the same nuclear family or of the same house, do not even accompany the corpse to the grave but remain crying near the empty bier. The *krã-geti* or *pá-krã* should comfort the relatives or even reprove them gently if their mourning is excessive by reminding them that they have other sons or brothers and that they should think of the living rather than the dead. In this way they control those expressions of grief which, among the Apinayé, can sometimes become quite violent (Nimuendajú 1939:151). It is also the *krã-geti* who bring the period of mourning to an end.

Fourth, during initiation a boy is given a new *krã-geti* chosen for him by his adoptive parents. At the same time he gets another formal friend, *krã-djúa,* chosen from those of his age-class. The relationship with a *krã-djúa* is symmetrical and there is no exchange of gifts. The new *krã-geti,* however, has to make a new set of adornments consisting of three to six pieces. These are made up after the novice extends a formal invitation to a new formal friend by giving him a small cylinder of aroeira wood. Aroeira is a very hard wood, and in my view the cylinders not only represent the ideal of durability between *krã-geti* and *pá-krã* but also the virility of the *pēb,* who are now of age to be married and to control their sexual lives.

These adornments are noteworthy, for they indicate a dual division and not a division into four groups, as Nimuendajú suggested. The first is a cord for the forehead, from which a fringe hangs down to the middle of the back. Attached to the cord is an arára feather, "its length varying with the wearer's kiyê" (Nimuendajú 1939:48). The items that Nimuendajú numbers two, three, four, and five have nothing to indicate different groups, but the sixth, a pair of plaited anklets, has "short pendent arára feathers or deer hoofs, according to the wearer's kiyê" (1939:49). Hence two kinds of adornment are said to be distinctively associated with a *kiyê,* and it is obviously a binary, not a quaternary, distinction that is apparent. The distinction in the first adornment, long or short arára feathers, is clearly consistent with the distinguishing marks of *Ipôgnotxóine* and *Krénotxóine.* The last adornment opposes arára feathers and deer hooves. Among the Apinayé, aráras are closely associated with humans, since it is from these birds that men obtain feathers. This suggests that there is an association between the arára and the center of the village, and therefore with *Ipôgnotxóine*. The deer hooves would therefore be associated with the jungle and the periphery of the village and consequently with *Krénotxóine*. The adornments offer a binary contrast, and I must conclude that they distinguish two groups, not four.

Fifth, the *krã-geti* also make the clubs that the *pēb* are given during the second phase of the initiations, when their period of seclusion is over. Here again there is an exchange of garden products (collected by the *krã-geti*) and meat (hunted by the *pēb-pá-krã*), indicating a complementary opposition.[14]

Sixth, in a ceremony observed by Nimuendajú, the *krã-geti* stood alongside their *pá-krã* when the latter had their genitals examined by an instructor looking for signs of masturbation. The *krã-geti* were there to help the *pá-krã* overcome their fear so that the examination could be carried out in an orderly fashion. If the instructor found signs of masturbation, the child was beaten, but sometimes the *krã-geti* would take the punishment in place of the child (Nimuendajú 1939:74). The *krã-geti* are therefore important in a rite designed to curb unacceptable sexual activity. They help channel sexual activity toward its proper place in the system, that is, toward marriage.

Seventh, a *krã-geti* is expected to take the part of his *pá-krã* when complaints are voiced against the latter. His intervention is particularly important in the case of serious conflict. If, for example, the trouble reaches a point where a man wants to leave the village altogether, it is his *krã-geti* who will, as a last resort, try to prevent him from doing so. A *krã-geti* and *pá-krã* should never be angry with each other, for the physical consequences would be very serious indeed.

And eighth, at the end of the *pēb* ceremony the radial paths of the village (the paths that the *pēb* take when they are reintegrated into the social system) are swept by the *krã-geti*. This also takes place among the Canela (Nimuendajú 1946:103).

The Structure of Formal Friendship

The question now arises whether there are any common denominators underlying the above series of obligations. Such invariant elements would constitute the underlying structure of the institution of formal friends.

The Apinayé of today make no reference to the obligations of a *krã-geti* during initiation rites. These rituals are gradually being lost and the age-classes no longer exist. But the Apinayé do point out the obligations of a *krã-geti* with respect to funerals, as well as his important role in preventing someone from leaving the village and breaking away from the community. They also mention how dangerous it is to be angry with a *krã-geti*. Nimuendajú's and my observations together point to two common elements. First, the *krã-geti* are always involved in making adornments. Giving these adornments marks their identification with their *pá-krã*.

Second, the *krã-geti* have a fundamental role to play in those critical, marginal situations: when someone wishes to leave the village, when someone dies, when the novice is going through a dangerous liminal stage during the initiation rites. It is during the closing, reintegrative stages of the rites that the *krã-geti* prepare adornments. During the first phase, the *krã-geti* prepare the second set of adornments (Nimuendajú 1939:48 ff.), and at the end of the first phase, the *krã-geti,* in a mischievous way characteristic of *Ipôgnotxóine,* throw garden produce, bananas, sweet potatoes, and peanuts at the boys' feet (ibid.:52). Throwing down the garden produce like this may be a way of representing the separation of the *pēb-kaág* from the agricultural and domestic areas of society. The message is that now they are ready to be hunters and enter the adult male world.

During the second phase of the rites, it is again the *krã-geti* who prepare clubs for the *pēb.* This takes place just before the final ceremony. Furthermore, the set of adornments that the *krã-geti* prepare during this phase indicates the final stage of a man's integration into society, where he joins a class of men who are of age to be married. Also at this stage, the young men's hair is cut, and plugs are inserted in their ears. Perforating the ear and inserting the ear-plug probably represents sexual intercourse, as it does among the Shavante (Maybury-Lewis 1967:248). The Apinayé think of the ear as a social "organ" because it links the individual and the outside world. A person whose behavior is antisocial is called *ambâ-krõ,* "rotten ear." The perforation of the ear, symbolizing "the penis piercing the vagina," indicates that from this point on the *pēb* must exercise self-control and pay proper attention to social matters. Finally, it is always a *krã-geti* who stays close to a boy when he has to undergo those procedures that may involve pain, such as the examination of the genitals or the piercing of the ears and lower lip.

In structural terms formal friendship consists of a relation between one position that is within the system and another that is outside it. Bearing in mind that the individuals involved are of different ages and that the avoidance behavior between a *krã-geti* and a *pá-krã* indicates a hierarchical relationship, it is clear that the structure of formal friendship includes a hierarchical or concentric component. The relationship is the ultimate social link that gives every individual a position within the society. If this link is broken, the individual will be completely outside society. Hence, when an individual dies, the involvement of the formal friend in the burial rites places the deceased in the appropriate category: a corpse that is no longer part of society. This resolves the ambiguity of a lifeless body, which is still something of a social being.

In summary, the relationship between formal friends is activated whenever one of those involved finds himself in a critical situation regarding the community as a whole: when a person dies and has to be segregated from the society; when a person wants to leave the village; when he needs encouragement to endure a physical ordeal, as during initiation rites; when he is reintegrated into the community after a period of marginality, such as those following rites of passage or periods of mourning.

Conclusions: Ideology of the Ceremonial Groups

In this section I shall compare naming and the *Kolti/Kolre* moieties with formal friendship and the *Ipôgnotxóine/Krénotxóine* moieties. Let us look first at the following details:

Naming	*Formal friendship*
Indicated by names.	Indicated by adornments.
Prescribed in terms of the relationship system: names must be given by someone in the category *geti* or *tui.*	Not prescribed in terms of the relationship system. The formal friend must be someone outside the kin group.
Age not important.	Age of crucial importance.
Joking behavior indicates that name-giver and named person are identified.	Avoidance behavior indicates a separation between formal friends.
Incorporation into groups that are considered symmetrical.	Incorporation into groups that are seen as asymmetrical.
No mystical aspect.	Mystical aspect: a *pá-krã* cannot be angry with his *krã-geti* since this would produce illness.
Relates domestic and public areas of society.	Relates marginal and normal areas of society.

Naming and formal friendship are clearly similar institutions in the sense that they produce the same structural results, namely, they relate two individuals from different areas of the social system. But naming remains within the theoretical limits of the bilateral system of kin relationships while formal friendship is outside these limits. The first case results in complete social identification: the name-giver passes on to the child both a ceremonial role and a name that is an intrinsic part of his social personality. In the case of formal friendship, the adornments that are given are external indicators of social personality. Again, since names involve positions already defined in terms of the relationship system, they establish ties between households already related by that system; by contrast, formal friendship, having nothing to do with the relationship system, establishes ties between households that are opposite each other on the village circle and that would not, usually, have much to do with each other. Along with this, formal friendship includes avoidance behavior, reflecting the hierarchical nature of the relationship. This is the most important feature that distinguishes the two institutions.

Avoidance behavior between formal friends emphasizes the relationship and strengthens the ties between the individuals involved. These ties are activated whenever one of the "friends" finds himself in a position that is out of order with the system of classification. Furthermore, anger or disagreement between formal friends can produce physical disorders. There is, therefore, what Leach calls a mystical component in this relationship that is to some extent uncontrolled and from which we can infer an aspect of "affinity" (Leach 196:22 ff.). Since formal friendships are established between households that are not directly related to each other, an individual will look for a formal friend in the same direction that he looks for a wife. This may account for the association made by one of Nimuendajú's informants between *Ipôgnotxóine/Krénotxóine* and matrimonial groups.

In terms of the Apinayé social system, the two pairs of moieties reflect the two kinds of dualism by which society and the cosmos are classified and organized. Incorporation into both pairs of moieties is always done by persons outside the nuclear family in a position classified by the Apinayé as "godparents" or "adoptive parents." Hence the process of incorporation shifts the emphasis first from nuclear family relationships to relationships within a wider kin group, and then to relationships that involve the village as a whole. A child is born in a house on the periphery of the village and is gradually involved in new relationships that are progressively further from the household where he was born. The idea that this is a gradual process or progression is clearly marked. What takes place is not a complete separation between parents and children but a gradual shift of emphasis from certain relationships and social roles to others.

A newborn child consists of a mixture of body and blood and is still not differentiated from its parents. When it is older it is given godparents, who arrange names. The shift of emphasis is from biological parenthood to social parenthood. Names are given by a person in a category outside the nuclear family, and in this way a link is established through the child between the nuclear family and the bilateral kindred. After this, when formal friendship is established, the child becomes related to another person who is completely outside the circle of kin. The process is schematically represented in Figure 17.

This figure is no more than a model (in the precise sense of the word) of a set of social rules and does not attempt to represent the complex social reality of Apinayé life. Hence, although it shows a clear separation between the various domains, these are not so obviously distinguished in

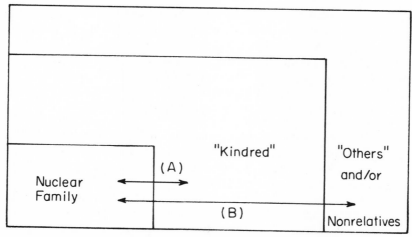

Figure 17. *The process of developing relationships.* A = *names, such as* Krã-tum (geti)/tui-re; B = *formal friendship.*

practice. The diagram does, however, represent the following points clearly: first, a given Ego always looks for a wife in the same category as that of formal friends, that is, in the category "non-kin."

Second, naming is associated with a social field that surrounds the nuclear family, and the act of naming establishes important links between the family and that surrounding domain. Here the term "nuclear family" should be understood in, one might say, the Apinayé sense, since it includes the same sex siblings of Ego's parents who are structurally and terminologically equated with the parents. This is illustrated in Figure 14.

Third, it can be seen that name-givers and formal friends are mediators between domains that are, to some extent at least, kept separate and distinct. The passage from one to the other is always expressed dramatically through those rites of passage typical of all the Gê groups.

An important feature of Apinayé ceremonial groups is that they operate in a way that avoids duplicating the social ties that they establish. In other words, relationships that are important in one domain are not carried over to the next. Although the real parents are the most important figures when a child is young, they lose much of that importance in the juridical area of the social system where, as we saw, it is the adoptive parents who intervene in quarrels. And if the adoptive parents have a mediating role in this area, where they arrange names and come to the child's defense when necessary, they are unimportant when it comes to the child's incorporation into the *Kolti/Kolre* moieties, where the role of the name-giver is preeminent. The same happens in relation to formal friends and the *Ipôgnotxóine/Krénotxóine* moieties.

The logical principles that underlie the system of ceremonial moieties are the same as those that organize the relations between social groups in everyday life. That logic is based on the principle of *dividing* domains and keeping them distinct so that one does not permeate the other. Unlike unilineal systems, in which one dominant sociological principle pervades throughout (all social relationships referring back to the link between father and son or mother and daughter), the Apinayé and Timbira social systems inhibit the dominance of a single principle.

The sociological model that I am suggesting for the Northern Gê and the Apinayé is already well known. In 1919 A. L. Kroeber showed that the Zuñi system could not be properly understood if it was assumed that the groups making up that society were all congruent with one another and functioned according to the same social principles. His account of the society shows how it operates on the basis of various intersecting domains and ties. Later, Radcliffe-Brown, in a similar (though independent) study (1924, [1952]), showed that some societies divide rights over children between various adults. Hence in unilineal societies MB or FZ may have a role that compensates that of the father and mother. We can now add that bilateral systems such as the Eastern Timbira and Apinayé give MB or FZ a role in the transmission of social rights from one generation to another. This is illustrated in the way naming is carried out among the Northern Gê and in the institution of adoptive parents among the Apinayé.

In unilineal social systems it appears that connections established through the marginal relative (MB or FZ, depending on the rule of descent) tend to be tenuous, whereas in bilateral systems both MB and FZ are points that support more firmly structured connections. In both cases we are presented with a continuum and, apparently, complementary distribution. However, the point made by Kroeber and Radcliffe-Brown stands, since in neither case does the system operate in such a way that the entire system of relationships is permeated by a single principle, as the theories of the 1950s would suggest. This kind of permeation can take place in different degrees and in different systems. Describing these systems adequately can be done only by locating and distinguishing these differences.

The African examples we know of seem to bear out this hypothesis since relations established with marginal relatives also follow a unilineal principle. In these cases, although the individuals involved may be different, the same basic principle permeates the system to a considerable degree. By contrast, the Timbira and Apinayé examples show that different relationships and domains are quite independent of one another, each one being based on a different social principle. The Northern Gê are therefore closer to the Zuñi than to the African examples.

These theoretical considerations suggest that we might look again at those well-known complex cases of double descent, especially those reported from Africa (Forde 1950). It is possible that societies with double descent are examples of a single unilineal principle being applied to different people. The individuals who transmit rights are different, but the logic of the system is the same.

Following Victor Turner (1969) one can conclude that all social systems allow multiple readings of their sociological reality and that societies based on rigid principles must indeed be rare. Even in examples of unilineal descent such as the Tallensi case, which Turner reinterprets, the MB has a loosely defined role in the system, which allows lineages to be integrated with one another through links on the mother's side and not the father's. Similarly, among the Shavante, proper names create loosely defined personal connections between MB and ZS which, to borrow Victor Turner's terms, we might call relationships of *communitas*. Among the Timbira and Apinayé, by contrast, proper names classify and are important both as juridical and structural features, the links between parents and children being relationships of *structure*.

The ideology of Apinayé ceremonial groups reveals a logic that divides domains, relationships, and social principles and that is just the same as the logic operating in the social groupings of their everyday lives.

4

The Relationship System

*T*HE APINAYÉ SYSTEM of social relations is embedded in the composition and ideology of their domestic and ceremonial groups. In turning now to the relationship system, the main question is not how Apinayé society is divided into groups but how these groups relate and interconnect with one another, and how the Apinayé think of these divisions and make sense of their society.

When we approach a relationship system we are dealing with a set of terms that the members of a society use to classify their social relations. It is a code that defines the internal divisions of the society and locates the principal connections between these divisions. It also provides a general classification of statuses and roles. The code can be understood only when the anthropologist discovers what the internal divisions are and how they are related.

In our society, for example, the expressions "X is my friend," "Y is my employer," and "Z is my confessor" use three different terms to indicate three different social relationships, operating in three different areas of social life, family, employment, and religion. These different contexts reflect internal divisions in our society, and a study of our relationship system would have to take into account how each term is used in its particular context. Not only does each different domain of a society have its own specific terminology, it also has a particular ideology associated with it. The anthropologist's first task is to find which domain each term belongs to, and then to look for the particular terms that serve as links between domains. Terms that relate domains in this way are of a kind that transcend their specific context and that can be used to define social relationships metaphorically and paradigmatically.

We are familiar with the metaphorical use of our own relationship terms when we say, for example, "God is our Father" or "My boss is such a close friend that he's like a brother to me." In the second example the speaker first indicates that in the case of this relationship the roles "boss" and "friend" are synonymous, suggesting that the relationship is symmetrical, and then the synonym is extended so that "boss = friend = brother." If one found that the role of "boss" is thought of in terms of an elder brother's role, one could assume that the terms "boss" and "brother" are being used as mediators between distinct, separate, and perhaps contradictory social domains. One would not be trying to show that "boss" and "brother" meant the same thing. That is clearly not so. The problem is to show how, in this equation, the terms are being used metaphorically to establish a connection between two different domains, family and work, and to show how, in so doing, they indicate a specific interpretation of the social system.

Whereas the statement "God governs us" is straightforward, inverting the formula to "the government is our God" would indicate an anomaly in the political system, just as inverting the expression "God is our Father" to "Father is our God" would suggest an abnormality in the usual system of family authority. In ordinary language use, metaphorical connections of this kind, grammatical and ungrammatical, show how certain relationship terms are used to link different domains of the social system. In this way many specific relationship terms can be transformed into sociological categories.

If we look at Radcliffe-Brown's explanation of so-called Crow-Omaha systems, and if we consider it in terms of the approach I have outlined, we can see that he discovered the following characteristics of these relationship systems: (1) certain terms are always used by members of one domain (Ego's lineages); (2) certain other terms are always used by members of another domain (the lineages related to Ego's); and (3) the link between these domains is established by means of certain individuals who act as intermediaries: MB in Crow systems and FZ in Omaha systems. These individuals leave Ego's lineage but remain members of it (Radcliffe-Brown 1952:chap. 3).

Radcliffe-Brown's explanation was inadequate in that it chose to emphasize "the unity of the lineage" and did not give sufficient weight to these "connective positions." The notion of the "unity of the lineage" then became reified into the distinguishing characteristic of these systems, producing a circular argument in which lineages implied Crow-Omaha systems and Crow-Omaha systems implied lineages.

Many relationship terms in our society, such as "companion," "friend," "brother," "wife," "mother," "boss," and so on, can be understood as part of a system only when it is realized that although each term refers specifically to one domain, some terms can be used to indicate connections between domains. To put it another way, all societies are composed of a number of different domains each of which has a particular relationship terminology appropriate to it. Understanding a terminology requires that we discover how it is used within the appropriate domain and how different domains and their corresponding terminologies are related to one another. In our society, the army is an institutionalized domain with its own system of values and its own relationship terminology. This does not mean that military terminology is completely isolated from other relationship systems within our society. We can quite naturally use expressions such as: "My father is like a sergeant-major in our house" or "our sergeant-major is like a father to us." Given two parallel terminologies, any suggestions of an equivalence between specific terms should be investigated, for we might discover similarities between the positions covered by those terms. But we must be careful not to indiscriminately attribute the values associated with a term in one system to a term in the other, seeing one as secondary or as an "extension" of the other. The systems are related by transformations and permutations, and although our inquiry may well reveal important differences between the various systems, what we should look for is the basic code common to all the relationship terminologies and classificatory systems operating in the society.

We have already seen that the Northern Gê peoples have a number of different terminological systems that coexist side by side. Each is appropriate to its own domain, but they can also overlap with one another. In some cases the sets are similar, and we can see functional equivalencies among the terms. For instance, the Apinayé say that terms for affines are similar to terms for the formal friends *krã-geti/pá-krã*. Other systems make clear distinctions between different groups of people, as in the case of the two sets of moieties. Sometimes terms are used to establish explicit connections between different domains, as in the case of terms used for instructors and the forms of address used between initiates, who call each other *krã-txúa*, "friend," "companion." But in all cases the terms are used within specific social fields that can all be interpreted on the basis of the distinction between village center and village periphery. Dualism entirely permeates the Apinayé system, and all the principal groups that constitute the society are discriminated according to this principle. But the question here is how the Apinayé establish links between distinct social fields. Are there particular categories of people who can effect these links? What is the terminology that an Apinayé turns to when he defines his relationship with all other members of the village?

We are dealing here with the most inclusive area of Apinayé society, and it is the code associated with this domain that I describe as the relationship system. I have already examined those terms associated with specific, discrete domains and shown how those terms classify and distinguish the social universe. We are now going to look at the relationship terminology as a mechanism that links the center and periphery. It is a set of categories that allows the Apinayé to integrate all social relationships into a single, coherent scheme.

General Categories

Apinayé relationship terminology provides a set of categories that can include all the inhabitants of a village and can be extended, in certain circumstances, to include the whole society. Initially it is difficult to understand how these general terms are used since the categories appear to be only vaguely defined. The best way of explaining this system of classification is first to describe the terms, then contrast the categories so that the distinctions between them will become clear.

Kwóyá is a general classificatory term used by any given Ego, male or female, to refer to those persons who are members of Ego's community and with whom Ego may or may not establish a familiar relationship involving, for example, exchanging food, asking for support in a dispute, or asking for help with work. The Apinayé always translate *kwóyá* into the Portuguese *parente* (relative) or *meu povo* (my people). The connotations of the Apinayé term are the same as those of the Portuguese equivalents used by Brazilians of the surrounding region. *Parente* according to this usage does not necessarily refer to links that involve categorical or prescriptive obligations. The concept implies a loose and flexible sense of solidarity, as does the even vaguer notion of *meu povo*. Similarly, the Apinayé equivalent *kwóyá* indicates a social field rather than a clearly distinguished group with its own well-defined area of corporate action. Indeed, it is extremely difficult for the Indians as well as the anthropologist to locate the actual group of people that this term incorporates. An Ego's *kwóyá* often includes persons from another village as well as people in Ego's own village. It can refer to those in the same residential group as well as those who share the same house. Thus *kwóyá* covers a *field of relationships* and does not refer to a specific corporate group.

Kwóyá két (*két* is a particle that indicates negation) is the opposite of *kwóyá*. The Apinayé translate the term as *não-parente* (nonrelative). Again, it does not refer to any specific group, but to Ego's relationship with particular persons, and can include people of Ego's village and from other villages. It negates the positive implication of the previous terms and describes a kind of relationship that is inhibited or that cannot be established directly. Included in this category are people whom Ego does not know well. He does not know their names, and he cannot trace any precise genealogical connections with them. He does not exchange food with them nor visit them, and so on. This is the category of his potential enemies and of his potential affines.

Although an Apinayé might say that his wife is *kwóyá két,* he would not use the term if he was referring to the relationships established by marriage. Marriage involves certain specific obligations toward his wife and toward a number of her relatives. Hence when he actually marries, the obligations that he undertakes are enough to place these affinal relationships in another category which will be described later.

The category *kwóyá két* does not admit of subdivisions. *Kwóyá*, however, can be subdivided into two categories, which allows a distinction to be made between the kinds of relationship involved: (1) *kwóyá kumrendy* (*kumrendy* meaning "true," "real," "genuine"); and (2) *kwóyá kaág* or *kwóyá purô* (*kaág* and *purô* meaning "false," "synthetic," "distant"). The Apinayé translate these into Portuguese as *parentes de perto* (near relatives) or *parentes legítimos* (literally, "genuine relatives"—a common usage in Central Brazil to refer to close relatives) and *parentes de longe* (distant relatives). Although these subcategories are sometimes used to refer to other Apinayé who are not of Ego's village, they usually refer to a field of relationships in which Ego is closely involved in everyday life. *Kwóyá kumrendy* are those who live nearby, "true relatives" with whom Ego can easily trace a precise genealogical connection.[1] They are Ego's coresidents; he exchanges food with them; he knows them well; they support him in disputes; he will gossip with them and exchange confidential information (on such matters as sorcery accusations and the killing of cattle belonging to Brazilian ranchers); he will see them every day and he will eat with them. A distinctive feature of the relationship is the constant exchange of food, which is carried on without the need for explicit demands. One of my informants put it that: "People who are *kwóyá kumrendy* do not have to ask—they always receive." This is a clear indication that the relationship involves categorical obligations.

Kwóyá kaág (or *purô*) refers to those who are *kwóyá* but who fall outside the *kumrendy* category. This includes adoptive parents. An Apinayé may exchange food with his *kwóyá kaág* or may ask them for help with work, but such arrangements are usually transitory and unsystematic. My informants said that when a *kumrendy* relative gets involved in a quarrel, "we immediately take sides with him," but if the quarrel is between two *kaág* relatives, "we try not to take sides."

The distinction of *kwóyá* into *kumrendy* and *kaág* makes it easier to see how the categories fit actual groups. Although the Apinayé often speak of their *kwóyá kumrendy* in general terms, giving the impression that the category includes many individuals, when pressed to say specifically who these people are, they quickly reduce the catetory to the informant's own nuclear family. The tendency to equate *kwóyá kumrendy* with the nuclear family, which I confirmed on a number of occasions, is understandable since this is the only group in which categorical obligations are unambiguously defined. The point is made clearly in the following statements by several informants: "One can trust only one's father, mother, and brothers and sisters." "The most important family is my natal family because I can go there, take what I please, and eat without having to be invited."

"The closest ties are those between the family inside the house ['house' in this context meaning 'nuclear family'] because with other relatives there are often misunderstandings and quarrels. Among the family in the house, even if there is a mix-up of some kind, nobody gets angry." "I ask for things only from my father, my mother, and my brothers and sisters—only from close relatives—I don't like asking things of the others." I noted numerous statements of this kind that made the same point, but even more significant is the fact that all adult Apinayé always send food to their parents and siblings.

Kwóyá kumrendy and *kwóyá kaág* are often explained as being *kãbrô apten burog* (same blood) and *kãbrô apten nikzé* or *purô* (different blood).[2] One informant, using Portuguese, described his "genuine relatives" as *parentes de parto* (relatives by birth). Such expressions denote a biological connection, and although this does not exclude their metaphorical use as a means of establishing a firm relationship between people who are not members of the same nuclear family, it is nevertheless the case that blood relationships are considered links of substance and that these constitute the only clearly defined group in Apinayé society: the nuclear family. The importance of these relationships is confirmed if we remember that birth restrictions and precautions associated with illness can be correctly understood only in terms of the way individuals are linked by blood ties.

We can quite properly equate *kwóyá kumrendy* with blood relatives and those closely related by blood ties, a category that includes both family of origin and family of marriage. But the equation requires qualification. That this particular group of people is arrived at by a process of reduction suggests that the limits of the category are not rigidly defined. The distinctive features associated with the category *kwóyá kumrendy* are the obligatory and systematic exchange of food and the fact that blood is considered a common substance among those related in this way. The exchange of food indicates how an individual should behave toward his *kwóyá kumrendy* and symbolizes the strong bond between them. While this clearly involves the nuclear family, an individual often establishes a systematic exchange of food with his name-giver or with a friend. This is particularly obvious in the case of chiefs and faction leaders, who always exchange food with people outside their nuclear families. Similarly, the Apinayé say that "blood is dispersed throughout the village."

An accurate definition of *kwóyá kumrendy* must include the notion of degree, which underlies the category. This is why I have described the nuclear family as a *paradigm* of blood relationships in opposition to ceremonial relationships, whose *paradigm* is the relationship between name-giver and named person. Those who exchange food systematically and who support each other in disputes are establishing both kinds of relationship even though they may not fall into either category. *Kwóyá kumrendy* should therefore be defined as a class consisting of a center and a periphery. At the center, individuals are linked by strong ties of common substance (blood), whereas toward the periphery blood ties weaken and become less important as a guide to an individual's behavior. It is in the peripheral area of the category that a person's ceremonial relatives are found. As blood ties weaken, exchange relationships also tend to become more tenuous. They depend more on the individuals themselves than on systematic, formal obligations.

Kwóyá kumrendy includes both the members of Ego's nuclear family and the category of people related to Ego by ceremonial ties. It involves both relationships of substance and those marked by constant exchanges (exchange being a prominent aspect of all Apinayé and Northern Gê ceremonies). It appears, then, that outside the nuclear family, the distinction between *kwóyá kumrendy* and *kwóyá kaág* becomes blurred and can be clearly distinguished only when it is used to justify particular social arrangements or particular kinds of behavior.

We can therefore define *kwóyá kumrendy* more precisely if we think of blood ties (relations of substance) and ceremonial ties as the contrasting extremities of a continuum composed of genealogical and terminological dimensions. The nuclear family is located at one extremity and the relationship between name-giver and name-receiver at the other. If one focuses on the nuclear family, social relationships appear narrow and exclusive since they are limited by biological ties defined in terms of blood. But if one focuses on ceremonial relationships, a much more open and integrative notion of social relationships appears. The Apinayé tend to refer to the notion of blood when they want to emphasize differences of degree between two or more persons referred to by the same term, that is, when they wish to make a distinction between close relatives and more distant relatives. If Ego calls two men *tõ* (B, FBS, MZS) he might say that one is *tõ kumrendy*, a "real" brother or, as they nowadays tend to say in Portuguese, *irmão legítimo*, while the other is *tõ kaág* or *irmão de longe*, a "distant" brother.

Whereas the biological dimension of the system allows the Apinayé to make distinctions of degree in the relationships between people, the ceremonial area accomplishes the opposite.[3] It allows for the integration of persons and groups that are originally quite clearly differentiated. We saw how an individual becomes incorporated into one of the moieties by means of his name. We can therefore regard ceremonial ties among the Apinayé (and indeed among all the Northern Gê tribes) as mechanisms that establish strong ties beyond those established by relations of substance. Ceremonial ties cut across the various domains, groups, and classes and thereby integrate fundamentally different areas of the social system. In other words, they are a mechanism that transforms social relations by creating openings in the boundaries of more or less well-defined domains.[4] Hence a name-giver might previously have been classified as *kwóyá kaág* or even *kwóyá két* (a nonrelative), but once the naming relationship is established he can be considered *kwóyá kumrendy,* since naming is considered something that can initiate a relationship of close solidarity between those involved. If the name-giver's relationship with his namesake is merely formal he will remain *kwóyá kaág,* but if he visits, exchanges food and labor, and offers support in political disputes, he will gradually become a *kumrendy* relative and will be classified along with the other members of his namesake's nuclear family. It is therefore through the name-giver's behavior in transforming a distant relationship into a close one that his position in the general system of classification is altered.

A similar sort of change takes place in marriage when a woman and her relatives come to be considered *kwóyá* by her husband once children appear and the marriage has proved stable. Initially these relationships are typically ceremonial and are described in terms of social distance (*piâm*). But as the ties between a man and his affines grow stronger, he and his wife come to be considered of the same blood and, as the Apinayé say, the two families become "one and the same thing." Hence while the wife and her relatives are initially classified as *kwóyá kaág,* they eventually become *kwóyá kumrendy.* At any point in the process an individual may have the choice of two or more terms by which to classify relatives, and, correspondingly, he may be able to choose different modes of behavior toward them. For example, an individual may address several people of a certain residential unit by terms that correspond to their being classified as *kaág* relatives. He may have no categorical obligations toward them although he may sometimes send meat to that household. But if his uterine brother then marries into that household he can choose either to use the same terms in addressing members of that household and maintain his traditional relationship with them or change to a set of affinal terms that classify them according to criteria of respect and social distance. This kind of duplication of social ties is so common in Apinayé society that I am inclined to see it as part of the structure of their relationship system. The opportunity to choose between two terms for the same person is not limited to those cases in which affinal ties are superimposed on *kwóyá* ties but occurs within the *kwóyá* category itself. It appears that the choice of one term rather than another depends on which relationship is considered the more important in any given situation. In the case of naming practices, the term associated with the ceremonial relationship replaces any other that could be used as a term of address, just as superimposing ties of affinity on former ties produces a corresponding change in the form of address. For example, one of my informants addressed the wife of his *geti* (in this case an FF) as *itõdy* (Z, MZD, FBD) and not as *tui-re* (FM) since, as he said, "she is my foster sister." She had been adopted by the man's mother in order to receive her names. Another informant called a certain person *geti* and was addressed in turn as *ikrá* (S, BS, and so on) but not as *tamtxúa* (SS, ZS), since this person was also his adoptive father and his arranger of names. A third informant called his mother-in-law *inā* (M), explaining that she was a "distant sister" (*itõdy kaág*) of his mother and that this relationship was stronger and more advantageous to him. There were numerous cases of this kind, and they all revealed the same pattern: a ceremonial relationship or a recently established relationship is always preeminent and determines the use of certain relationship terms. The use of these terms can therefore be seen as indicating the informant's situation at a particular moment in his life as well as representing the social alignments of the community at a specific time. Hence changing a social relationship may also involve a change in terms of address and a consequent reclassification of a set of social relationships.

It is factors such as these that create the so-called flexibility of Apinayé and Northern Gê relationship systems. A transformation of the relationship between people initially situated in different social fields may or may not provoke the terminological reclassification that would indicate the social realignment. I would therefore argue that Apinayé social classification depends upon the dynamic and shifting quality of the various realignments that take place in their social life. The biological dimension of social relations is always present, however, and can always be used to justify distance or proximity between people. I am convinced that many of the apparent confusions in the usage of Apinayé terminology are the result of our failure to grasp these underlying factors, especially the way that gradations are established along the dimension of substance.

I became aware of the importance of the notion of substance underlying the relationship system only when I began to examine Apinayé food prohibitions and birth precautions: the so-called couvade. When I saw that these are rationalized in terms of blood proximity I was then able to understand relationship terms systematically by taking blood as a crucial dimension. The Apinayé say that one undertakes these precautions only on behalf of *kwóyá kumrendy* (close relatives), whose blood is "strong." They also explain that "the blood of an *ikrá* [son, daughter] is stronger because it is closer to the parents' blood. *Itamtxúa* [grandchildren, or sister's children] have weaker blood because they have already moved off and are far away." One informant put it that "precautions stop at the *tamtxúa* because blood is far away and weaker."

These are important facts, for it is through the dimension of substance that the Apinayé are able to explain their relationship system in abstract terms. For example, I have heard some Indians compare their network of relationships with a tree: the roots (*me ô pó kráti*) are like the old people whose blood becomes weaker as it spreads throughout the whole kindred. One informant said: "The person who gives blood weakens it. The person who receives blood gets stronger and stronger. If a couple have a child and this child in turn has a child, the grandparent's blood is getting weaker and weaker." This implies not only that the old people are getting weaker through losing their blood (that is to say, they are aging) but also that their relationships with their descendants are becoming ever more tenuous in terms of substance. Another informant compared relations of substance with a stalk of maize, which produces its newest ears at the top. Ears representing the youngest members of the community are produced by the older ones lower down. The same informant drew an image of the system as he saw it (see Figure 18), with lines representing blood and circles, with small dots inside, nuclear families. An Apinayé therefore has an abstract conception of relationships consisting of a complete system of connections in which small groups give blood to other small groups of the same type. The notion of substance is therefore critical if we are to understand the system. As the Apinayé explain, "blood is spread throughout the village." Furthermore, adjacent groups have more blood (or stronger blood) in common than groups that are separated from one another.

In summary, the subcategory *kwóyá kumrendy* has two basic components and, depending on which is emphasized, the category can operate in different ways. In terms of substance, *kwóyá kumrendy* can be reduced to the nuclear family. This is the group most strongly connected by blood, and it is the primary model on which the category is based. In terms of ceremonies, *kwóyá kumrendy* is essentially constituted by a number of ceremonial ties and, as such, is only tenuously separated from *kwóyá kaág*.

The Apinayé also refer to a category of *iprom kwóyá* (that is, the *kwóyá* of one's wife). As in the case of the terms previously discussed, this refers to a category of people and not to an actual social group. The category is formed a posteriori following a marriage. When asked where his *iprom kwóyá* actually are, an Apinayé will do no more than indicate the houses on the other side of the village that are opposite his own and where, ideally, his sons should find their wives. But the expression does not refer to any specific group in which a man must find his wife. Since marriage is explicitly prohibited between *kwóyá kumrendy* (close relatives),[5] one might say that *iprom kwóyá* (affines) are always categorized a posteriori from those previously classed as *kaág*, the category of nonrelatives. This explains why it is possible for a man and a woman designated by any relationship terms to marry, as long as they are considered to be distant (*kaág*) relatives, and it is also consistent with the appearance of the various terminological alternatives that I have already discussed. Hence an affinal relationship among the Apinayé (as in Krahó society) is one that has been transformed in one of two directions: either those desig-

Figure 18. *An Apinayé representation of their relationship system. Circles are houses and lines are ties of substance.*

nated have been brought closer (if they were nonrelatives), or they have been placed at a distance (if they were *kwóyá kaág*) (cf. Melatti 1970). This kind of transformation is quite consistent with the notion of incest since the Apinayé say that to copulate with a mother or a sister or a *closely related tamtxúa* transforms the person into a thing, an animal (*me-bóyá*). This theme is made clear in a myth in which a group of boys are transformed into birds after copulating with their sisters (Nimuendajú 1939:182).

The categories are represented in Figure 19. The diagram reveals a number of fundamental features of the Apinayé relationship system. It indicates the distribution of the categories and how they are related on various levels of contrast. Areas I and II (*kwóyá*) can be contrasted with area III (non-*kwóyá*). This could express the contrast between the Apinayé and another people, or the same distinction could be used to differentiate one Apinayé village from another. The Apinayé of São José might consider themselves *kwóyá* in opposition to the Apinayé of Mariazinha, whom they would regard as *kwóyá két*. Such contrasts can be unambiguously established only when they are referring to a group that, potentially at least, could function as a unit and, as I have emphasized, the terms characteristically do not refer to specific social groups. But in this case, should a dispute arise between villages, an individual's ties within his residential community will be emphasized at the expense of any ties he may have with persons of the other village and thus allow him to make a clear distinction between the two groups that are in conflict.

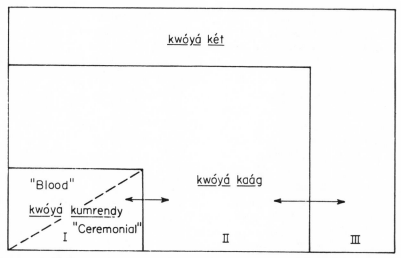

Figure 19. *Distribution of Apinayé general relationship categories in the social space.*

The diagram also indicates that *kumrendy* relatives form a fairly small class, as do those classified as nonrelatives. This is quite consistent with Apinayé descriptions of their own society: "One has few *kumrendy* relatives, many *kaág* relatives, and few nonrelatives" (see Da Matta 1979).

We can see in the diagram how the field of ceremonial relatives is penetrated by the field of *kaág* relatives and how a relationship is established between the central group, formed by relations of substance, and the peripheral group, formed by ceremonial relations that are formalized by exchanges and mutual support. One could also include in the diagram the category of *iprom kwóyá* (affines) by placing it in an area that overlaps the boundary between *kwóyá kaág* and nonrelatives.

Finally, the diagram offers a simple visualization of the areas where relationships and social domains interpenetrate. The arrows indicate how individuals or relationships can be transformed by passing from one area to another.

From this perspective we can now isolate two basic features that account for the flexibility of the Apinayé relationship system. First, the terms do not strictly refer to social groups but to fields or spheres of social relations. It is these fields that are defined with precision and not the persons or groups that can be included within them. Hence the terminology indicates conjunctions and disjunctions of domains and social relations.

Second, although social relations can be defined prescriptively in terms of classes, the prescription does not refer to actual persons or specific groups but suggests only a specific field of social relations. For example, a man knows that his name-giver cannot be his genitor and must be a *geti* (*krã-tum*), but he cannot precisely say who will be covered by this category. In the other Northern Gê groups the statistical possibilities of what can and cannot be included in a category are reduced. Among the Kayapó, the normative category of name-giver is the mother's brother. Statistical evidence conforms with the categorical rule. This is also the case among the Eastern Timbira (Canela, Krahó, and Krĩkatí); in addition, there is a significant emphasis on reciprocity: a man gives his names to his sister's children, and she gives her names to her brother's children. Reciprocity is apparently an important feature of the Timbira system, indicating that naming has a classificatory function. (This feature is absent among the Kayapó.) Among the Apinayé, however, statistical evidence reveals a great deal of variation, although there are still informants who speak of the mother's brother in terms of a categorical norm when they attempt to define the name-giver with precision. The importance of this lack of fit between the categorical norm and the statistical evidence will become clearer in the discussion below.

A basic feature of the Apinayé relationship system is that categories are determinate but persons (and groups) are indeterminate. That is to say, many terms obtain their sociological content only in the context of social practice. In a sense, Apinayé social life can be described as a process that is constantly transforming strangers into relatives, nonrelatives into affines, and false relatives into true ones. A person who arrives from another village or another tribe is initially classified by most, if not all, of the residents as *kwóyá két*. But over time, depending on the kind of relationships he manages to establish, more and more people will begin to classify him in a different way until he may well become a *kumrendy* relative of a large number of people, especially if this is established through ceremonial ties. This happened, for instance, when two Sherente Indians came to live in the village of São José. Through marrying Apinayé women they established stable relationships in the village. The integration of a third Sherente, however, was not as successful, and he was always distinguished as a stranger—a *kwóyá két*. The success of the first two was due to their stable marriages, the birth of children, and good relationships with their affines. The third constantly found himself in matrimonial difficulties.

The reverse process takes place for an Apinayé child during the cycle of his social life. The child is brought up in his natal household within an exclusive circle of *kwóyá kumrendy* relatives. When he later receives names and formal friends he becomes associated with people who represent ever more inclusive social fields. Finally, when he marries he obtains another set of *kumrendy* relatives (his wife and children). This is why the Apinayé refer to their affines as *iprom kwóyá*. Marriage is initially a ceremonial relationship, but the birth of children and the maintenance of a stable marriage involves the partners in relations of substance. Hence the transformation of *kaág* to *kumrendy* is realized.

I do not claim that the explanation offered here is an exhaustive account of the complexities of the Apinayé relationship system. Indeed, I do not think it could operate quite as simply as I have presented it. But the virtue of using models of this kind is that a complex situation can be presented in its most elementary terms. I am therefore convinced that my account is sufficiently correct to be accepted as a minimal translation of the system used by the Apinayé. I would further suggest that the general classificatory schemes found among the other Northern Gê peoples follow the same principles as the system presented here.

The corresponding terms in Krahó classification are: *meikhuampéimã* (which Melatti translates as "close consanguineal relatives"), *meikhói'nare* ("nonrelatives") and *meikhúa* ("relatives in general") (Melatti 1970 and 1979). The prefix "me" is probably a collective particle. If this is the case then the Krahó terms are cognates of the Apinayé terms. The corresponding Krīkatí terms are: *khwá* (relatives defined by precise genealogical connection), *kjwá mpe* (*mpe* = true), and *khwá kahák* (*kahák* = false) (Lave 1967:206). The Kayapó terms are: *õbikwá* (relatives in general), *õbikwá kaág* (adoptive and affinal relatives), and *õbikwá kumren* (true relatives) (T. Turner 1966:300). The Krĩkatí and Kayapó terms are obviously cognates of the Apinayé terms.

There is an unresolved question in Melatti's, Lave's, and Turner's accounts in that the authors do not explain how these terms operate as a classificatory system. They stress only their extreme flexibility and integrative value. Melatti and Lave emphasize that relatives are considered those with whom one regularly exchanges food (Melatti 1970:chap. 6; Lave 1967:211). Turner, by contrast, mentions the problem of defining Kayapó relationships on a biological dimension but does not go on to explain how this is an essential factor in understanding the Kayapó system (T. Turner 1966:302–303). Indeed, he seems to be arguing that it is incorrect to define Kayapó terms genealogically. Yet these accounts are interesting in that they emphasize the two aspects that I have distinguished. While Turner mentions the biological dimension, Melatti and Lave concentrate on what I have called the ceremonial domain, pointing out that the systematic exchange of food and mutual political support are essential indications of how the kinship system operates. All three explain that the terminologies are subject to a great deal of manipulation and that the classes they refer to are extremely flexible.[6]

I suggest that if one describes Northern Gê systems in terms of domains and if one explains the kinds of relationship that bring these domains into contact with one another, one can then construct a model that will account for all those features described as "flexibility," "absence of limits," "manipulability," and so on. The properties of the system become much clearer if one thinks of a biological component cutting across a ceremonial component, and vice versa. Choice and flexibility can then be seen as intrinsic features of the system and do not have to be dismissed as inconsistencies of some kind.

The Apinayé system is represented in the Venn diagram shown in Figure 20.

The circle P contains two smaller circles, A and F. Circle N represents the category opposed to P. Circle A contains two smaller circles, S and C, which represent the biological dimension of "common substance" and the ceremonial dimension. Circle A is basically defined in terms of circle S, of which the paradigm is the nuclear family. But S overlaps with C, which in turn links circles A and F (nonrelatives). And it is this circle F that links "relatives" (P) and "nonrelatives" (N).

It is the overlapping of the various areas that is crucial. That blood relatives overlap with ceremonial relatives is consistent with the fact that ceremonial relatives (name-givers and formal friends) are related to a given Ego through the mediation of adoptive parents. Adoptive parents are in turn directly related to Ego by parallel ties, that is, they are same sex siblings of Ego's genitors (FB or MZ). It is immediately evident that

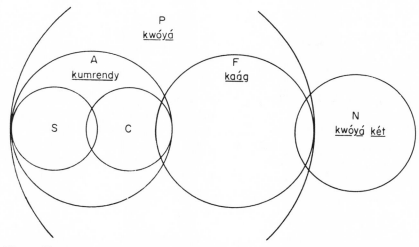

Figure 20. *Diagram showing the working and overlapping of the Apinayé general relationship categories.*

ceremonial relations are mechanisms that mediate between relatives classified as "true" and others referred to as "false." Ceremonial relatives are either linked to Ego through cross ties (MB, FZ) or they are persons located on the grandparents' genealogical level. Thus name-givers link areas *A* and *F* just as formal friends quite explicitly link the domestic area and the most distant social area represented by the circle *N*.

With the help of the diagram we can also visualize two further features of the Apinayé system. First, we see how an individual can define relationships according to the criteria he wishes to emphasize. For example, if I wished to distinguish between my relatives and my nonrelatives, I would focus on circles *P* and *N*. But if I wished to distinguish between close relatives and more distant relatives, I would use the opposition between circles *A* and *F*, ignoring the subclasses included within *A*. A distinction within class *A* is made only when there is some reason to place members of that category in polar opposition. Second, the diagram clearly indicates the possible choices open to an Apinayé when he is referring to someone else who might be situated in any one of these circles.

Finally, the Venn diagram resolves the difficulties of establishing the limits of Apinayé terms and explains their flexibility and how they are manipulated. The two important features here are: first, that the terms do not refer to specifically defined groups and second, that a specific term used in one context to define a relationship with Ego can, in another context, be equated with a different term. An examination of what is called the "kinship system" will make this clearer.

Specific Categories

In addition to the general categories described in the previous section, there is another set of terms used to classify specific relationships between members of Apinayé society. They are principally used within the general category *kwóyá* and not within the opposite category *kwóyá két*. Persons classified as *kwóyá két* are addressed either by their proper names or by one of another set of terms appropriate to the relationship established. If, for example, a person was classified as a formal friend, his circle of relatives would be designated by the appropriate terms explained in Chapter 3. A spouse's relatives are also addressed by a set of terms designating affinal relatives. It should be remembered, however, that affinal relations can be superimposed on the *kwóyá kaág* category.

1. *pam:* F, FB, MH, MZH

This word is a term of reference. The word *txún* and its variations *txún-re* and *txún-ti* (where *re* is a diminutive and *ti* an augmentative) are used both as terms of reference and as terms of address. Some informants use the Brazilian form *papai,* but only for their actual father. Both *pam* and *txún* are used with the categories *kumrendy* and *kaág* if the speaker wishes to indicate the exact position of that *pam* in relation to himself. The descriptive term *nipeitxó* is also used to distinguish the actual father from others in the category. It is best translated "the one who made me" (*nipeitxe* meaning "to make" and *txó* a particle indicating action). This last term emphasizes the "substantial" aspect of the relationship between father and child whereas *pam* reflects the sociological aspect. Someone in this category who has died is referred to as *pam pinrog,* the second word, according to the Apinayé's own translation, indicating death. The term *me-papam* (our father) refers to the sun or, today, to God. The term *tõ-re* (*tõ* meaning "brother") may be used by a man as an affectionate term for his actual father, and women use the corresponding brother term *kambû.*

2. *nã:* M, MZ, FW, FBW

This is also a term of reference. The word *dyil* is used both as a term of reference and as a term of address. The particles *ti, re, preké* (old), *kumrendy,* and *kaág* can be added to the term to indicate physical or social aspects of the person being referred to. The descriptive term *katortxô* (*katóro* meaning "to leave"; *idkatóro,* "I leave"; and *txó,* a particle indicating action) can be translated "the one from whom I came out" and refers to the actual mother, again emphasizing the relation of substance between a person and his *nã*. When a *nã* dies the term *pabotxói-ti* is used.

3. *tõ:* B, MS, FS, MZS, FBS

4. *tõdy:* Z, MD, FD, MZD, FBD

These are used both as terms of reference and as terms of address. The particles *ti* and *re* may be added to indicate physical size, whereas *kumrendy* and *kaåg* indicate social distance. *Preké* and *prin* indicate old and young. Two terms of address, *pigkwá* and *kambû*, are used by male and female Egos respectively. The addition of the word *pinrog* indicates that the person is dead. The expressions *kro-ti* and *kro-re* refer to older and younger brother.

5. *krà:* S, D, BS, BD (man speaking); S, D, ZS, ZD (woman speaking)

This is both a term of reference and a term of address. In addition, the terms *akatxóiti* and *akantê-re* may be used to distinguish a male or female *krá*.

6. *geti* (*ngeti*): FF, MF, MB, FZH

This word is both a term of reference and a term of address. *Krã-tum* is used when a *geti* becomes a male Ego's name-giver (the reciprocal form being *krã-dúw*). A *geti* who has died is referred to as *geti pinrog*. *Geti* and *krã-tum* are used as synonyms except when the informant is specifically asked to explain the difference; then he will make the distinction mentioned earlier. Some Apinayé use the Brazilian word *vovô* (grandfather) in place of this word.

7. *tui* (*tukatui*): MM, FM, FZ, MBW

This is a term of reference and of address, and again the particles *pre, ke, prin, ti,* and *re* are used to distinguish between persons in this category. Similarly, *kumrendy* and *kaåg* indicate social distance. But in this case, when a *tui* gives her names to a girl in the category *tamtxúa* (see term 8) there is no change of term corresponding to the change from *geti* to *krã-tum* in term 6. *Tui pinrog* again refers to someone who has died.

8. *tamtxúa:* SS, SD, DS, DD, ZS, ZD, WBS, WBD (man speaking); SS, SD, DS, DD, BS, BD, HZS, HZD (woman speaking)

This is also a term of both reference and address. As with term 5, *partxóite* and *apare* distinguish male and female *tamtxúa*. *Pinrog* indicates a person's death.

AFFINAL TERMS

9. *imbré-geti:* WF (reference, man speaking), HF (reference, woman speaking)

Tukóyá is the term of address.

10. *papam-geti:* (reference and address) WM

11. *iprom:* (reference and address) W

12. *papany:* (reference and address) WZ, BW

13. *imbré:* (reference) WB

14. *idpienhon-ti:* (reference) ZH

   Tukó is the term of address.

15. *txóiti:* SW, BSW, ZSW, BW (woman speaking)

16. *tukó-ti:* (reference) DH

17. *idpien:* H

18. *ponmre-geti:* HM

19. *ponmre:* HZ

Analysis

Three features of this terminology are immediately apparent. First, apart from certain affinal terms, particles can be added to the terms to indicate specific social relations (*re, ti, prin, kumrendy, kaág, prege/preke*). Hence, when the terms are used by themselves they can refer to very broad categories and can classify people indiscriminately both inside and outside the category of *kumrendy* relatives. I have therefore called all these terms "categories of consanguineal relatives" since they refer both to those related to Ego through primary ties (maternal grandparents, for example) as well as to those whose relationship to Ego is distant and difficult to trace with any precision.

Second, it is again apparent that the categories indicated by those terms consist of fields of relations and not specific corporate groups. The terms are used to integrate a series of diverse social fields, and it is in this sense that they reveal their systematic quality.

Third, the terms for Ego's parents' genealogical level are of the bifurcate merging type, which distinguishes cross and parallel relatives. Cross uncles and aunts (MB, FZ) are distingushed from parallel uncles and aunts (FB, MZ) and equated with grandparents. The features of the terminology can be accurately represented in Figure 21 (which was designed by Lave to illustrate Krĩkatí terms; see Lave 1967:207; see also Lounsbury 1964).

The cross/parallel distinction is more important in defining certain positions than distinctions of sex and genealogical level. Following Lave's original diagram, it will be noted that here also I have not indicated the position of cross-cousins. This is because the Apinayé use terms for these positions that vary depending on a number of factors. The important point to note here is that I do not take an examination of the cross-cousin terms as the most important starting point in my analysis of Apinayé terms.

Since the work of Tylor and Rivers, cross-cousin terms have tradition-

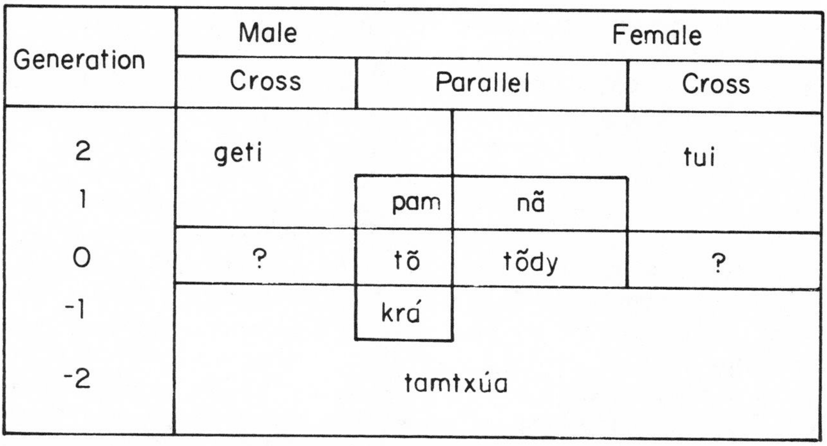

Generation	Male		Female	
	Cross	Parallel		Cross
2	geti		tui	
1		pam	nã	
0	?	tõ	tõdy	?
-1		krá		
-2	tamtxúa			

Figure 21. *Relationship terms.*

ally been considered the focal point in the analysis of relationship terminologies, but in fact there is no particular justification for this approach, especially in those cases where one is dealing with a system in which there is no prescriptive marriage rule (Maybury-Lewis 1967:214). Among the Northern Gê, there is an obvious difficulty in isolating a category of cross-cousin since these are the only genealogical positions that vary from society to society, and even within the same society in the case of the Krĩkatí and the Apinayé.

All Northern Gê societies have the same repertoire of terms, which varies only according to the dialect of the group. The first eight terms described in the previous section could be used quite simply to define the same genealogical positions among the Kraʼ∂, Krĩkatí, Kayapó, Gaviões, and Canela (Nimuendajú 1946:104; Crocker 1962; Keesing n.d.). But the definition of Kayapó cross-cousin terms produces equations of the Omaha type in which matrilateral cross-cousins are classified as *nã* and *geti* and patrilateral cross-cousins as *tamtxúa*. Among the Gaviões and Krahó the equations produce a Crow-type terminology in which matrilateral cross-cousins are called *krá* and patrilateral cross-cousins *pam* and *tui* (Laraia and Da Matta 1968:108; Melatti 1967:72 and 1970:197). Among the Krĩkatí there are various terms for these same positions, except when one looks at cross-cousins in relation to the transmission of names (Lave 1967:197). Melatti has also found among the Krahó that there are variations in these positions when they are associated with name transmission (1967:75).

Variations in cross-cousin terminology are therefore a normal feature of these systems.[7] Furthermore, among the Northern Gê it is only these terms that show variations, the Kayapó showing an Omaha pattern and the Timbira a Crow type. Since cross-cousin terms are the variant features of these terminologies we should properly assume that they cannot be of fundamental importance in understanding the systems. The invariants are the equations in Figure 23 (see below). The initial problem is therefore to interpret these invariant equations and then to look for an explanation of the variant cross-cousin terms.

I have already pointed out that in the Apinayé terminology the distinction between sexes is equivalent to the distinction between genealogical levels. Figure 21 shows that the parents of *pam* and *nã* as well as their opposite sex siblings (Ego's MB and FZ) are designated by only two terms, distinct from the two terms that cover parents and parents' same sex siblings.

The sociological and ideological reasons for this distinction are twofold. First, the nuclear family is independent. Indeed, it is the only clearly discernible social group in an Apinayé village. It has its own gardens and often its own house, and it is the basic unit of economic cooperation and social reproduction. I showed earlier that there are several social practices that emphasize the unity of the nuclear family and that these are based on an ideology of relations of substance. These features are clearly expressed in the terminology, in which the terms for genitors virtually describe these biological connections by distinguishing between biological and social relations and between genitors and their same sex siblings (see terms 1 and 2).

Second, the rule of uxorilocal residence is also consistent with the distinction between same sex siblings and opposite sex siblings. Women remain in their natal household, but a man, following marriage, is obliged to leave and take up residence elsewhere. Residence rules therefore reinforce ties between sisters and separate women from their brothers who have left the natal home. The emphasis on the distinction between same sex and opposite sex siblings is also clearly reflected in the behavior between members of a nuclear family. The Apinayé say that between father and son, and between brothers, relationships are extremely relaxed and intimate whereas between mother and son, brother and sister, or father and daughter, relationships are characteristically marked by *piâm* (social distance and respect). The institution of adoptive parents further reinforces the relationship between parents and their same sex children since the arranger of names acquires jural authority over his or her adopted children. Father/son and mother/daughter relationships are therefore relieved of jural content and become symmetrical in that they are like a relationship between siblings of the same sex. Looking at term 1, we see that a man calls his father *tõ-re* (*tõ* meaning "brother," and *re,* a diminutive), but this does not mean that he will take his father's place in a certain role or succeed to membership in any specific social group (as would be implied in a system of parallel descent). The explanation is that between a son and his father there is no distance because authority over the child is transferred to an adoptive parent, who becomes responsible for him in disputes outside the nuclear family.

If we again consider the Apinayé idea that links of common substance exist between members of the nuclear family, we can understand why a man distinguishes between his own and his sister's children by referring to close and distant blood relatives. Indeed, the distinction between same sex and opposite sex siblings is clearly expressed in a biological idiom, which can be detailed as follows.

First, there is an axiomatic distinction between the sexes. A woman is said to be weaker, slower, and physically more fragile than a man because she has more blood. The diet of young initiates consists of the meat of certain animals, well roasted to avoid blood, so that the young men will be made lighter and become more agile runners. Symbolically, this is consistent with cutting the ties between the young men and the female world of the periphery of the village, preparing them for entry into the male world after the initiation process is completed.

Second, when this absolute distinction between the sexes is translated to the level of terminology, the result is the following: the distinction between a sibling of the same sex and a sibling of the opposite sex is, in structural terms, a distinction between an equal and someone different. Same sex siblings occupy structurally similar positions and establish symmetrical relationships whereas opposite sex siblings establish relationships that are equivalent to a distinction between genealogical levels, hence the use of the term *tamtxúa* for sister's children (or brother's children from a woman's point of view).

Taken together, these features explain both how the nuclear family is clearly distinguished from the rest of the kindred and why a distinction between cross and parallel relatives appears. Indeed, anyone situated outside the nuclear family or outside the immediate group constituted by blood ties is, actually or potentially, a cross-relative, that is, a ceremonial relative. It is the father's brothers (or mother's sisters) who should ideally be a child's adoptive parents and arrangers of names, while grandparents and the mother's brothers (or father's sisters) should be the child's name-givers. Hence father's brothers and mother's sisters enlarge the social field of the nuclear family, while grandparents, father's sisters, and mother's brothers relate the nuclear family to a different social field. This is represented in Figure 22.

This is an alternative representation of Figure 20. Three areas are distinguished, but areas I and II are closer in terms of substance—a fact reflected in the terms of reference where the Apinayé do not distinguish genitor from pater nor from adoptive parents (arrangers of names). The

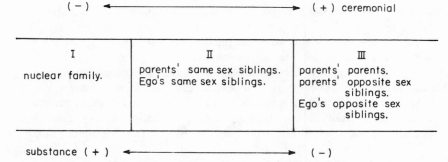

Figure 22. *Diagram of the connection between substance and ceremonial relationships in Apinayé society.*

ideology of area II is therefore an extension of that which is so strongly marked in area I. In area III (the category of *geti* and *tui-re/tamtxúa*), blood is considered weak and is therefore not a significant feature in determining social behavior. Relationships in the third area are therefore peripheral. They indicate the theoretical limits of Ego's kindred in terms of effective relationships based on blood ties. But if that is so in terms of substance, when we consider the matter in terms of the ceremonial dimension, it is this peripheral area that emerges as the most important, for it is here that a person will find his name-givers. Thus in the very area in which blood relationships become weak, people in those categories are turned back toward Ego in the form of ceremonial relatives. And in fact when the Apinayé explain those features that we describe as Crow-Omaha cross-cousin terms, they say of relatives referred to by such terms that "they are returning." From a sociological point of view, the phrase is perfectly intelligible since they do indeed "return" in terms of ceremonial relationships.

The Apinayé relationship system can therefore be regarded as a cyclical process in which relations of substance are exchanged for ceremonial relations. The inherent dualism of the system is quite clear: when blood ceases to be a significant criterion of classification, relationships become ceremonial. It is specifically through the ceremonial groups that a person is integrated into the most inclusive categories of society, but although this domain certainly involves an individual in a network of relationships different in kind from the domestic domain, both domains are essential in the formation and definition of the Apinayé individual.

The characteristics of the two domains of the system can now be summarized.

Domestic sphere	*Ceremonial sphere*
nuclear family (corporate group)	classes of persons and relationships

substance (blood)—internal, bio-logical criterion	ceremonial (exchanges, names, adornments)—external and social criteria
same sex relatives	relatives of opposite sex and those of different genealogical level
distinctions of degree	absolute distinctions between persons and groups
pam and *nã/krá*	*geti* and *tui/tamtxúa*
limited by relationships surrounding the nuclear family	indeterminate limits that can include the entire village

It could be argued quite simply that the terminological equation *mother's brothers and father's sisters = maternal and paternal grandparents* is precisely consistent with the rule of uxorilocal residence and the ideological and symbolic differences between men and women. This point of view is supported by the fact that in the set of affinal terms there is a correspondence between the terms for WF and WB. It is the men referred to by these terms who control the affinal group into which a male Ego marries and for whom he has to work. (This is particularly so in the case of the father-in-law, *imbré-geti,* who remains resident in Ego's wife's house.) Although a man's female affines are distinguished from his wife, they are all classified under the same term, *papany* (the term for WM being *papan-geti*). Just as the terminology distinguishes a man's own nuclear family, so it distinguishes a man's wife from her sisters (although the wife's sisters' children will be called *krá*). Similarly, the husband calls his father-in-law *tukóyá* and is in turn called *tukó-ti,* the reciprocal form of address indicating the husband's incorporation into his affinal household. With the exception of the wife (*iprom*), a man's relationships with all people referred to by these terms are characterized by *piâm* (respect and shame), which is most pronounced between husband and wife's parents and between husband and wife's brother. *Piâm* is characteristic of the boundaries between nuclear families and indicates that area where affines are transformed into close relatives—an important mechanism in the Apinayé system of classification.

The transformation takes place gradually. When a man first goes to live in his wife's house he is considered a distant relative and must behave accordingly. Following the birth of his children, and as his brothers-in-law move out, he gradually gains more influence within the group. Since his own blood has now been mixed with his wife's he will become sufficiently close to his affines to be able to consider them *kumrendy* relatives. The process can be described in two stages. First, affines are strangers and initial relationships are marked by an exchange, that is, the wife's sexual services for service carried out by the husband for the benefit of his affines. This is, in essence, a daily, systematic continuation of the marriage ceremony itself, in which an initial exchange was established between the two domestic groups. This is emphasized at a certain point during the Apinayé marriage ceremony, when a gigantic meat pie is exchanged for the wife.

Second, following the birth of children, who represent the union of the couple and the mixing of their blood, the exchange relationship becomes one of common substance. The process transforms a ceremonial relationship into a blood relationship. In other words, it is the reverse of the process that incorporates an Apinayé into ceremonial groups, when he receives his names and formal friends and enters the political life of the village.

The Problem of Cross-Cousin Terms

The analysis so far has concentrated on the invariant features of the system, that is, those terms that informants agree on, which, apart from a few minor corrections, correspond with Nimuendajú's evidence (1939:111–112) and which are cognate with terms used by other Northern Gê societies. In considering the cross-cousin terms the analysis becomes difficult, for these conditions do not obtain.

Nimuendajú's presentation of Apinayé cross-cousin terms was not at all coherent (1939:111; see also Maybury-Lewis 1960). If the facts were correct, it was not only an unusual system but it allowed for a number of terminological possibilities all of which were difficult to understand. The terms were presented as follows:

MBD = *id-pigkwá* (= *itõdy,* see term 4)
MBS = *id-krã-túm-re* (or *geti,* see term 6)
FZD = *tui-re*
FZS = *id-krã-túm-re*

Alternatively, all four positions can be classified as *tamtxúa.*

The pattern is typical of a Northern Gê system since the terms indicate equations between positions on different genealogical levels. But the first two terms do not correspond with their reciprocal forms. If Ego calls his MBS *krã-tum* he should call his FZS *tamtxúa,* and if he calls his FZD *tui-re* he should call his MBD *tamtxúa.* But according to the evidence neither of these possibilities actually occurs. A major difficulty in interpreting Nimuendajú's evidence is that there are no genealogical tables in his book, and he does not state how he collected the evidence. When I asked the Apinayé where Nimuendajú might have collected his information, they said that he worked only with the chief of Bacaba (now São José), with the old counselor of Bacaba, and with the counselor's daughter—as Nimuendajú himself indicates in the opening chapter of his book (1939:16).

When he published the Brazilian version of the book, in an edition "revised, annotated, and corrected" by the author (1956:viii), the cross-cousin terms appeared in a simpler, clearer presentation (p. 141):

MBD = *tui-re*
MBS = *id-krã-tum*
FZD = *i-tamtxwú*
FZS = *i-tamtxwú*

Here there are no alternative or inconsistent terms. As a "solution" it follows an Omaha pattern similar to the Kayapó terminology described by Terence Turner (1966:452ff.). But the matrilateral cross-cousin equations present certain difficulties since there are two siblings designated by terms that in the first and second ascending genealogical levels designate affinal relationships: MBW, MM, FM = *tui-re* and FF, MF, FZH = *geti* (*krã-tum*). Such equations are inconsistent, but they are not uncommon in South America.[8] Also, in the Apinayé case, one can see how the terminological pattern is consistent with the sociological identification between genitor and son and between genetrix and daughter, which stresses the unity of the nuclear family within the cognatic kindred. Hence, as Turner suggested, the equations could be indicative of the way husbands are integrated into their affinal households (T. Turner 1966). And by using the term *tui-re* for MBD instead of *nã*, the Apinayé give even greater emphasis to the unity of the nuclear family than do the Kayapó.

This is not the only way in which the Apinayé express these genealogical ties. Before we examine the others we can conclude that these particular ones are intelligible in precisely the same terms as Turner's account of the rationale behind Omaha cross-cousin terms among the Kayapó. Given the importance of the nuclear family in Apinayé society and the emphasis placed on the link between genitor and son, the equations are a solution to the problem of uxorilocal residence where a man must be integrated into the household of his affines.

I collected twenty-seven examples of cross-cousin usages among the Apinayé from genealogies gathered through interviews with both men and women. Of these, eight follow an Omaha pattern (FZS, FZD = *tamtxúa*; MBD = *nã*; MBS = *geti*). But eight follow a Crow pattern, three show cross-cousin terms of a Hawaiian type (that is, cross-cousins identified with siblings and parallel cousins), and four appear to be quite anomalous. (The anomalous cases are from material collected by missionaries from the Summer Institute of Linguistics.) The final four examples are indeterminate but suggest either Crow or Omaha equations (see Lounsbury 1964).

If one wished to classify the Apinayé terminology one might argue either that it was an anomalous type or that the anomalies are the result of social change. The first suggestion is not helpful since the anomalies concern only cross-cousins. For the same reason the second is not of particular theoretical significance, but it should nevertheless be taken into account. But neither suggestion approaches the principal problem, which is to explain the apparently inconsistent usages of cross-cousin terms. Let me then recapitulate the principal features of the argument so far.

The invariant equations of the Northern Gê systems are:

$$\text{FZH} = \text{FF} = \text{MF} = \text{MB} = geti \qquad \text{reciprocal} = tamtx\acute{u}a$$
$$\text{MBW} = \text{MM} = \text{FM} = \text{FZ} = tui$$

All informants are consistent in their use of these terms to indicate these positions, that in itself being an indication of the importance of the equations in the system.

From a formal point of view these equations hold in all Northern Gê terminologies. They are indeed typical of what Lounsbury calls a "complementary Crow-Omaha" system (1964a) since they equate genealogical levels, including those positions indicated by affinal terms (where WB and WF = *imbré* and *imbré-geti,* man speaking; and HZ and HM = *ponmre* and *ponmre-geti,* woman speaking). Hence *geti/tui,* and the cognates in other Northern Gê terminologies, have a number of "generative" possibilities.[9] The specific male and female cross-cousin categories indicated in Figure 23 could appear as either *nã* or *tui* in the female case and as either *pam* or *geti* in the male case. Since all *geti* and all *tui* are potentially important in the ceremonial domain they are classified together without distinction. The resulting equations across genealogical levels have within them *the inherent features required to produce both Crow and Omaha cross-cousin terms.* That is, the invariant equations, which are the most important in Northern Gê terminologies, can produce both Crow and Omaha solutions for cross-cousin terms without any terminological inconsistency.

The problem presented by cross-cousin classification among the Northern Gê is that the Kayapó fix these cross-cousin categories in an Omaha pattern whereas certain others (the Krahó, Gaviões, and Canela) fix them in a Crow pattern. And it is the difficulties and anomalies of

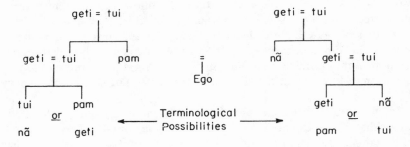

Figure 23. *Terminological equations across genealogical levels.*

the Apinayé system that give it a privileged position in clarifying this problem, for it oscillates between the two possibilities.

When I was collecting cross-cousin terms in the field I found at least three cases in which it was quite clear that the various terminological alternatives could be offered by the same informant, depending on the emphasis he gave to particular relationships. In response to a question about naming, one Indian told me that the relationship between name-giver and name-receiver was like that between siblings of the same sex. They were socially identical because they shared the same name. I then questioned him about cross-cousin terms, asking how his *krã-dúw* (the person he gave his names to) would address his (the informant's) children. His response was unusually clear—generally the Apinayé have some difficulty answering this sort of question—and he immediately gave me a Crow-type classification of cross-cousins. I later put the same questions to two other people and got the same answers. But if I subsequently rephrased the question in an abstract way, asking about the same categories of people but without mentioning names and name-givers, the response was quite different.

It seems that when an informant offers Crow terms for cross-cousins, he is concentrating on the specific relationship of naming at the expense of all others. The result is the solution that is also found among the Krahó and Gaviões. It could be argued that this is simply coincidental. But there is similar evidence from the Krahó and Krĩkatí: the women explain their relationship with their name-givers in terms of Omaha equations, that is, FZ is structurally identified with Ego, hence the female Ego calls FZS and FZD "children," revealing the typical imbalance of an Omaha terminology. Melatti writes: "The Omaha pattern only appears when names are actually transmitted by a particular father's sister. The Crow terminology remains unaltered with respect to the children of any other father's sisters" (Melatti 1979:72). This important example corroborates my argument. Even in a society where variations among cross-cousin terms are minimal, a variation of this kind can appear because of an institutional arrangement. In other words, when there is a certain lack of equilibrium in the system of institutions, giving a particular institution a privileged place, the system of terminology acknowledges this by making appropriate changes. These changes can always be accommodated by using either one or the other type of cross-cousin classifications.

The Krĩkatí case offers an even better comparison with the Apinayé material since cross-cousins can be defined only by referring to the relationship between name-givers and name-receivers. Outside the context of naming, cross-cousin terms show the same variations as in the Apinayé system (Lave 1967:chaps. 6 and 7).

Among the Eastern Timbira, therefore, it is the institution of naming that accounts for the Crow-type classification of cross-cousins. This is consistent with the fact that there is a clear preference for the MB as name-giver and also that there appears to be a reciprocal exchange of names through opposite sex siblings. Hence, among the Canela and Krĩkatí, if a man gives his names to his sister's son, she will give her names to her brother's daughter (Nimuendajú 1946:77; Keesing n.d.; Lave 1967). There are therefore three factors that explain the pattern of cross-cousin terms in these societies: (1) the institution of naming as a way of classifying men; (2) the role of the mother's brother in the transmission of men's names, which tends to take precedence over other categories that could also fulfill the role (Melatti 1979); and (3) a more complete integration of nuclear families within the extended uxorilocal residential groups. Variations in the pattern appear only when there is a disproportionate emphasis on the name-giver, as in the case of the transmission of female names among the Krahó.

The adequacy of this explanation can be tested by comparing the Apinayé variations, which appear in an Omaha pattern, with the Kayapó case, where the Omaha pattern is constant. Among the Kayapó, the Omaha pattern is consistent with the process whereby men are integrated into their affinal households, with the consequent emphasis on the nuclear families. It is also consistent with the important role of the adoptive father in the classification of men in that society. Among the Timbira and Apinayé the relationship between name-giver and name-receiver is public and ceremonial, leading to the creation of clearly defined groups. But among the Kayapó it is a private relationship between two individuals. Here it is not the *geti* (or name-giver) that establishes a young man's membership in the different groups within the Men's House, but a person addressed as "father" (*pam kaág*) who assumes the role of an *adoptive father*. The mediation between the domestic area and the ceremonial area is thus effected by a *symbolic* father, as opposed to the real father or the *geti*. Hence the classification of cross-cousins is based on the terminological identification of adoptive father and adopted son. The result then parallels the Krahó case. Among the Krahó, although there are many instances in which the name-giver is not MB, it is the MB/ZS relationship that is preeminent. Hence a Crow terminology consistently appears. Similarly, among the Kayapó, although pater is distinguished from genitor, social relations are classified on the basis of pater being the principal public figure. His social role represents a domestic, nuclear family role being projected into the ceremonial domain, and the preeminence of the adoptive father/adopted child relationship results in the appearance of the Omaha pattern of terminology. Kayapó Omaha terms are consistent with the fact that it is pater who mediates between the public and private spheres. Timbira Crow terms are consistent with the fact that a similar mediating role falls to the name-giver.

The same reasoning explains the appearance of Apinayé Omaha terms as presented by Nimuendajú (1956:141). Having resolved that problem, we can now see that the variability of Apinayé cross-cousin terms is the result of two factors. First, the institution of name transmission in this society is peculiar because it is a synthesis of both Kayapó and Eastern Timbira institutions.[10] Although Apinayé naming establishes a link between a *geti* (name-giver) and a *tamtxúa* (name-receiver), it also involves parents' same sex siblings (real, false, or putative). And it is these relatives, the "adoptive parents," not the true parents, who arrange names for the child. Furthermore, adoptive parents are given jural responsibilities over the child. Hence among the Apinayé these two institutions, naming and the adoption of children, are bound up together. The transmission of names takes the same form as among the Eastern Timbira, while the adoption of children takes the same form as among the Kayapó. Variations in cross-cousin terms depend on which aspect of this composite institution is being emphasized. If the relationship with a name-giver is being emphasized, the appropriate terminology for cross-cousins will be of the Crow type; if it is the relationship with the adoptive parent, the appropriate terminology will be of the Omaha type.

The second factor is a corollary of the first. If the Apinayé can choose to emphasize either the name-giver relationship or the parental relationship (with genitor and pater), then the appearance of a particular set of cross-cousin terms must indicate the relative importance of the relationships in question. It cannot be predicted a priori which set of terms will appear, but it might be possible to make such a prediction if one knew how a given Ego regards the two kinds of relationship. In theory, this sounds like a useful experiment that could be carried out in the field, but in fact it is extremely difficult to test the hypothesis because demographic factors and social arrangements are constantly changing. And indeed it may well be the case that these changes are the very reason why Apinayé terminology appears to be so flexible.

In summary, the variations found in Apinayé cross-cousin terms are not anomalous. On the contrary, they fit perfectly well within the general ethnographic picture of the Northern Gê. The oscillation of Apinayé terms between apparently contradictory possibilities is clearly explained by taking into account the relationships and institutions of these other societies. Apinayé relationship terminology is not a distinct type, nor does it reveal any peculiar anomaly or inconsistency. It can be understood in terms of certain relationships and certain institutions that are not peculiar to the Apinayé but that are found throughout all Northern Gê societies.

The Apinayé relationship system is based on a dichotomy between a private, domestic sphere and a public, ceremonial sphere. The terms for *kwóyá* relatives can be understood in terms of a binary matrix, where the pair *geti-tui* and its reciprocal *tamtxúa* are in opposition to the pair *pamnã* and its reciprocal *krá*. The first set characterizes ceremonial relationships while the second characterizes relationships justified by links of common substance—blood. But if one looks at the system as a whole, it becomes apparent that all these categories establish links that integrate the two basic domains of Apinayé society.

The relationship system operates as a technique that resolves the contradiction between the public and private domains. Some terms are primarily centered around relations of substance, others around ceremonial relations, but taken together, they establish a systematic *continuum* and a coherent language. It is a language that allows the Apinayé to conceptualize and classify their social relationships and integrate those domains that are so radically separated in everyday life.

5

The Political System

IN THE PREVIOUS CHAPTERS I described the set of norms and rules that forms the basis of Apinayé society. This was not intended as an exhaustive account but only as an indication of the minimum that a stranger would need to know of the rules in order to have some understanding of the Apinayé universe. Having understood the basic rules that order daily life, as well as those that govern ceremonial life and the continuity of the society, a stranger could then find his way around Apinayé society with a certain sense of security.

Thus far I have said little about the application of these rules in everyday life. I have, for example, described the nuclear family and the residential groups (and also the way these are conceived) as basic units of the society, but I have not described how they are actually organized, how they actually communicate, nor how, as groups, they influence the behavior of their members.

Here I will be looking at how these rules are manipulated, extended, contracted, and reformulated, and for what reasons. My justification for calling this a study of the "political system" is quite straightforward. "Politics" is simply the study of themes such as "control of conflicts," "competition," "disputes," and other such divisive processes of social life, and we know that such discontinuities between groups and individuals result from the difficulties in applying norms, rules, or cultural ideals to the processes and situations that occur in everyday life. Rules of behavior are necessarily less flexible than the situations to which they are applied, just as in linguistics the question as to whether a certain phrase is grammatical or not may first require the consensus of grammarians as to what is and what is not a correctly formed phrase. We know that such decisions are often arbitrary (hence the debates among linguists). Similar problems arise in cultural systems, but here the grammarians are those who have power, and the application of rules in difficult or ambiguous cases is called jurisprudence.

"Power" and "authority," then, indicate the capacity of an individual or group not only to decide which types of behavior are undesirable or "ungrammatical" but also to change the very rules of the social game. In both cases the question becomes one of applying cultural codes to actual situations. Power and authority therefore address themselves directly to the public and collective aspects of behavior, and the critical problem then becomes finding a way of legitimizing the decisions that are made.

In this chapter I will first describe those who have political power in Apinayé society. They are the groups and group leaders who, because of their position in society, can decide which kinds of social behavior are "correct" and which are "incorrect" in terms of the interests of the group (which are, of course, considered to be the interests of the whole society). I will show how these groups are composed and organized, and I shall explain their invariant properties. I shall then look at the way social coercion is directly applied and discuss the power and position of the chief within the community. Finally I shall examine the competition for power: how competing groups are politically related and how "opposition" groups (those without political dominance) operate within the system. The object here will be to show how political power is threatened.

Residential Groups and the Political System

The political life of the Apinayé (and the Timbira in general) can be contrasted with that of the Shavante-Sherente and the Kayapó. Whereas the latter have institutions that channel political life by organizing men into well-defined groups, such as the Shavante lineages and clans and the Kayapó Men's House, similar institutions in Apinayé and Timbira societies do not have that function. Indeed among the Apinayé and Timbira the essentially male groups such as the age-classes, the plaza groups, and the named groups play an integrating role in society. They are formed especially during initiation rites and their functions are quite clearly communal, by which I mean that both ideally and in practice they are motivated by collective values. We have already seen that the Apinayé moieties *Kolti* and *Kolre* are complementary. It is an absolute division that reflects the Apinayé view of the cosmos and has nothing to do with those groups that are formed for some practical activity in everyday life. The moiety division refers to transcendental aspects of the social order and unites the two groups through a series of oppositions that permeate the whole Apinayé universe and are the basic principles of order.

In everyday life the residential groups are the permanent units. Depending on his matrimonial status, each man lives with his family of origin or with his family of marriage (or perhaps, in certain circumstances, with both). Whereas a Kayapó man can always discuss political matters formally or informally in the Men's House, an Apinayé can do so only when a leader calls a meeting—a measure taken only in exceptional circumstances. The Kayapó institution mediates between domestic life on the one hand and political and ceremonial life on the other, but in Apinayé society the role fulfilled by Kayapó Men's Houses (or Shavante lineages and clans) can usually be carried out only within the residential unit.

Residential units are composed of nuclear families linked by uxorilocal marriage and the relationship between parents and daughters. They are formed in an ad hoc fashion, and their composition depends largely on how stable the relationship is between the women and their husbands who have come to live in that part of the village circle. The boundaries of these groups are, therefore, diffuse, and their definition as units emerges more in terms of their opposition to other groups rather than through any intrinsic principles of organization. Although there is no principle of unilineal descent in Apinayé society, the groups tend to assume a matrifocal character since the rule of uxorilocal residence removes men from their natal households. Hence the diffuse nature of group boundaries is in large part attributable to the fact that a man is linked to at least two households. This tends to inhibit the appearance of functioning corporate groups.

During my first field trip to the Apinayé, it was not at all clear to me that residential segments played an important part in the political life of the village. The Indians themselves do not explicitly recognize them as a source of coercive power, and when questioned on political matters they tend to refer to the formal institutions of social control. They would talk about the chief, *paí-ti,* and his auxiliaries and also about the village counselor, *kapel-txúm,* and describe their functions in fairly abstract terms with hardly a mention of residential segments and the conflicts that the chief found himself involved in.

Formally, the political structure is quite simple. The basic political unit is the village, with one chief and one counselor. The chief organizes any kind of collective work that is carried out for the benefit of the whole village. He also adjudicates quarrels and disagreements. The counselor's role in organizing collective effort is more symbolic than instrumental. He is the central figure in organizing rituals; he calls people from their houses and advises on how to carry out the ceremony properly if the participants have forgotten details. It is said that the counselor should be a *pinget,* an old man, or a man with grandchildren, since he must be an expert on Apinayé traditions. In São José, where I collected most of my data on the political system, the counselor was indeed an old man, but I suspect that others of the same status could fulfill his role equally well. I was present on a number of occasions when another old man took Velho Estêvão's role in organizing naming ceremonies and dances.

Given the counselor's importance as a kind of human national archive, it is obvious that he should be on cordial terms with the chief. Although the counselor has no authority in the adjudication of disputes, if he refuses to cooperate with the chief, he can remove an important part of the collective life of the village, which the chief has an interest in preserving. This once happened in São José when Toim was chief, but today the chief and the counselor are father and son, and they get along with each other very well. The relationship between counselor and chief seems to have been equally cordial in Nimuendajú's time when Matúk was chief and Nicolau Velho was the counselor (Nimuendajú 1939:20). When they talk of these roles, the Apinayé give the impression that they see them as complementary. The counselor appears as a kind of symbolic judge, the guardian of legends and historic traditions, while the chief has an executive role, like a small-scale minister of planning, organizing collective activity and arbitrating disputes.

The chief has a number of auxiliaries called *paí-ti pêb*. Today the Apinayé translate the expression as "the chief's soldiers" or "the chief's secretaries." There are two *paí-ti pêb* in São José. They are men in whom the chief can confide. They are his "eyes and ears," keeping him informed about what is going on in the other residential segments. Unlike the counselor, these men are not chosen because of their age and their knowledge of traditions. They are simply men the chief trusts. In São José one of the chief's auxiliaries was an Apinayé who had been brought up among the Krahó, yet the chief considered him his *krã-txúa* ("friend," "companion": a title used between those who have been initiated together). The chief's brothers were not asked to be auxiliaries partly because they were too young to be involved in political life, but more significantly because it is considered proper that the office of chief be kept impersonal and detached from family ties. Kinship ties are not important in choosing auxiliaries. What interests the chief is the man's loyalty and his alertness in recognizing incipient problems that might cause the chief difficulty. Hence it is extremely important that the auxiliaries live at a distance from the chief, in other residential segments.

The man who was chief of São José in 1966 drew Figure 24 to explain the layout of the village. The diagram illustrates many of the points explained in the above discussion. The counselor is linked directly to the village plaza, indicating that his position transcends the ordinary arrangements of houses and individuals. And we can see how in São José the auxiliaries live in houses on the opposite side of the village from the chief. Villages such as Botica and Cocal, which no longer exist, also had auxiliaries who were similarly located. Without the information from these "eyes and ears," on the other side of the village, it would be almost impossible for the chief to govern the village effectively.

The Apinayé tend to describe these roles as if they had nothing to do

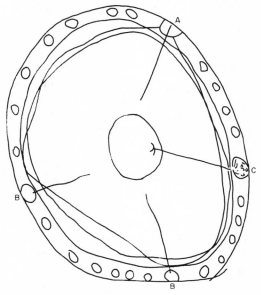

Figure 24. *Diagram of a village with emphasis on the positions of* (A) *the chief;* (B) *the chief's auxiliaries; and* (C) *the counselor's house. The lines show how they are connected.*

with any other aspects of the social structure. They say only that "the chief has to be good"; that "he must help everyone"; that "he must know how to give good advice"; and so on. They have very little to say about what lies behind the chief's position and what gives him his power and prestige. But if one spends some time in an Apinayé village one soon finds out that the source of the chief's power lies in his residential segment and in the links he may have with other segments. When I asked specific questions on the nature of political support (and I questioned most adult males in São José and Mariazinha), they always said that it depended on the number of people in the chief's residential segment. First they would refer to the number of *kwóyá* (relatives) living there with the chief and only then would they consider these relationships in a more precise way. For example, a young brother-in-law might first be considered part of the chief's *kwóyá* and therefore one of those who would give the chief support. But if asked to specify the young man's relationship precisely, the informant might explain that the man only recently married into that segment, and that should a dispute arise, he might well take no part in it at all. This kind of situation in the political sphere is, of course, quite consistent with my description of the relationship system.

In general, residential segments are groups within which there is economic cooperation, and which operate as political pressure groups. In a word, they are factions.[1] If one of these is large and well organized, it may even be an exogamous group that establishes systematic affinal relations with others.

Residential Segments as Factions

The Apinayé use the Portuguese *famílias* ("families" of the village) to describe their residential segments. They say that São José is composed of three families (or "big" families): the family of Velha Joana Kokôti (also called "the family of Chiquinho Grebaú"); the family of Pedro Viado (also called "the family of Estêvão Velho" or of Grossinho, the chief); and the family of Toim, leader of the faction opposed to the chief. Anyone familiar with the use of the word "family" in Central Brazil will appreciate that the Apinayé category is broad and not clearly defined. To find out how the faction is composed one has to ascertain who has prestige and use these people as points of reference. When some informants described Toim's family, they included the families of Pedro Xavito and Velho Dionísio. But at other times they would say only that Toim's family was opposed to Grossinho's or Estêvão's, emphasizing the two factions in the village most involved in the struggle for power. In 1962, when factionalism was less intense, many more people were mentioned as heads of big families than in 1967, when factional disputes had intensified. In Mariazinha also, in 1962, leadership was firmly in the hands of one person, Zezinho, who later died. When I returned there in 1967, two names, "Zezinho's family" and "Júlio's family," indicated the factions that were involved in the competition for power. This was so despite the fact that Zezinho and Júlio were *krã-tum* and *tamtxúa* to each other. The number of recognized residential segments therefore depends on the degree of political polarization in the village, and the alignment of factions, as in the case of social relationships, depends on the changing political context. When we also take into consideration the rules of marriage and residence, it becomes even more difficult to delineate these groups with any precision.

But when a chief comes under pressure from a group that challenges his leadership, a polarization of interests does tend to appear, and the remaining residential segments, if there are any, tend to take sides with one or the other of the two principal groups who are competing for power.[2] Let us look at this situation as it developed in São José.

Figure 25 indicates the residential segments of São José; the letters correspond to the diagram of São José presented in Figure 1. For the purposes of exposition it is more convenient to represent the village as a circle although, as I explained, it does not in fact have this form today.

Segment I, formed by domestic groups *E, F, G, H, I, J,* and *K,* is a compact political group. This is the chief's segment, and *F* indicates the chief's household. Directly opposite is segment II: *O, P, Q, R,* and *S.* This

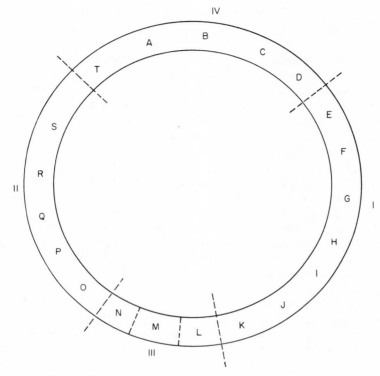

Figure 25. *São José village—1967. Residential segments.*

is also a compact, effective political group, led by Toim (in household Q), who was at one time chief of the village. Segment IV, T, A, B, C, and D, is linked to both segments I and II. Men of this group say that theirs is a group that "stays in the middle," although, in fact, its links are stronger with segment I. In segment III, the two households L and N are occupied by men who do not participate in the political affairs of the village. They are in fact connected with segment I, but this is not of political significance. The head of household L is considered miserly, prone to drunkenness, and far too concerned with his own affairs. Much the same is said of household N. But the head of household M is in a peculiar situation. His son is the head of household O in segment II. But although O is part of faction II, M is aligned with faction I. (Because of this peculiarity, the figure separates L, M, and N with dotted lines.)

With the exception of the three families in segment III, the Apinayé generally refer to a segment in terms of a "big family." Segment I is referred to as the family of Estêvão, of Pedro Viado, or of Grossinho, depending on which man the speaker wishes to single out. Segment II is associated with Toim's family, and segment IV with either Maria Joana's

family or Chiquinho Grabaú's (resident in house *T*). Segments I and II
are both veterans in the art of gossip and are constantly pointing out the
defects of the other. Segment IV (and segment III to some extent) tend to
mediate and control the confrontation between the other two.

In São José there are thirty-two politically active men. They are all
married and have children. Since they are regarded as men who have
been initiated, they can therefore take their full part in public life.[3] These
men spend a great deal of time building and repairing their houses, hunting, collecting babassu nuts, and generally providing their wives, children, and other relatives with food. They have to resolve cases of disagreement, theft, violence, adultery, defloration, and so on, not just when
they are directly implicated but also when their own children and grandchildren are involved. In other words, they have to apply cultural codes
and rules of conduct to concrete cases and "separate the wheat from the
chaff." It is they who have to distinguish between what is legitimate and
what is improper, inadequate, or immoral. Ultimately it is they who decide whether village life is going to be peaceful or turbulent, their decisions being the foundations on which the political system and jural order
rest.

This does not imply that Apinayé women are totally passive in the political process. Indeed, women have two extremely important roles. First,
they get to know about matters which a particular group of men might
prefer to keep secret. The women pick up this kind of news at the river or
in the gardens, where all the women gather to fetch water, to wash
clothes, or to plant and collect garden produce. The information is duly
passed on to other men of the village.

Second, when there are disagreements between men, it is often the
women who intercede on behalf of their husbands, brothers, or sons, and
avert the threat of open conflict. Although it is difficult to judge the
women's political role with any accuracy, it is certainly significant, especially in the light of the effectiveness of gossip.

Figure 26 presents diagrams of the most important genealogical relationships between members of the four residential segments. It must be
emphasized that the genealogical connections set out here are those
which the Apinayé themselves held to be the most important. In Apinayé
society persons are often related by a number of genealogical connections; in such cases, one tends to be singled out as preeminent. The diagrams are not, therefore, complete genealogies but are those offered by
informants. Each position is given a letter that corresponds to the domestic groups represented in previous diagrams, and also a number indicating a name which, in many cases, is mentioned in the text.

There are two important points regarding the composition of these
groups. First, some marriages do not follow the rule of uxorilocal residence. They are: 7 and 8 (domestic group *B*); 9 and 10 (group *C*); 36 and

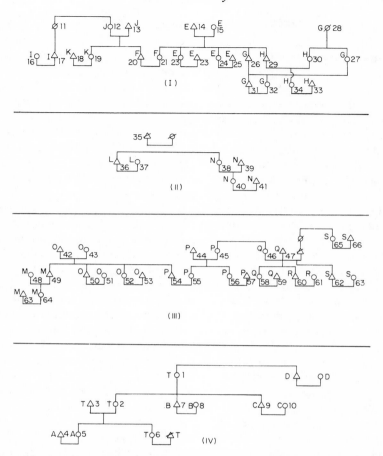

Figure 26. *Genealogical distribution of the residential segments in São José village, 1967.*

37 (group *L*); 50 and 51 (group *O*); 60 and 61 (group *R*); 62 and 63 (group *S*). When I pointed this out the Apinayé explained that this was quite normal. In some cases (61, 10, and 37, for example) it was explained that the women came from another village and that their parents did not live in São José. In other cases it was said that the parents did not want their son to leave home and therefore arranged a marriage with a woman who had no parents in the village. Both explanations are of the same kind, and such marriages possibly reflect a tendency for segments to split up into household groups. This suggests that factionalism is increasing, but I lack sufficient data to confirm that this is so.

Second, in the older generation of segment leaders these discrepancies are not so obvious, but they are present. The main reason for discrepancies in this case is that many of the older men now living in São José came from villages that no longer exist. For example, when Dionísio (number 42, group *O*) came to São José, he was already married. He established himself and his wives at a certain location on the village circle and became involved in relationships with neighboring houses. People who arrive like this often change their place of residence as a result of disagreements and, by moving to another part of the village, set up new alignments. Furthermore, divorce or new alliances with people of another faction can also cause people to move. One man (7; *B*) left his father-in-law's house (44; *P*) because he quarreled with Toim (47; *Q*). He and his wife left that area of the village to live in a house near the wife's mother. Similarly, Estêvão (13; *J*) quarreled with his brother (66; *S*) over a litter of pigs belonging to the latter and moved to the house he now occupies. Sometimes these disagreements result in an entire residential group moving from one part of the village circle to another, or even moving to another village. In 1963 a family moved from São José to Mariazinha because the wife was accused of sorcery. In 1967–68 group *I* (16 and 17) left faction III and joined faction I. Since it is usually quite easy for an Apinayé to find a kinship link of some kind with any other person, changes of residence cause little difficulty. It is simply a matter of emphasizing one's relationship with the group one joins and ignoring relationships with one's former group. One can use the distinction between "close" and "distant" relationships to justify what one wants to do. Given the possibilities of reckoning kinship ties cognatically and given that each nuclear family remains independent within the residential group, it should now be clear that these two aspects of the relationship system facilitate the movements and realignments that take place.

The political power of a segment depends largely on the prestige of its leader. The Apinayé define prestige as a man's capacity to keep his sons-in-law within his own household (or at least in neighboring houses) and to maintain a harmonious segment. This is what Pedro Viado (14; *E*) has achieved. He is not physically impressive; he is thin and appears to be shy, rather like a Brazilian backwoodsman. (Indeed, his father was a Brazilian who married an Apinayé woman.) But through the marriages of both his sons and his daughters and through his capacity to keep friction to a minimum, he has maintained a large, well-organized kindred. It is said that Pedro Viado is a strong and effective operator behind the scenes in village politics because he has so many men in his segment on whom he can count. In addition to his own sons and his married daughters with their children (indicating stable marriages), he can also include in his segment the village chief (20; *F*) and the counselor (12; *J*). But Pedro Viado's name is not the one always associated with the segment. Velho Estêvão (12; *J*) is also mentioned, and in recent years Grossinho (20; *F*) is often held to be the leader. Pedro Viado seems to be most effective in holding the alliances together and resolving those frequent outbursts of disagreement that arise particularly between father-in-law and son-in-law and between brothers-in-law. Velho Estêvão and Grossinho are, respectively, village counselor and village chief. They are much more involved in the broader political life of the village, adjudicating disputes and organizing collective work.

The composition of segment III is much less secure. There is an astonishing incidence of divorce, which means that men tend to join this segment for a time and then leave it. I discovered that every woman associated with this segment had been divorced at least twice in the past eight years. Women 55 and 56 (group *P*) were both married to various men and are now considered extremely unreliable wives. But the divorce rate is also quite high in other segments, and, indeed, unreliability is a characteristic attributed to all women by Apinayé men. I do not think, therefore, that the divorce rate is in itself a particularly significant indicator of why this segment is unstable. A more probable explanation is the demands made by older members on newly married men who join the group. The relationship between 44 and 45 (group *P*) and 54 and 57 (the men who married their daughters) was particularly fraught with difficulties of this kind, as was that between 46 and 47 and their affines. There were constant arguments and complaints, usually on the part of the parents, who complained that their daughters' husbands were lazy, bad hunters, and so on. Filomena (46) seems to be a particularly difficult woman. She makes excessive demands on her affines and also interferes in the affairs of her children's families. I have seen her punish her daughter for having struck one of her *tamtxúa,* and it was she who prevented her son Vicente (62; *S*) from leaving the village after he had murdered Joãozinho (husband of number 6, group *T*).

Another cause of instability in this segment is that three of its members are potential leaders: Dionísio (42; *O*), Pedro Xavito (44; *P*), and Toim (47; *Q*). They are old men, and all three have ambitions to be village chief. In segment I, Grossinho is unquestionably the leader. The two old men, Pedro Viado and Estêvão, do not interfere with his decisions. Indeed, Pedro Viado avoids practical matters altogether and leaves Grossinho to coordinate the activities of the group. But in segment III, the three old men are all said to be powerful, and to make matters more difficult, Toim's wife, Filomena, is also considered to have significant influence behind the scenes. Many Apinayé say that factionalism in São José is particularly bitter because Filomena constantly stirs things up with her interminable gossiping. To complete this picture of tension and instability there are three adult men, Vicente (62; *S*), Permino (60; *R*), and Romão (54; *P*), who also have strong personalities and who are always

involved in quarrels. Theft and drunkenness are the usual causes of these
disturbances. Vicente's notoriety for fighting grew over the years and cul-
minated with his murder of a man in 1956.

It is clear, therefore, that the political power of a segment depends on
how well the mature men get along together. If they cooperate with one
another their segment will be more effective in the political affairs of the
village as a whole. The structural factors that have to be taken into account are uxorilocal residence and the relative independence of nuclear
families. The first, by separating men from their natal group, is responsible for the difficulties of coordinating a segment in which there are a
number of potential leaders, as in the case of segment III. The second
allows a man to leave the residential group if he thinks that his affines are
not treating him well. He can either divorce his wife or move his nuclear
family to another part of the village. If men can harmonize the residence
rule with their political ambitions, then the segment will emerge as an effective political group, such as segment I, in which a division of roles
successfully unites old men and younger adult men—Pedro Viado is the
focal point of most of the important relationships, Estêvão is the counselor, and Grossinho is the undisputed political leader of the group.

We know that among other Gê societies uxorilocal residence imposes
certain restrictions on the way men can be aligned into effective political
groups. Each society reveals a different solution to the problem. Among
the Shavante, men try to maintain the unity of the sibling group by marrying sisters. Hence uxorilocal marriage does not split the patrilineage
(Maybury-Lewis 1967:88). Among the Kayapó, uxorilocal marriage also
tends to disperse men, but the institution of the Men's House unites them
again. Among the Apinayé, and possibly among the other Timbira, the
basic political unit is not preformed by institutions such as lineages or a
Men's House. It has to be established by affinal ties among a group of
men, each of whom is in control of his own nuclear family. The core of
the residential unit is the relationship between father-in-law and son-in-
law (and between brothers-in-law), and it is on the basis of such relationships that political groups emerge.

The Chief and the Interrelations between Residential Segments

The Apinayé see their chief as someone who should resolve disputes,
deal with gossip and witchcraft accusations, and maintain harmony and
order in the village. In this section I shall examine the extent to which he
can fulfill this role. When the Indians say that the chief can govern only if
he has the support of his relatives (*kwóyá*), their explanation appears
quite adequate until one takes into account the complexities of the relationship system. Since an Apinayé can trace his kin cognatically, there is
a great deal of flexibility in what he can consider his *kwóyá*, and indeed if
he wanted to, he could find some sort of kinship tie with anyone in the

village. The problem is therefore to explain how the Apinayé use the relationship system for political purposes.

Let us first remember that the relationship system can operate on a purely formal level such that a political leader (or any mature man, for that matter) can claim that everyone is his relative and can justify his claim genealogically. This is not difficult to understand when we reflect that our own kinship system can be used in the same way. In many areas of Brazil, when two strangers meet it is quite common for them to look for kinship links in order to discover a social "infrastructure" on which to base their new acquaintance. They look for a common relative in preceding generations who may have been an important point of reference for a large number of related people. Although this person may be barely remembered now, he may still prove useful as a basis on which to rationalize their relationship. This is also what the Apinayé do, but in both cases it does not necessarily follow that the common relative is actually instrumental in social or political terms. That is to say, even if the relative is still alive, he himself may not recognize his relationship with the parties. Hence this process of establishing relationships depends initially on the fact that everyone can potentially be related to everyone else in some sort of way. Recognizing this, we can then look at the kinds of links that are singled out in this complex web of interconnections. What we find is that sometimes two informants can disagree completely on their relationship to each other or that an agreed relationship may be appealed to only in certain contexts and for certain specific purposes.

The Apinayé always said that everyone in the village was related, and they could always support their assertions with examples. But when I asked who actually gave help to a specific person, the reply was limited to a much smaller number of people: those, in fact, whom the informant would classify as *kwóyá kumrendy*. In other words, everyone is a relative from the point of view of the solidarity of the village group. But in the variable contexts of "who gives political support" or "whom one exchanges food with," those included are limited to the domestic group or the residential segment. Residence depends on marriage, and marriage translates people from a distant category (*kwóyá két* or *kwóyá kaág*) to a closer one (*kwóyá kumrendy*). It is in this process that the role of the chief or segment leader becomes so important. Given that the group is composed of men originally from other residential groups, it is up to the leader to see that it functions as a cooperative unit.

A residential segment is an effective alliance of a number of domestic groups. When a man has a stable marriage and is well treated by his affines, he transfers his loyalty from one segment to another. But it should also be noted that a man's relationships before marriage are never completely terminated. There is indeed a shift of emphasis to a new set of relationships, but this does not imply severance of old ones. Indeed some, such as those between parents and children and between name-giver and name-receiver, remain prescriptively defined by explicit rules. They are marked relationships that carry an important ideological message. But there are many others that are totally dependent on contingent factors. Informants refer to them by the same terms used for people directly related to Ego, even though it may be a tenuous connection. Some will be selected and used (those arising from marriage and residence will always be important), and others will be forgotten or reactivated only for limited purposes.

A segment leader—and the village chief particularly—constantly tries to keep all his relationships operating. To gain prestige it is important for him to make all efforts to keep alive secondary or tertiary links with people in "distant" categories. When he has already established his position, many of those distant relatives will themselves choose to keep the relationship active since it is advantageous to be related to a strong chief. In São José, Grossinho was always worrying about keeping up relationships and, correspondingly, many people in both villages spontaneously mentioned that they were related to him before I even questioned them on the matter. In addition, many of those related to faction II in São José would take pains to point out that they also had relatives in Grossinho's group.

A leader's prestige therefore depends on his ability to take advantage of his relationships, translating distant links into close ones and making them effective in terms of political support. He can do this in two ways: first, he can keep up regular exchanges of meat and other foodstuffs. This indicates his attitude toward those he exchanges with and establishes that they are "true" relatives. Second, when he organizes the work force he must be careful to satisfy everyone in the village. The Apinayé are quick to complain when a leader arranges a work team for something that will benefit only his own kindred or his own segment. It is always easy for the chief to do this since his segment contains the greatest number of active men, and work teams can be organized without the help of other segments. But if he consistently behaved like this, he would quickly polarize the village. Other segments would organize their own work teams and in so doing would undermine the chief's authority to supervise the whole work force. In São José, a common complaint of those in segment II was that Grossinho lacked impartiality and that the teams organized to fell trees or fence gardens never included them. Grossinho would deny this and defend himself by saying that if he did not organize a team from faction II it was only because the men there never came along to volunteer for work.

Exchanging food and organizing the work force are the means by which the chief tries to obtain effective political control of the community. Complete political control could be attained only through a tyrannical use of force. The very nature of the system prevents this, for if the chief organized a very strong faction of his own, he would provoke the kind of conflict that would result in the fission of the village.

Fissions in Apinayé villages are due partly to decisions made for practical reasons and partly to an increase in village size. My demographic data are limited because it is impossible to reconstruct the situation that existed prior to the disruptive effects of contact with Brazilian society. But I think it is reasonable to suggest that an increase in population (which enlarges the social network and increases the incidence of conflict) is a limiting factor on a chief's capacity to control the group. This is certainly a reason given in the myths that refer to themes of political control. According to the Apinayé, the linguistic, cultural, and geographical homogeneity of the Northern Gê tribes exists because they were originally all part of one huge village, which split after a log race when the two teams broke up into quarreling factions. There is also a half-legendary story of a village called Bonito, which split into two after a series of fights between its two leaders, Dokô-re (who represents established authority and the abuse of power) and Nindo-pó (his rival, representing wisdom, who is a paragon of how to seize power and overcome oppression). Dokô-re is older and abuses his seniority. Nindo-pó is young and shows complete control of his emotions. The dramatic power of the narrative lies in a series of episodes in which Dokô-re tries to get Nindo-pó prematurely involved in open dispute before the latter is prepared either physically or socially, that is, before he has the guaranteed support of all the members of his faction.

There are two chiefs within living memory who behaved like tyrants and built up a strong faction in order to do away with their rivals. One was Pedro Corredor, or Pĕbkôb, of the village of Botica (Gato Preto) (Nimuendajú 1939:12). When Nimuendajú visited the Apinayé, families were already leaving Botica for the other villages. Of the present residents of São José (then called Bacaba), Jacinto (group *N*), Grossinho (group *F*), Augusto (group *L*), and Pedro Xavito (group *P*) all left Botica to get away from Pedro Corredor. The Indians regard the end of Botica as a tragedy. They say that it finally broke up through sorcery—a clear indication of the extent of social unrest caused by the chief and his faction. The other noted tyrant was José Dias Matúk, who is responsible for the factionalism now present in São José—Toim is his son, and Grossinho was part of the group opposed to him.

The extent to which a chief can gain power is limited by properties of the social structure. Although he can make every effort to gather around him a large group of followers, he can never absorb them completely into his group since they will always be related in some way to people in other factions. This is assured by the rule of uxorilocal residence, by the relationship system, and by the system of ceremonial relations. The chief's role in the political process must, therefore, work within these limitations, and his most effective avenue for exploiting the system is to make use of the established relations between residential segments. He can, perhaps, try to attract domestic groups away from their own segment and into his own. This is in fact the way segment I was formed, when the original large domestic group, Pedro Viado and his children, were able to attract and absorb members of other domestic groups, but such a process of fusion is difficult to accomplish, especially if the group that the chief tries to attract is itself quite large.

If political organization were to be strictly based on kinship, segment IV would support segment II. But this is not the case, partly because there was a serious disagreement between Paraibano and Toim during a feast that resulted in Toim attacking Paraibano and wounding him with a knife. Furthermore, segment IV and segment I established a strong ceremonial relationship. In 1962 one of Paraibano's sons (the boy 23 in group *E*) married one of Pedro Viado's daughters and has lived quite happily with his brothers-in-law since then. Also, Grossinho, the chief, always sends food to a number of people in segment IV and puts his work force at their disposal. If Grossinho has not succeeded in making them part of his segment, at least they are not politically hostile. Hence men of segment IV always say that if there is a dispute between factions I and II, they will "stay in the middle" and act as mediators.

It is difficult to be sure if the exchanges between segments I and IV were established purely for political purposes. But the evidence does suggest that the chief's attempt to neutralize segment IV was at least implicit in the process. The chief made an obvious political decision when he went on to choose Alcides (4; *A*) as one of his auxiliaries. The choice had nothing to do with kinship links or any other kind of obligation. Indeed, choosing auxiliaries is always a political decision. The second auxiliary up to 1967 was Permino (group *R*), a member of faction II, but since he was always involved in drunken brawls, Grossinho dismissed him and chose instead Toim, the leader of faction II. Initially I did not understand this choice, and I thought that perhaps Grossinho had been forced into it by political pressure, but I later realized that this was a very clever political maneuver on Grossinho's part, as he himself later confirmed. I am similarly inclined to view the exchanges between segments as maneuvers to gain political advantage.

The Apinayé political process follows two distinct directions. The group in power makes every effort to see that its relationships with other groups are not disturbed or "forgotten" (hence it exchanges food and labor and gives offices to members of other groups), while the "opposition" group tries to hinder these relationships and break them up. Although the chief knows that the group "in the middle" is at present on his side, he is also aware that it could easily swing back to the other faction given the strong links between them.

The nature of the political process leaves its mark on the way the chief goes about resolving disputes and controlling conflict. His manner is cautious and his oratorical style is inspired by an attempt to emphasize the cohesion of the community. Apinayé oratory avoids emotional outbursts. In his speeches the chief, like the English, does not let his own sentiments intrude. His tone of voice and his gestures are modulated to be in keeping with his theme, which dwells on the values of the whole community. The speeches I heard (translated for me by other Indians) always began with careful proclamations of how everyone in the village was related, that relatives should not fight, and so on, and the real problems of the moment were introduced only as a counterpoint to the theme of consensus within the community. In 1967 I heard Grossinho address the village in this way when members of faction II were killing cattle on one of the ranches in the area, and in Mariazinha I heard Zezinho, the chief there, take up the matter of the deflowering of a girl—an incident that had caused considerable bad feeling in the village. The rhetorical technique is not to go directly to the heart of the matter but to proceed by circumlocutions that present the sensitive points within a clearly established context of community values. If the chief were to follow the style of Catiline and make violent accusations, he would undermine his power and put in jeopardy the support he requires from those groups only tenuously related to him. He must conduct himself in a way that avoids exacerbating the divisions between the various groups, and he must try to create a sense of community. As the Apinayé put it, the chief gives "advice" and "lessons" (*kapenre* = "talk") but does not give orders.

The chief tries to resolve disputes calmly. If there is a specific disagreement he will, as far as possible, try to avoid making it public. The more a disagreement is brought into the open, the less his chances are of controlling the group interested in its solution. It is said that the chief "should kill gossip as it is born." Hence he often simply calls the parties in the dispute to his house to give them an "audience" (as it is called nowadays). By isolating the problem in this way he avoids getting relatives involved and prevents the disagreement from spreading throughout the village. Any kind of large-scale polarization in the community damages his prestige. In fact, the opposition's most powerful weapon is to create such problems and to challenge the chief's ability and prestige as often as they can.

The Political Process

The problems of everyday life always impinge on the political process. Individual cases of theft, adultery, and aggression are always in danger of being transformed into disputes that affect the whole village. Hence in his role as adjudicator, the chief must always emphasize his impartiality and must make every effort to cure the causes of discontent that lie behind the quarrels. In doing so, he can rely only on his powers of persuasion. He has no army or police force to implement his decisions by force or to contain groups that challenge his power. His only weapon is his power of oratory, which he uses when he "gives counsel" in public or in those private audiences where he analyzes a case in the presence of the disputants. As the Apinayé say, "a chief must speak well" since his authority depends more on example than on institutions directly linked to his office.

Just as the chief "speaks well" in order to resolve conflicts, so those opposed to him speak to effect the contrary. All discussions that do not please those who support the chief are classified as "gossip" or "lying talk" (*me-êdji: me* being a collective particle and *êdji* meaning "a lie"). Any kind of disagreement can give rise to gossip. If X steals maize from Y's garden and if Y complains to the chief, there will be gossip about the incident. If X and Y both go to the chief and he advises X to return what he stole, there will be gossip about that too. Any incident can start it off, from the breach of a rule to simply a comment on a relationship between two persons. What is common to all gossip is that the attitude that the person or group has taken up with respect to the incident is revealed. Gossip is therefore most virulent in cases where rules have been breached or where someone's behavior is considered to be abnormal. In São José, much of the gossiping concerns the history of the chieftaincy as it relates to factional struggles. In other words, it mostly takes the form of arguments supporting or denigrating a person's or a group's capacity to lead the community.

THE HISTORY OF THE CHIEFTAINCY IN SÃO JOSÉ

In Nimuendajú's time São José, then known as Bacaba, was firmly under the control of José Dias Matúk. Although there had already been considerable problems with Brazilian settlers, the focus of the friction was always outside the village. There had been trouble over land claims, the killing of cattle, and the destruction of babassu resources, but the internal organization of the Apinayé villages was not significantly affected. When Matúk died, the chieftaincy passed to Velho Estêvão, an Indian from Cocal who had in the past shown considerable talent in dealing with Brazilians. It was Estêvão who had gone to Tocantinópolis to see Padre Velho and arranged the demarcation of Indian territory that is still more or less respected to this day. But Estêvão consolidated his power with the help of the first Indian agent to be sent to the Apinayé—a certain João Felix. During this time it appears that although Velho Estêvão was astute in negotiating with Brazilians, he lacked sufficient support within the village. São José apparently had two factions, one composed of Estêvão's relatives and the other of Matúk's. During the 1940s a second Brazilian, Zé Fábio, took charge of the Indian post, and Matúk's relatives convinced him that Matúk's son Toim should replace Estêvão as chief. With

Zé Fábio's agreement this was duly accomplished. Toim and his group governed São José until the 1950s, when the village was visited by the chief inspector from Goiânia, a man named Iridiano. On this occasion Velho Estêvão and Pedro Viado managed to arrange that the chieftaincy be given to one of their group, and the office was given to Grossinho, Estêvão's son.

This summary of events is enough to explain the factional division between Grossinho's group and Toim's, although its history can be traced back even further to Matúk's time, when the old chief had one of Estêvão's nephews, Aníbal, killed. But the significant points behind the story are these: first, the factional division has a long history and probably dates back to Estêvão's arrival from Cocal to take up residence in a village firmly controlled by Matúk and his group. Second, this factional struggle shows how Brazilian society eventually came to interfere in the internal politics of the Apinayé village. Every time the chieftaincy changed hands, the group taking over sought the approval of a Brazilian government official. But it would be incorrect to attach too much importance to the role of the Indian agent in Apinayé politics. Certainly his approval was always sought when the new chief was chosen, and this did affect the internal process to some extent. But their desire for external approval of the appointment is better seen as an indication of problems inherent in the Apinayé political organization itself. We have already seen that the group that has power at any one time is not clearly defined. This makes it difficult to consolidate political power and leads to the vacillations we have been looking at. Appealing to the Indian post official for support every time power changed hands was an attempt by each group in turn to solve a chronic problem implicit in the political structure of Apinayé society.

São José did not split up because the population felt insecure in the face of territorial pressure from the encroaching settlers. The group who lost the chieftaincy preferred to stay where they were rather than move to a new site and lose the support of the SPI or FUNAI. Given this state of affairs it cannot be said that the SPI agents had direct power to decide who the chief was going to be. They only consolidated a decision that was about to be made whether or not they were there to give support to it. Indeed, one could argue that rather than being coerced by the agents, the Apinayé used the SPI. The agents did no more than give their support to the various results of a continuing political process that had always been going on in the village.

The events outlined in the above discussion are always brought up when there is factional conflict. If the chief is accused of not organizing a feast properly, or if he is said to have failed to resolve a quarrel adequately, the gossip will begin and those in Toim's group will accuse Grossinho and his followers of being usurpers. "They are outsiders: they are from Cocal" and "Grossinho is chief only because of Iridiano" are typical comments. Those in Grossinho's faction in turn bring up Toim's behavior when he was chief: "He never stayed much in the village"; "He was a drunkard"; and so on. It is interesting that Brazilian backwoodsmen confirm that Toim did not take much interest in the external problems that threatened the village and was not at all good at dealing with the settlers. Nowadays Toim's opposition to Grossinho's faction must show itself capable of dealing not only with internal village politics but also with external difficulties, particularly the relationship with Indian agents.

<h2 style="text-align:center">Gossip</h2>

Gossip is one of the most important techniques in the manipulation of factional disputes. The Apinayé say that gossip "is the friend and companion of sorcery." In other words, they themselves see it as a good measurement of social maladjustment. If disagreements within the community were rare there would be no gossip and no sorcery accusations. In terms of the political process, both gossip and sorcery can be seen as the means by which a weaker group expresses its discontent and disapproval. Gossip can arise out of trivial events. A daughter of Zezinho (the chief of Mariazinha) once lost a bracelet of beads in the village of São José. Immediately there was talk that the bracelet had been stolen, and speculations were made about the identity of the thief. Zezinho even threatened to take the case up with Grossinho, the chief of São José. The gossip continued for a few days, then died down, and the incident was forgotten. A much more serious event was when Vicente (62; *S*) murdered Joãozinho (*T*). The murder was immediately transformed into a serious factional dispute. Toim was accused of being responsible for the murder. It was said that he did not like Joãozinho and had therefore ordered Vicente to carry out the killing. Toim's faction (to which Vicente belonged) had a quite different version. They said Joãozinho was a sorcerer who had tried to seduce Vicente's wife on a number of occasions and had also caused the death of two of Chiquinho's daughters. Chiquinho (62; *T*) was Joãozinho's father-in-law. By spreading this version of the story, Toim and his faction were not only trying to justify the actions of Vicente, one of their own group, but they were also trying to attract Chiquinho to their faction. A similar case was when Permino (60; *R*) had a fight with Santana during a feast at which they both got drunk. Permino wounded Santana with a knife. This produced a wave of factional gossip. Faction I said that Permino was always provoking fights. Faction II, to which Permino belonged, accused Santana, saying that he had seduced Permino's wife. The chief was asked to mediate and an indemnity was paid, but even after being settled in this way the case is still brought up by one or the other faction as an example of how treacherous the other is.

The incident with Estêvão's horse is a further example of how a straightforward situation can turn into a factional dispute. In 1962 Estêvão's horse was found dead on the outskirts of the village. The cause of death was not clear at the time (although later some nearby settlers explained to Estêvão that the horse had died of illness and old age), and Estêvão openly accused Vicente of killing it. According to Estêvão, Vicente hated him and was envious of him. Since Vicente could not harm Estêvão's son (Grossinho, the village chief), he had killed his horse instead. An alarming rumor immediately spread through the village that Estêvão was going to kill Vicente, despite the fact that Toim's faction kept pointing out that there were no wounds of any kind on the horse's body. Both factions were prepared to fight. But after a few weeks, during which Grossinho refused to do anything about Estêvão's complaints, the latter was finally convinced that his horse had died naturally. Yet he went on saying to me that Vicente "was still a bad Indian."

In these cases the significant sociological feature is that even the most insignificant events can become part of the political process by being turned into a factional dispute. The opposition can transform the event into a collective issue and use it to create dissension among the groups that support the chief. This is what Toim was trying to do in the case of Joãozinho's murder when he claimed that it was in fact his group that was being victimized by the chief's faction through their accusations and malicious gossip. It is therefore in the chief's interests to "kill gossip" before it spreads and becomes a public issue, for when this happens, the chief's competence is called into question even by those segments that are not competing for power. In 1967, following Joãozinho's murder, when factionalism in São José was extremely intense, a favorite maneuver of Toim's faction was to go off and kill ranchers' cattle. The idea was to create problems in the village that would force Grossinho to call public meetings.

If we look at the function of gossip within a single faction, we can agree with Gluckman (1963) that it acts as a catalyst of social cohesion. But in the broader context of Apinayé society this is not the case. Here, gossip is a powerful source of propaganda against the chief. All sorts of difficulties can produce gossip, which in turn can lead to open conflict. The relationship system is not conducive to the appearance of well-defined, cohesive groups, and when open conflict breaks out, the result is village fission. If the chief is to hold the village together, he must eliminate gossip insofar as possible. Part of the power of gossip is its anonymity. It may be considered "a lie," but it carries partly true and partly false information, and no one can be held responsible for it. It is a private conversation that becomes transformed into public discussion, even though it may not be generally accepted as true. But a major disadvantage of using gossip as a political technique is that it may have the opposite effect from that intended. When Zezinho's leadership in Mariazinha was getting weaker and was being strongly contested by Júlio, gossip was quite effective in hastening the decline of Zezinho's power. But in São José, where Grossinho's leadership was very strong, gossip was often taken as clear proof of his rivals' bad faith.

Gossip appears in those situations that are thought to contravene established convention. In other words, it is an attempt to interpret ambiguous situations in the real world when it is difficult to understand them in terms of the dominant social code.[4] Initiating a rumor can be an effective political maneuver to challenge established authority, but the Apinayé are well aware that it is a dangerous game since it can rebound on those who began it. They have a similar view of sorcery (*me-o-txú*) since it is an activity that can give power to the sorcerer but that can also result in his being killed. They do distinguish between gossip and sorcery, but it is a distinction of degree rather than of kind. Gossip is considered normal as long as it does not reach such a pitch that community life becomes intolerable. But sorcery is always a grave matter, and its function in the political process tends to be more obscure. Both gossip and sorcery are effective partly because they are protected by a veil of anonymity and uncertainty. Inveterate gossips are known because they are always roundly criticizing others, but it is never known for certain who began a particular rumor. In 1967 the well-known gossips were generally held to be in Toim's faction, since these were the people who had most reason to create difficulties for Grossinho. They were considered malicious, but their behavior conformed with the attitude of a whole residential segment.

The identity of a sorcerer is even more difficult to establish since the characteristics of his personality are vague. He is said to be a miser and a scrounger. He will not reciprocate any gift. Hence if a person makes any exaggerated requests, coming into a house, for instance, and asking for a great deal of meat or other valuable articles, he is suspected of being a sorcerer. It follows that if the person who is asked does not comply with the request, he will be bewitched. But what makes it particularly difficult to identify a sorcerer is that he acts on his own. His motives are personal, not factional, and he may even act against his closest relatives. Joãozinho, the man who was killed, was always cited as an example of this sort of behavior. He practiced sorcery against his wife's parents, who were particularly close relatives since he and his wife had by then produced a family. In short, a sorcerer behaves as an individual, not as a member of a community. It is as if relationships and obligations do not exist for him. He will break any convention. He will always want to seduce old women who are sexually undesirable or married women who are faithful to their husbands. If his desires are thwarted he will strike down his victims with incurable illnesses (as Joãozinho is said to have done to an old woman,

Velha Mariquinha, who had an incurable disease of the throat). He does his "work," as the Indians say, by introducing some sort of foreign body into his victim, perhaps by putting a thorn or a piece of bone in someone's heart or by placing the *me-karon* (image) of a spider or a toad in a person's head. The Apinayé believe that sorcerers neutralize the cures for illnesses and therefore that any illness that does not respond to treatment is caused by sorcery. That is to say, anyone who dies of an incurable illness has been bewitched.

In terms of the political process, the difference between gossip and sorcery is that the first acts in the interests of a group or faction whereas the second does not. The sorcerer rejects the obligations and privileges of belonging to a group, and in this sense he is an extreme case of a marginalized person. But from a moral point of view gossip and sorcery are similar in that the factional emphasis of the first and the individual interest of the second are both opposed to the collective interests of the village as a whole. The collective aspect of Apinayé morality is strongly pronounced. A good man or a good leader is he who gives more than he receives, who fulfills all his social obligations, and who subordinates his personal interests to those of the community at large. In the various myths of Sun and Moon, the paragon of Apinayé virtue is Sun, whose behavior is always contrasted with that of Moon.

Gossip is the first step in the breakdown of collective values. Sorcery takes the process still further. The meaning of the Apinayé saying "gossip and sorcery are friends and companions" is therefore quite clear. They are both part of a *continuum* that moves increasingly further away from collective interests. We could therefore expect sorcery to appear as part of the political process when the struggle for power becomes so intense that it seriously threatens the values of the community. In other words, we could expect explicit sorcery accusations in a village that was on the point of breaking up. This was not the situation in São José, although accusations of a kind were made against a Sherente Indian (25; *E*), a member of Grossinho's faction, and against Vicente in Toim's faction. These accusations were extremely guarded and did not become explicitly involved in the political struggle. The Apinayé deny that a chief or a faction leader would use sorcery to increase his power. Nevertheless, the accusations were tinged with political implications. Vicente participated enthusiastically in factional disputes and had considerable influence on Toim's decisions. It was he who killed Joãozinho and justified the killing by saying that the murdered man was a sorcerer. The other faction therefore responded by making a counteraccusation against Vicente. It is not so obvious why Moacyr Sherente was accused, but it was said that he was a troublemaker, that his marriage was most unstable, and that he was always ready to protest if he thought his affines were taking advantage of him.

I cannot offer a convincing demonstration that witchcraft accusations play an important part in the Apinayé political process. When the person is extremely antisocial and pathologically selfish, the sorcery accusation has no political implication. But it is quite probable that if a situation of extreme political polarization developed, the protagonists would appeal to supernatural resources to further their aims, even though the Apinayé deny that their leaders would do so. We know that this happens in Shavante society, where sorcery accusations are used by those in power against weaker groups as well as by the weak against the strong (Maybury-Lewis 1967:275).

Among the Shavante the groups that are important in everyday life are far more involved in the political process than they are among the Northern Gê. The Shavante social universe is divided by the opposition kin/affine, which is conceptualized in terms of strong and weak, especially when marriage first takes place. The dichotomy is a result of their organization into patrilineal descent groups. Given this opposition, it is not surprising to find that sorcery accusations follow the same lines. We would expect groups in opposition to accuse one another of sorcery. And, in fact, sorcery accusations are frequent between affines as well as between strong and weak lineages and clans.

Among the Northern Gê, by contrast, the composition of groups is less clearly defined since they are not formed on the principle of unilineal descent. In Apinayé society, the important political groups are residential segments that are composed (by the rule of uxorilocal residence) of alliances between men living in neighboring houses. Group boundaries and areas of political influence are therefore diffuse. Correspondingly, witchcraft accusations tend to appear more randomly, and it is more difficult to see how they are associated with political disputes. The Kayapó are the only Northern Gê group among whom we might expect an association between sorcery and politics as found among the Shavante, since here too men's groups are apparently well defined. But according to Terence Turner (1966) the situation is in fact similar to that of the Apinayé.

The evidence suggests that the location of supernatural power is correlated with the way a society organizes its segments in terms of political power. Among the Shavante, political power rests within well-defined lineages and clans. Political maneuvering consists of alliances between the clan that is dominant and those that wish to share that power. Hence sorcery accusations follow a clear pattern. This situation does not obtain among the Apinayé and the Kayapó since the residential arrangements and cognatic kinship reckoning are not conducive to the appearance of clearly defined groups. In other words, since those groups that compete for power are not clearly marked, it is very difficult for the Northern Gê to find ways of legitimizing power within any specific group.

In conclusion, then, I would argue that in Northern Gê societies political power is relatively free and is not contained within clearly defined areas. Similarly, supernatural power is also free and is not confined to any clearly defined category of person. It can have such precise categorical definition only if village factionalism produces an unambiguous polarization in the community. In normal circumstances, then, sorcerers are marginal people, not affines or members of another faction. The Northern Gê do not conceptualize their universe in terms of "us" and "them," and neither can they say precisely who their sorcerers are. If factionalism were to grow more intense, sorcery would gradually become associated with precise categories of people, but both tendencies would indicate that the social code was being subverted. Only at such a point would the groups competing for power separate into discrete units and destroy the network of relationships that holds the whole society together.

We can argue, therefore, that Shavante sorcery is very much like witchcraft,[5] that is, it is an involuntary evil influence. It is sufficient that a person be categorized as "them," as opposed to "us," for him to be suspect. By maintaining the distinction between kin and affine and between "our group" and "those opposed to us," the accusation, as Mary Douglas suggests, "enables guilt to be pinned on the source of ambiguity and confusion" (1966:107). If we also remember that the political segments of Shavante society are clearly distinguished by the principle of unilineal descent, we can see that sorcery accusations together with the political process follow a consistent pattern that makes it easy to establish which groups have power and why that authority is invested in them. But among the Northern Gê the situation is the reverse. Group boundaries are blurred, and there are difficulties in establishing where authority should properly be invested. The history of the chieftaincy in São José illustrates this well, and I am sure that the situation is similar in those other Gê societies where there are reports of two or more chiefs in the same village. In such situations in which political power is diffuse, magical power will also be diffuse. That is to say, sorcery will take place in the marginal areas of society. It will concern kin as well as affines, and strong groups as well as weak ones.

The localization of sorcerers among the various Gê groups is correlated with the different social structures of each society. Where dominant groups are well defined, so is the area from which sorcerers will appear. Where dominant groups are not well defined, sorcerers are seen as being on the extremities of social life. They are marginal individuals who refuse to be incorporated into the web of relationship that holds the community together.

Conclusion: The Lessons of
the Apinayé Case

*M*Y PRINCIPAL AIM in this book was to uncover the ordering
principles that underlie Apinayé social structure. As a counterpoint to this theme I also wanted to describe the dialectical relationship between social rules (the formal aspects of the social order,
which are explicitly recognized) and those concrete situations to which
they are applied. Although it may be said that all human societies can be
interpreted in terms of this dichotomy, I also hope to have shown that the
Apinayé themselves clearly distinguish these two aspects of their social
reality.

When the Apinayé describe their own society, they always begin by referring to the oppositions "center/periphery" and "house/plaza." As well
as indicating the topography of the village, these oppositions also refer to
the way their cosmos is organized. Beginning with this physical opposition one can move on to more abstract binary oppositions that are more
relevant to the interpretation of the Apinayé system, namely, the structural contrast between *public* and *private* and the corresponding distinction between *ceremonial life* and *everyday life*.

I have interpreted Apinayé society as a world divided by means of
these oppositions. But it is a division of a special kind. It is not historical
in the sense that one could explain its development from an initial ideal
situation of inequality. On the contrary, the oppositions are absolute and
are conceived of as complementary. One side of the opposition makes
sense only in relation to the other. The Apinayé (like the Gê-Timbira)
never refer to an initial moment when their world consisted solely of the
domestic groups of everyday life, onto which was superimposed another
secondary world of ceremonies and the public life of the plaza. This kind
of explanation in terms of historical process may be appropriate for our

society, but it is irrelevant in the case of the Apinayé. What interests the Apinayé is the harmony revealed by the relations between things. They do not consider any group, person, or category to have some sort of pre-eminence because it emerged first. Consequently, their world is not one in which distinctions imply privileges nor one in which people can exploit one another.

It is a divided world in which divisions do not imply privileges. In Apinayé society, to divide is basically to produce an order wherein the dualism implies absolute equality and symmetry among its terms. The dualism we are familiar with is based on opposition and asymmetry: God is superior to the devil; a dominated class is morally superior to the class that dominates it; and woman is basically superior to man. But Apinayé dualism is absolute, and instead of making certain categories, actions, groups, or individuals inferior, it produces a balanced, symmetric classification through which to construct the world.

The most complete expression of this world view is found in the cycle of myths that deals with the adventures of Sun and Moon, the two culture heroes who created the universe of the Timbira and the Apinayé. They are two men, linked by a relationship of formal friendship, who decide to come to earth to create the world. They come from the heavens (from "above") to "put things right" and invent the world. There follows a series of episodes in which their relationship produces a dialectic that not only differentiates them into opposite characters but also produces the opposite and complementary nature of the things of this world. While Sun makes the animals, Moon adds his own inventions of jaguars, poisonous snakes, and wasps. When Sun sees this, he objects and says that all their future children will be killed by the jaguars and the snakes and stung by the terrible wasps Moon has invented. Moon's response is Hegelian. He says that this is just the way things should be because if there were no animals like jaguars and snakes, men would have no fear of the jungle and would never return to their villages. In other words, if there were no features to make clear the distinctions in the nature of things, men would not be capable of distinguishing nature and culture. Furthermore, through the dialectical interaction of the two characters, the myth implies that to the extent that nature is invented so too is culture invented. To the extent that Sun creates "cultural animals" (which men will use to sustain themselves and their society), so too does Moon invent "natural animals" such as snakes and jaguars, which still compete with men. (The jaguar is a carnivore and a hunter, armed with teeth and claws. He is also the master of fire in Timbira mythology.) In another episode Moon divides up the animals because those invented by Sun had no fear of men. He also invents work; he creates ugly people, black people, and lame people; and he finally creates death.

All the episodes of the cycle reveal the same principles of a "native

Hegelian dialectic"; Sun initially establishes something, Moon establishes the antithesis, and in a third, final movement Moon produces a synthesis of the episode by arguing against Sun's doubts and objections. For example, Moon explains that separating animals into those who fear men and those who do not (whereas formerly all the animals lived *with* men) is necessary to avoid cannibalism. His argument is that if the paca, the deer, the armadillo, the queixada, the caitetu, and so forth did not fear men and run away from them, men would soon kill off all the animals and end up eating one another. He uses a similar sort of argument to justify the creation of death. If men did not die, how would it be possible to have one generation succeeding another?

Moon's role is to defend the antihistorical mechanisms of Apinayé society. By maintaining the equilibrium between men and nature, he tries to prevent the invention of *refuse* (or residue) as a social category. We know that systems which, through history, produce internal distinctions of class, are those in which human and cultural *refuse* was finally invented. In other words, we can say that Moon prevents the appearance of abundance in the Apinayé system. Hence his inventions are just as ingenious as Sun's. In this cycle of myths Sun's role is that of someone whose vision is limited to regularity and certainty. Sun represents the tranquility of nature, which does not have the capacity to question itself. It is a pure and inert object. Moon, by his questioning, introduces distinctions and divisions, and creates a human logic. And in establishing this human logic, a circular and reflexive movement simultaneously creates the logic of nature.

The myth of Sun and Moon reveals the complementary dialectic that permeates the logic of the divided world of the Apinayé. Analysis of the myth has shown that it encodes what Lévi-Strauss called diametric dualism based on symmetries, like those produced by the diameter of a circle. Apinayé society demonstrates that this dualism is operating on various levels.

How is this "dualism" revealed in the world of social rules and practices? This is an important question, for in the anthropological literature the question of "dual organization" has been approached with very little attention being given to native ideology. Theoretical discussion of the phenomenon has been limited because the dualism detected by the anthropologist is not explained as a conception of the people themselves. In this book I have tried to develop a theory of dualism side by side with Apinayé conceptions in such a way that their thought has become increasingly important as the argument proceeded.

In the case of the Gê-Timbira in general and the Apinayé in particular, the problem was to find out how these societies implement the dual structure, revealed in their cosmology, mythology, and ceremonies, in their social practice. Briefly, the problem can be summarized in the following points, which were all taken up by Lévi-Strauss in his articles of 1952 and 1956 (1963:chaps. 7 and 8):

1. Dual organization is realized in social practice through systems that prescribe (or prefer) marriage with the bilateral cross-cousin. This was one of Rivers's discoveries (1968), which was later elaborated by Lévi-Strauss (1969).

2. Marriage with the bilateral cross-cousin is the most logical and economical way of implementing dual organization in practice. The village would be divided into moieties, and the members of those moieties would exchange sisters. Given a unilateral residence rule and a unilineal descent rule, this system would be the most "simple" and the most "perfect."

3. Among the Timbira, however, although there were moiety divisions, these did not regulate marriage. Marriage with the cross-cousin was prohibited. This is why Lévi-Strauss, in his article of 1952, says that the Canela (Timbira) mystify themselves: they have a moiety system but they regulate marriage according to other principles. Since the Apinayé were described by Nimuendajú as having a prescriptive marriage system of four classes, Lévi-Strauss took this as evidence to support his hypothesis that the Timbira moiety system could not regulate marriage. What, then, did regulate marriage in these societies?

4. It is an important question given that for many anthropologists the marriage systems of primitive societies are total systems that have political, economic, domestic, mythological, and cosmological aspects. The structural study of a kinship terminology in a preferential marriage system allows a complete, simultaneous decoding of the entire social system. This is the theoretical and methodological import of Lévi-Strauss's *Elementary Structures of Kinship* ([1949], 1969), which draws on the example set by Marcel Mauss (1950).

5. How then do these premises relate to the Gê-Timbira? Is dualism in these societies in some way incomplete, or mystifying, as Lévi-Strauss would put it? Or can we find other principles that are at the root of Gê-Timbira and Apinayé dualism?

The answer I have offered in this book is that the basis of Apinayé (and Gê-Timbira) dualism is to be found in other principles. It is not a phenomenon associated with an exogamic marriage system, which necessarily entails marriage with the bilateral cross-cousin and a corresponding relationship terminology. It is associated with a certain conception of the world that I have tried to explain in the course of this book.

The Foundations of Gê-Timbira Dualism

Following a suggestion of Melatti's (1970), I showed that the basis of Apinayé and Timbira dualism is a radical distinction between two types of social relations: those conceived of as genetic or physiological, which concern physical reproduction, the production of food, and domestic life; and ceremonial relations, which involve the transmission of status from one generation to another through the institutions of naming and formal friendship. There is an explicit ideology corresponding to each of those kinds of relations.

Physiological relations are centered around a social group that the Apinayé themselves define in terms of *substance*. The nuclear family is the paradigm of such relationships, and the most obvious ideological features associated with them are ideas of the mixing of substance, of physical identification, and of suppressing boundaries between categories. The couvade, eating precautions, and restrictions on behavior are the clearest practical demonstrations of these relationships.

Relations of substance involve a "reading" of social relationships in physiological terms. That is, the Apinayé use a physiological idiom to define, justify, and reify a certain set of individual relationships. They use this language of the body to institutionalize a certain set of social ties and to demarcate an important "area" in their social system. The logic operating in this area is one of mixing and of physical generation, and its basic components are blood, sperm, sweat, flesh, and bones, together with the essential qualities (or sensible qualities, as Lévi-Strauss would say) of food, liquid, and individuals.

Ceremonial relations are marked by exchange obligations that begin when names are passed on from one person to another of the same sex according to explicit rules. Their ideological basis is a dualistic logic, the names indicating an absolute division of people in Apinayé society. As I have indicated, names in Timbira and Apinayé societies are classificatory devices. They do not individuate (as they do in our society) but are a vehicle by which status is transmitted from one generation to another. It is through their names that members of Apinayé society are incorporated into the ceremonial moieties and into ritual roles. Since moieties and ritual roles are absolutely complementary, we can say that ceremonial relationships are centered around reciprocity and complementary opposition. The area of ceremonial relations is clearly marked by a public logic that has juridical and political aspects. The paradigm here is not a domestic group (the nuclear family) but the ceremonial groups on which the most important rituals are based.

Comparing these two sets of relationships, I suggested that underlying the nuclear family was an idea of unity through links of common substance, in other words, an ideology of *communitas,* whereas relationships established through naming were based on an ideology of *structure* (cf. V. Turner 1969). Hence in the domestic area (the domain of the nuclear family), distinctions of sex and age are canceled out by food prohibitions and restrictions on behavior, while in the domain of ceremonial relationships distinctions between ritual roles are fixed and clearly defined.

The dialectic between these sets of relationships, seen in abstract terms, can also account for the dynamics of Apinayé social life and, by extension, that of the other Northern Gê. The basis of Gê dualism therefore appears as an axiomatic opposition between physiological relations and ceremonial relations. From this perspective one can give an adequate account of the relationship terminologies as well as a more complete theoretical integration of the various domains of the social systems of these societies. The dualism of the Northern Gê is not, therefore, strange or problematic. The complementary opposition between "those who form the body" and "those who form the social *persona,*" which is expressed in terms of links through substance and links through names, is also found in Western society in the contrast between parents and godparents as well as in the contrast between blood relatives and "legal" relatives or affines (on this last point see Schneider 1969).

It could be said that the dualism of Apinayé society is based on two possible perspectives of social reality. One emphasizes social relations by using a physiological code that allows distinctions of degree to be established between those who have more substance in common and those situated on the opposite pole of the *continuum* who have no substance in common. The other arranges social relations in terms of a ceremonial idiom based on the transmission of names. Names, which are instruments of social classification, are impersonal masks transmitted from one generation to another. These perspectives are complementary and both are essential for an understanding of the Apinayé world view.

Dualism and Disjunctions

The dual universe of the Apinayé (and Timbira) is not based on a system of exogamic moieties, codified in a terminological system of two sections—as current theories suggested and to a certain extent predicted (Maybury-Lewis 1960). It is based on a conception of the world in which, in the final analysis, there is a radical opposition between nature and culture. The human world is not thought of as contained in nature nor as containing nature. On the contrary, *natural things* and *cultural things* are complementary and offer two opposed ways of "reading" the human and nonhuman universe.

Consequently, in the Apinayé world, a reading of social relations can be carried out either by starting from their physiological nature or by seeing the organizing principle in the ceremonial relations, which begin with the exchange of names and the exchange of goods and services. This results in a disjunctive view of the social reality, making a high degree of social manipulation possible and, therefore, a high level of uncertainty in the political field.

When the Apinayé order the social world by means of substantive links between people (blood, sweat, flesh, and so on), they enter a universe ruled by degrees. There are those who share my blood and those whose blood is different from mine to a greater or lesser degree. Hence the physiological *continuum* allows for a *hierarchical* arrangement of social relations since it is situated along the axis of a *concentric* dualism—that is to say, at the limit between full hierarchy and inequality, and absolute symmetry, as Lévi-Strauss suggested (1963:chap. 8). It is obvious that, at this level and with this logic, a triadism could easily be institutionalized. In the case of the Apinayé and Timbira some important social relations are distributed along this "natural" axis, and the age classes can in fact be a hierarchical arrangement that is complemented by a symmetrical arrangement, as the Canela case shows.

The conclusion is that on the axis of physiological relations, or better, from a certain view of the social world where relations are defined along a physiological axis, *degrees* and *hierarchy* appear.

Exactly the opposite takes place in the case of social relations marked by the transmission of names, that is, when the Timbira order their world in terms of ceremonial relations. Here, the social universe is placed in perspective through relations of symmetry, equality, and identity. Names incorporate people into one of the ceremonial moieties, and a person either is or is not a member of one of the groups. A person cannot be *more or less* a member of a moiety. The moieties are seen as symmetrical and as having the same social weight. This is the level of the ceremonial or ritual world of the Timbira universe, and it is here that everything makes sense, being complementary and balanced.

But it would be wrong to see the ceremonial world as the Apinayé or Timbira *reality,* just as it would be wrong to see the world of natural links as their only reality. And it would also be misleading to say that there is a basic incompatibility between these two worlds. In fact, if hierarchy tends to exclude symmetry and the two maintain a precarious balance, it is precisely this balance that creates the dynamism of the Apinayé and Timbira social world.

One of the principal aims of this book is to show that the world of the Northern Gê is a divided world and that a dual ideology allows multiple readings of their social reality. Hence instead of presenting the classic view of a tribal society as being highly coherent and functional, this study offers a perspective from which reality can be interpreted in different ways, either as one based on a *continuum* and obeying a logic of degrees or as a totality that is divided equally and absolutely, like a circle divided diametrically. To live in such a system is to be involved in a perpetual game between a hierarchical and a symmetrical view of the social system. It is not difficult to understand why all the Northern Gê can maintain an extremely complex ritual life, even after a devastating period of contact with pioneering fronts of the national society, and why without their complex rituals their social life would certainly lose much of its dynamic quality.

Like other so-called primitive societies, the Gê-Timbira-Apinayé systems demonstrate the use of multiple codes in such a way that reality is never completely constrained by the "rule of custom." The kinship system is based on an opposition between genitors (relations of substance) and name-givers (ceremonial relatives), but even in this area there is considerable room for manipulation, and we can now recognize this as one of the basic elements of these social systems.

The data from the Northern Gê suggest that so-called Crow-Omaha systems are systems of attitudes and terms based on disjunction and that they can appear in unilineal societies, in cognatic societies, and in societies where descent is organized along other institutional axes. Among the Northern Gê the so-called Crow-Omaha systems seem to express possibilities of complementary readings offered by the social system. It is possible to emphasize both relations based on the link between father and child and those on the mother's side brought out by the link with the name-giver. The Kayapó emphasize the adoptive father/child relationship; the Timbira do exactly the opposite, emphasizing the link between MB and ZS. Also, among the Kayapó, name-givers and name-receivers establish firm relationships of solidarity through "symbolic patrilineages," while among the Timbira, it is the relationship between genitor and child that intensifies sentiments of *communitas.*

My suggestion is that Crow-Omaha systems express the disjunctive multiplicity of these societies and that they are a way of reconstituting categories on a terminological and ideological level that were previously broken down on other levels. I am referring particularly to the division of sexes (which follows the logic of concentric dualism: man = center; women = periphery; children = the space between) and to the age distinctions. Thus, in systems in which men and women are rigidly separated and in which distinctions of age separate parents and children, the passage from childhood to maturity is equivalent to leaving the world of women and entering the world of men, that is, the passage between generations is equivalent to the separation of the sexes. As I explained elsewhere, this is a significant feature of those systems, since, conceptually, men become older than their sisters. The distinction between brother and sister (the basic moment of the sexual division of labor) takes place at initiation when the brother is placed in an age-class and is separated from his natal family. The separation of the sexes is therefore equivalent to a change of age status such that boys become symbolically "older" than girls and men symbolically older than women. Hence two brothers think of their relationship as closer than that between them and their sisters. Correspondingly, the term for sister's children is the same as that for grandchildren (Da Matta 1979).

It appears that Crow-Omaha systems were always viewed as the result or expression of a single social principle. The early theorists saw them as based on jural links determined by unilineal descent. Later there were several attempts to explain these systems as products of a certain kind of marriage relation. But a study of the Gê groups reveals that such systems can exist without these correlations. We now know that Crow-Omaha systems can be based on several different principles, and that such systems cannot be explained by reducing them to a single set of social relations.

This is precisely what is discovered among the Northern Gê, where a certain relation that is basic to one domain does not operate with the same force in another. The result is a set of intersecting links based on various social principles. In these societies everything is reordered and reintegrated by an ideology of complementary oppositions, where the principle of dualism can be seen as a way of uniting the integral parts of a system that is deeply divided. While other theories of dualism prefer to emphasize its divisions (and there is certainly a level on which such a division is realized), I prefer to emphasize the inverse aspect. Thus, instead of thinking of dualism as the result of a division of one into two, I think it is more fruitful to see it as a technique that can unite two into one. This is exactly what is revealed by a study of the Apinayé case.

Notes
References
Index

Notes

Introduction

1. For an account of the Shavante, see Maybury-Lewis 1967; for the Kayapó, see Moreira Neto 1959, Terence Turner 1966, and Bamberger 1974; for the Gaviões, see Da Matta 1963, and Laraia and Da Matta 1967.

2. The Gê groups are classified as follows: Central Gê (Shavante and Sherente) and Northern Gê (Kayapó and Timbira). The Timbira are in turn divided into Eastern (to the east of the Tocantins River) and Western (the Apinayé). See Map 1, and cf. Nimuendajú 1946 and 1939:1.

3. Crow-Omaha terminologies are those in which generational discriminations are not made and in which Ego classifies cross-cousins along with other members of ascending or descending generations. For a fuller consideration of this system, see Chapter 4.

4. The most recent attempts to "solve" the Apinayé anomaly (as a system of prescriptive sister-exchange or cross-cousin marriage) are those by Robin Fox (1967a:143–145) and T. Zuidema (1969). Both interpretations contradict the ethnographic evidence. Claude Lévi-Strauss, in the most recent edition of his classic work, *The Elementary Structures of Kinship,* also refers to the Apinayé system but adds nothing to previous interpretations (Lévi-Strauss 1969:228–229). Recently, Floyd Lounsbury and Harold Scheffler took up the problem and suggested a formal solution in terms of an extremely rich comparative inquiry. I assessed these interpretations in Da Matta 1979a.

5. The reader will note that I borrow this formulation from Max Gluckman (1965:111ff.).

6. It is commonly believed in the interior of Brazil that the only travelers who pass through are "foreigners," American, English, or German, hence the local people were most surprised to find that I was Brazilian and that I was there to study Indians. When I passed through Goiânia in 1966, one of the newspapers on the following day produced a rather excited headline that ran: "BRAZILIAN AN-

THROPOLOGIST goes to study the Apinayé" (*O Popular,* January 5, 1966, my emphasis).

7. This is not a rhetorical exaggeration. On various occasions, I tried to convince the locals that the members of the Summer Institute of Linguistics, who were working with the Apinayé, were interested only in languages and the Bible. Some local people insisted that they were spies who were turning the Indian language into a code and also prospecting for minerals. I was once furious to discover that a stranger who was passing through the village, having found out that I was there to study the Indians, decided that I was in some way mentally handicapped. This was clearly confirmed, in his view, by the contrast between my intelligent manner, on the one hand, and the obvious "waste" of my supposed talents, on the other: "Wasting his time in a village when he could be earning money in Rio or São Paulo."

8. The Indian Protection Service is now known as the National Indian Foundation. It is the government agency responsible both for controlling contact between Indians and Brazilians and for looking after the interests of the Indians. It will be referred to throughout by the appropriate Brazilian acronym: either SPI or FUNAI.

9. The "government" for the Indians and local people alike refers to a vague, all-powerful entity which sees and knows everything but which, like God, interferes only on rare occasions and then only through its agents. For example, although the Apinayé do not yet have their territory officially demarcated, nor receive any medical assistance, they nevertheless think of the "government" as something that is supporting them.

10. See, for example, the discussion between Claude Lévi-Strauss and L. R. Hiatt. Lévi-Strauss refers to contact and social change to defend his models of Australian kinship systems, which were quite properly challenged by Hiatt (De Vore and Lee 1968:210ff.).

11. The results of this study are published in Da Matta 1963, 1967a, and Laraia and Da Matta 1967.

12. The interruption occurred because I went to Harvard as a "special student" and also because I had difficulties in finding funds for the field trip after I had returned to Brazil.

13. It is with pleasure that I must remark the growing of this bibliography in the last ten years. See Melatti 1978; Carneiro da Cunha 1978; Vidal 1977; Seeger 1980 and 1981; Urban 1978; Bamberger 1974; Lopes da Silva 1980; and Maybury-Lewis 1979, where the reader will find a collection of articles on the Central and Northern Gê and the Bororo.

14. This seems to be an important problem in certain situations. Anthropologists refer to a "perpetual lack of privacy" (Maybury-Lewis 1967:xxv; Chagnon 1968:8), but it could be described as stress that results from conflicts inherent in the field situation. Fieldwork, like social or cultural contact, consists of unavoidable physical proximity with one's people together with a need to maintain a social or cultural distance. The attempt to maintain this distance (an attempt that violates one of the basic principles of the anthropologist's semiromantic ethic) makes the anthropologist particularly sensitive to physical proximity. It is interesting that SPI officials and missionaries find a much easier solution to the problem by simply establishing a hierarchical relationship with the Indians, thereby

avoiding the risk of being absorbed by the tribe. Hence they do not find themselves in that paradoxical kind of contact that anthropologists do. For further details on this question, see Chapter 1, and Da Matta 1976.

1. The Present Situation of the Apinayé

1. It is impossible to verify today if the names "José Dias," of the chief "Matúk," and of his son "Antônio Dias," have anything to do with the original José Dias de Mattos.

2. The tradition of the tribe gives a similar account; see Nimuendajú 1939:183.

3. For the same year, IBGE gives the following figures of production in the Marabá area: agricultural produce, 411,000 cruzeiros; extracted vegetable products (Brazil nuts), 48 million cruzeiros. There was little livestock in the area, and the production of milk was small.

4. Recent reports on the Brazil nut region suggest, however, that the extractive industry established there is beginning to diversify and invest in ranching. This was greatly encouraged and made considerably easier when the BR-14, Belém-Brasília Highway was built (Velho 1967 and 1972).

5. The dates are approximate, for both the municipal archives and those of the Indian post were burned for political reasons.

6. The legendary Padre João Lima known as "Padre Velho" was the former local boss, who controlled the political affairs of the town with an iron fist. He used all sorts of iniquitous means to deal with his enemies, bequeathing his style of petty politics to his successors.

7. In 1967 the Apinayé were producing about one thousand kilos of babassu nuts per month. But the figure varies a great deal depending on whether or not the Indians feel inclined to collect the product.

8. The collection of babassu nuts by the Indians was facilitated (and to some extent encouraged) when the SPI official managed to establish an area that was to be exploited only by the Apinayé. This was done on the basis of a verbal agreement with Padre João, the former mayor of Tocantinópolis. Each village has a small store that serves as a market. Here the Indians can exchange babassu nuts for those products they consider essential, such as salt, sugar, gunpowder, lead shot, paraffin, tobacco, and matches. The absurdity of the situation is that the money produced by the actual sale of the Indians' babassu nuts is sent to Goiânia and is never reinvested in the villages.

9. These settlements do not form compact villages. Their total population in 1967, according to figures from the National Malaria Service, was 1,052. In the immediate vicinity of the Apinayé village there were about 580 Brazilians.

10. Perhaps because they see the game as a ritual, the Apinayé are not concerned about winning. The Brazilians, for their part, do not understand the rules of the game very well. The way everyone took part in the event certainly suggested to me that it was more a ritual than a proper game, but I do not have the data to argue the point.

11. This was the only area of Central Brazil where I found Brazilians addressing older Indians as "senhor" or "senhora." Another occasion that brought the two communities together was the festival of São José. An event like this required the suspension of any latent hostility between Indians and Brazilians, since everyone was honoring the same saint, but dialectically the obvious result

was that the tensions between them were merely put in abeyance. The festival became a context wherein tensions were "domesticated" through an inversion of roles, the Indians sponsoring a saint's festival and inviting Brazilians to come to their village and take part. The carnival of Rio de Janeiro performs a similar function (Da Matta 1973 and 1976). In 1971 I returned to the village, hoping to make a detailed study of the festival as an interethnic ritual, but I found on arriving that it had been forbidden by FUNAI.

2. Domestic Life

1. In Chapter 3 I give a detailed account of the composition and function of these two pairs of moieties.

2. Terence Turner (1966) includes some Kayapó drawings, but these are his rough copies of what the Indians actually drew.

3. It was this idea of context that Maybury-Lewis wanted to emphasize in his well-known commentary on Lévi-Strauss's dualistic models. While I agree that the Winnebago, like the Apinayé, use both concentric and diametric dualism depending on what is being represented, I do not agree with the conclusions that Maybury-Lewis draws from this (Maybury-Lewis 1960; Lévi-Strauss 1960).

4. See Chapter 4.

5. In 1961 this happened to the Gaviões of the Praia Alta River, Pará. When their village was reduced to only four houses, they decided to build one large communal house divided into family compartments. When I revisited them in 1962, they declared that they wanted to continue living in this way (Da Matta and Laraia 1967:140).

6. In São José there are eleven extended families as against nine nuclear families. In Mariazinha the proportion is eight to seven. Compared with the other Timbira, the figures show a high proportion of nuclear families and probably indicate that the Apinayé tend to form nuclear families more readily than other groups.

7. Examples are given in Chapter 5.

8. I became interested in this problem while carrying out a comparative analysis of the "Myth of Auké," a Krahó and Canela myth dealing with the origin of the white man (Da Matta 1971 and 1973). The myth tells of a boy, Auké, later to become a white man, who has to be killed because he is a source of disorder in the community. In the Canela version, his killer (and therefore the person with domestic authority over him) is his mother's brother. Auké's father does not appear in the myth. This is a typical matrilineal solution. But in the Krahó version, Auké's father does appear, and the person who kills the child is his mother's father, an affine in a matrilineal system. This suggested questioning the term "matrilineal" as applied to tribes like the Canela and the Krahó. Earlier I had noticed in Nimuendajú's material that there seemed to be a great deal of variation in the way domestic power was structured among the Canela (Nimuendajú 1946:84, 125). In fact, the Canela, like the Apinayé, have no clearly defined structure of authority within the family but have a system which admits of various possibilities. The suggestion at the end of my article, written in 1964, that the Timbira have no clearly defined structure of authority, has since been confirmed by evidence from the Krĩkatí and the Krahó (Lave 1967; Melatti 1970).

9. The Apinayé do not make it clear how they think the mixing takes place.

The question requires further field investigation, but it is possible that when pregnancy does not occur, menstruation is seen as a kind of abortion.

10. Perhaps constant sexual intercourse is considered to be a way in which a man can make an equal contribution to the formation of the child, since the Apinayé say that the quantity of sperm given by the man is less than the menstrual blood given by the woman.

11. In other contexts, *me-karon* is more accurately translated as "image." Since everything has an "image," everything has a *me-karon*. The idea here is that there are two worlds, a real world and a world of images. But the Apinayé, not being Platonists, say that the real world is better than the image world since images are weaker and more ephemeral than their real counterparts.

12. This is consistent with the notion that souls first spend some time in the village of the dead before they finally die (see also Nimuendajú 1939:141). After this, the soul's soul is transformed into the stump of a tree or into an animal. When the animal dies, the soul's soul finally disappears. Animals that are possessed by a soul's soul are said to have little blood and are not eaten by the Indians.

13. I am grateful to Patrick Menget, who first pointed out to me the important associations of smell, soul, blood, and its volatile nature. He found similar associations made among the tribes of the upper Xingu.

14. At the same time, the child's soul is still weak and is not completely secure in its body. A sociological interpretation would suggest that this indicates the child's lack of a social personality, something acquired later, when the child receives its ceremonial names. Babies are thought to lose their souls easily if they are frightened. A fall or a sudden start can cause this, and it requires the help of a curer (*vaiangá*) to put matters right (see also Nimuendajú 1939:144). Naming is explained in Chapter 3.

15. This is the situation described in certain myths that are narratives of a person's transition from one part of the Apinayé cosmos to another. Certain conditions must be satisfied before the transition can be effected. The person must be alone. He must detach himself from his society and pursue his own interests with singleminded purpose (Da Matta 1971a, 1973). Apinayé omens also describe this transition clearly (Da Matta 1971b).

16. Lévi-Strauss makes this point in *The Savage Mind,* but whereas his observations are of a general nature—and his suggestions are excellent—I am dealing here with a particular case. I disagree with his statement that "in South America, the husband has to take even greater precautions than his wife because, according to native theories of conception and gestation, it is particularly his person which is identified with that of the child" (Lévi-Strauss 1966:195). Evidence from the Gê material as well as from a number of recent analyses of other South American tribes suggests that this kind of identification of father and child is rare. This is consistent with the absence of unilineal descent groups among these tribes and the importance of the nuclear family as a separate group within the village community.

3. Ceremonial Life

1. My use of the expression "relationship system" follows a tradition in the study of terminologies and kinship relations initiated by Kroeber (1909) and Ho-

cart (1937), which sees this domain as a technique of classifying relationships and social positions. In this way, as Maybury-Lewis has pointed out, it is hoped to free the expression "kinship system" from its biological and genealogical connotations. There are indeed terminological systems that can be adequately translated into genealogical terms, but there are others that are refractory to that type of translation *at the level of sociological analysis*. However, all so-called genealogical systems are at the mercy of redefinitions that have nothing to do with translating their relationships in terms of genealogies or consanguinity (Maybury-Lewis 1965).

2. My comparison of Apinayé dualism with Christian and Manichaean dualism is intended to draw attention to two points. First, there is a logical question to be considered in showing how dualism is a technique or a logical model that is capable of resolving the problem of uniting two elements within an organized, coherent totality. Second, in terms of what Weber called theodicy (1963:chap. 9), dualism emerges as a doctrine that gives a new and original explanation of deviant behavior (those acts that a theological discourse would call sinful). In this sense, it is interesting to look at Apinayé dualism as a form of theodicy.

3. This again reveals the potentialities of a dualistic classificatory system. The formula is so rich in its possibilities that, depending on the context, it can express both complementary opposition and hierarchy.

4. Left and right symbolism (*apke/ipogrum*) is found among the Apinayé. The association of north and south with right and left explains the direction the initiates take on their daily processions around the village as well as certain directions taken in the rituals: those of *Kolti* always turn toward the north (that is, to the right), while the *Kolre* people always turn toward the south (that is, to the left). This might explain the association found by Nimuendajú (1939:28, 43, 67, 134) between *Kolti* = north, *Kolre* = south. Although I did not verify this particular association in the field, I suspect that if one equates north with right and south with left, one would find that other Northern Gê groups do make these associations. It was Professor Evon Z. Vogt of Harvard who drew my attention to this problem, one that is also found in Chiapas, Mexico.

5. The tapir represents power, strength, and generosity. It is associated with men, and it helped them steal fire from the jaguar (Nimuendajú 1939:158). The rhea is the animal most closely associated with women since, according to the Apinayé, it makes the male hatch the eggs.

6. In 1966 I collected a myth concerning the origin of the Timbira tribes in which the episode of their separation into different groups was explained as being the result of a log race. The conflict began because the losing team did not accept their defeat and objected to people saying they had lost. In this case, at any rate, the competitive aspect overcame the ritual aspect.

7. The myth is that of Tetxôaré (Sharpened Leg). One of the principal themes of the story is his transformation into a skull that rolls about (*krã-grodgrôd-re*) attacking the Apinayé of the olden days (Nimuendajú 1939:175–177). In *peny-tág*, the rolling skull is symbolized by the balls of latex. In my opinion, the theme here is that the novices must be agile and alert (cf. Nimuendajú's comments, 1939:64–67).

8. I distinguish between *category* and *genealogy* as follows. A *genealogical position* is analytically defined in terms of a scheme that may or may not be per-

ceived by the people themselves. All relationships can be translated into genealogical terms. *Category* refers to the way the members of a society arrange the genealogical positions. It could be the case, as for example in certain systems of prescriptive alliance, that a category has no genealogical component, or one so vague that it is not an important factor in the sociological interpretation of the category. Here I am following Maybury-Lewis and others in equating the genealogical approach with etics and the categorical approach with emics (Maybury-Lewis 1965:211). But I do not agree, as some would argue, that there is an insuperable contradiction between these approaches. As in linguistics, they complement each other, being moments in a single process of understanding (see also Needham 1962).

9. The Apinayé have certain major names, such as Ireti, Tapklid, Tamgaága, and Amdyág, which have no opposite number in the opposing moiety. There are indeed certain ceremonies where only bearers of these names take part, and they do, therefore, form groups in the manner of the Timbira and the Kayapó, but even in this case they are always associated with one of the moieties—in this case they are all *Kolti* (Nimuendajú 1939:23–29).

10. It is interesting to note that Nimuendajú was aware of the importance of adoptive parents, but he saw the relationship in terms of the *kiyê* and left the matter there. He comments: "I have noted how the newborn or even at times the unborn child acquires the names of its maternal uncle or aunt, i.e., by a transfer within the moiety. But of greater significance is the foster-father or foster-mother assigned to each child immediately after birth in accordance with the kiyê organization. In case of a boy, a paternal uncle goes to the parents and declares, 'I will rear your son!' If it is a girl, her mother's sister 'rears' her. The term is not to be taken literally in most instances, although the foster-parents always do share some responsibility on the child's behalf" (Nimuendajú 1939:106–107). My examples show that these relationships are much less formal and that they have nothing to do with the exogamic rules of the so-called *kiyê*.

11. This is an example of "structural comparison" as opposed to "functional comparison." The latter does not make the distinction between *rules* and their specific *application* in the context of each society.

12. I collected five versions of the myth of Sun and Moon in both Apinayé and Portuguese. My versions are clearer than Nimuendajú's in two respects: (1) the dialectical opposition between Sun and Moon is more obvious, Moon always doing the contrary of what Sun does, and (2) the final episode usually has Moon in a synthesizing role. Indeed, the pattern of the myths is extraordinarily similar to a Hegelian dialectic. Although I cannot here explain the point in detail, it is clear that from a general point of view the cycle of myths is a codified expression of the most important relationships and events in Apinayé society. The myths involve the two pairs of moieties (Sun = *Kolti,* Moon = *Kolre* and Sun = *Ipôgnotxóine,* Moon = *Krénotxóine*). They also deal with formal friends (Sun and Moon are *krã-geti* and *pá-krã*) and with various critical themes such as death, burial, classification of plants and animals, adultery, and so on.

13. It is significant that Nimuendajú introduces the matter of formal friends when he is describing the *kiyê*. At one point, describing one of the ceremonies concerning formal friends, he writes: "Then Vanmengri conferred his own style of painting on the boy and henceforth refrained from putting it on himself"

(1939:35). This shows how a formal friend passes on the body painting style of his moiety to his *pá-krã*. Also, one can see in Nimuendajú's account (1939:31–35) a pattern of rules similar to that which I have described here.

14. The *pēb* receive these clubs during the second phase of initiation, *pēb-kumrendy*. Nimuendajú's description is similar to Maybury-Lewis's description (1967:242ff.) of Shavante clubs. In both cases, they are obviously phallic symbols. One end of the Apinayé clubs is shaped like the end of a penis, while the other is decorated with arára feathers. The symbolism suggests the dual nature of sexuality—its aggressive and creative aspects, the latter being associated with marriage and the family. Giving the clubs to the novices symbolizes that sexual energy is being controlled and that the *krã-geti* are directing that energy into its proper place within the society.

4. The Relationship System

1. Apinayé genealogies have little depth, and few informants can name relatives beyond the second ascending genealogical level. But their horizontal extension is considerable, and everyone can use genealogical connection to explain or justify a relationship or a certain kind of behavior (for example, "X is the brother of my father's mother and therefore he is my *geti*"). Genealogical connections are usually traced by using a particular relative as a point of reference.

2. One person described certain of my relationships in the village as being *apunhã kãbrô* (*apunhã* meaning "point" or "extremity," *kãbrô* meaning "blood") as distinct from those of his own, which were *kãbrô apten burog*.

3. These two dimensions are yet another aspect of the dualism that, as we have already noted, runs through Apinayé cosmology. Blood and ceremonial relations are in complementary opposition along various dimensions of contrast. But it is interesting to note that each operates according to either a logic of concentric dualism or a logic of diametric dualism. That is, blood relations follow a pattern of concentric dualism, establishing gradations and exclusions (and, consequently, distance and hierarchy among relationships when some are seen to be more important than others), while ceremonial relations establish integration and symmetry as is typical of the relationship between name-giver and name-receiver.

4. In Apinayé thought (and among the Gê in general) the notion that exchange creates strong links between differentiated persons or areas is clearly revealed in their ceremonies and myths. All Apinayé ceremonies involve exchanges of food (which, if my interpretation is correct, are symbolically consistent with the various domains described in Chapter 3) for adornments; of food for rights over a person; or of food for certain favors. In the myths, when something is exchanged, a strong relationship is established. Refusal to exchange destroys a relationship. This appears clearly in the myth of Fire (Nimuendajú 1939:154).

5. Clearly, one of the most difficult problems in understanding Apinayé relationship terminology is to establish the exact boundaries of the categories being discussed and in doing so, to establish precisely where marriage is and is not possible. Since relationship terms are not associated with specific groups, the general categories overlap. This results in a duplication of social ties and gives an individual alternative choices of terms that can be used. Although this is partly explained as one of the results of depopulation, it is nevertheless an integral part of the Apinayé system, as in other cognatic systems that are centered on the individ-

ual. Evidence from genealogies and interviews indicates that the Apinayé avoid marriage with persons who are closely related genealogically, that is, where the relationship can be established easily and without too many intermediaries. The most notable case of incest that I came across was of a man who had married his mother-in-law after his wife's death. One case of sister exchange was justified as being correct because the families already knew each other. The same justification was put forward to explain a case of marriage with a female patrilateral parallel cousin.

6. Melatti is the only writer who shows how practices associated with birth and illness can throw light on the terminology, and I have found his insight extremely helpful in my own work. But my criticism of his account is that the extremely rigid use of the notions of "consanguinity" and "affinity" causes him to lose sight of the way the categories of the system are interrelated. Hence he does not explain the possibilities of choice that the system offers.

7. Similar variations are found outside the Gê area in relationship systems classified as Crow-Omaha. Schneider and Roberts in their reanalysis of Zuñi terminology state: "At crucial points Zuni terminology is equivocal; it is neither clear-cut Crow type nor is it unambiguously generation type *by virtue of permitting alternate terms for cross cousins*" (1956:15, my italics). Sol Tax, also dealing with North American societies, says: "The Wintun and the Pomo have the Omaha form, too, but the most northern of the former *have terminology of a very peculiar sort—intermediate between Omaha and Crow*" (1937:6, my italics). Robin Fox found a similar state of affairs in his recent study of the Cochite (1967). I cannot compare all these systems here, but it is probable that the presence of alternative terms for cross-cousins in Crow-Omaha systems is extremely common.

8. Maybury-Lewis (1960b:208) also points this out in his analysis of the Apinayé system. A similar system was found among the Sirionó of Bolivia (Holmberg 1960:53). For an extensive discussion of this problem, see Lounsbury and Scheffler 1971.

9. An interesting curiosity is that in terms of behavior, we retain the equation: grandparents = uncles, although we make a terminological distinction between the genealogical levels. But according to Lounsbury, in Roman and Germanic societies, there were terminological equations exactly like those of the Northern Gê, that is, MB = *avunculus,* which is a diminutive of *avus* = grandfather, and correspondingly, "a man's sister's children were, like his daughter's children and his son's children, *nepos* and *neptis*" (1964:375). Lounsbury suggests that this bears the marks of an Omaha system. But bearing in mind that the Northern Gê equation *uncles = grandparents* results in two alternative solutions for the cross-cousin categories, the Roman system could similarly produce both Crow and Omaha solutions. This is an interesting point if we remember that European systems eventually became cognatic.

10. The geographical position of the tribe is between the Eastern Timbira and the Kayapó to the west of the Tocantins River.

5. The Political System

1. Cf. the characteristics of factions described by Ralph Nichols (1965).

2. Similar situations developed in the old villages. Velho Estêvão told me that in Botica (Gato Preto), chief Pēbkôbo was engaged in a factional dispute for the

leadership with another Indian, who was his classificatory brother. The challenger failed, according to Velho Estêvão, because he explicitly announced to everyone that he wanted to become chief. Pedro Viado told me that in the old village of Cocal there was a chief called Feliciano Katíre. He had the largest family in the village (that is, the largest residential segment) and had come to power after the death of the old chief Grekrú-ti (who was Pedro Viado's uncle). After Feliciano Katíre took over the leadership, a dispute developed that was to continue over the years between two residential groups.

3. In Chapter 3 I pointed out that the Apinayé no longer perform initiation rituals. A politically active man is nowadays one who is married and who has rights to a garden and a house (or a place for his family within a house).

4. For an excellent study of this point, see Allport and Postman 1974. See also Paine, 1967.

5. I am following the distinction established by Evans-Pritchard (1937:387). Briefly, the sorcerer uses magical techniques with conscious intent, whereas witchcraft is an unconscious activity beyond the practitioner's control.

References

ALLPORT, GORDON, and LEE POSTMAN. 1974. *The psychology of rumor.* New York: Russel & Russel.

BAMBERGER, JOAN. 1965. Ethnobotanical notes on Simaba in Central Brazil. Botanical Museum Leaflets, Harvard University, 21(2):59–64.

―――― 1967. Environment and cultural classification: a study of the Northern Kayapó. Ph.D. diss., Harvard University.

―――― 1974. Naming and the transmission of status in a Central Brazilian society. *Ethnology* 13:363–378.

BARNES, J. A. 1962. African models in the New Guinea Highlands. *Man* 62:5.

BARTH, FREDERIK. 1966. Models of social organization. *Journal of the Royal Anthropological Institute.* Occasional Papers.

BERGSON, HENRI. 1935. *The two sources of morality and religion.* New York: Anchor Books.

BOHANNAN, PAUL. 1959. The impact of money on an African subsistence economy. *Journal of Economic History* 19:491–503.

CARDOSO DE OLIVEIRA, ROBERTO. 1964. *O Índio e o mundo dos Brancos: a situação dos Tukuna do Alto Solimões.* São Paulo: Difusão Européia do Livro.

CARNEIRO DA CUNHA, MANUELA. 1978. *Os mortos e os outros.* São Paulo: HUCITEC.

CHAGNON, NAPOLEON. 1968. *Yąnomamö: the fierce people.* New York: Holt, Rinehart and Winston.

CROCKER, WILLIAM. 1962. *A method for deriving themes as applied to Canella Indian festival materials.* Ann Arbor: University Microfilms.

DA MATTA, ROBERTO. 1963. Notas sobre o contato e a extinção dos Índios Gaviões do médio rio Tocantins. *Revista do Museu Paulista,* vol. 24. São Paulo.

—— 1967. Grupos Jê do Tocantins. *Atas do simpósio sobre a biota Amazônica.* Rio de Janeiro: Conselho Nacional de Pesquisas.

—— 1971a. Myth and antimyth among the Timbira. In *Structural analysis of oral tradition,* ed. Pierre and Elli Maranda. University of Pennsylvania Press.

—— 1971b. Les pressage Apinayé. In *Echanges et communications: mélanges offerts à Claude Lévi-Strauss.* The Hague: Mouton.

—— 1973. *Ensaios de antropologia estrutural.* Petrópolis: Vozes.

—— 1976. Quanto custa ser Índio no Brasil?" *Dados: Publicação do Instituto Universitário de Pesquisas do Rio de Janeiro* 13:33–54.

—— 1979a. The Apinayé relationship system: terminology and ideology. In *Dialectical societies,* ed. David Maybury-Lewis. Cambridge, Mass.: Harvard University Press.

—— 1979b. *Carnavais, malandros e heróis: para uma sociologia do dilema Brasileiro.* Rio de Janeiro: Zahar Editores.

DEVORE, IRVING, and RICHARD LEE, eds. 1968. *Man the hunter.* Chicago: Aldine.

DOUGLAS, MARY. 1966. *Purity and danger: an analysis of concepts of pollution and taboo.* New York and Washington: Frederick A. Praeger.

EVANS-PRITCHARD, E. E. 1937. *Witchcraft, oracles, and magic among the Azande.* Oxford: Clarendon Press.

FOCK, NIELS. 1960. South American birth customs in theory and practice. In *Folk,* 2:51–69. Copenhagen.

FORDE, DARRYL. 1950. Double descent among the Yako. In *African systems of kinship and marriage,* ed. A. R. Radcliffe-Brown and Darryl Forde. London, New York, and Toronto: International African Institute.

FOX, ROBIN. 1967a. *Kinship and marriage.* Baltimore: Penguin Books.

—— 1967b. *The Keresan bridge: a problem in Pueblo ethnology.* London: Athlone Press.

GLUCKMAN, MAX. 1963. Gossip and scandal. *Current Anthropology* 4(3).

—— 1965. *Politics, law and ritual in tribal societies.* Chicago: Aldine.

GOODENOUGH, WARD. 1955. A problem in Malayo-Polynesian social organization. *American Anthropologist* 57:71–83.

—— 1964. Introduction. In *Explorations in cultural anthropology.* New York: McGraw-Hill.

—— 1965. Personal names and modes of address in two Oceanic societies. In *Context and meaning in cultural anthropology,* ed. Melford Spiro. Glencoe, Ill.: The Free Press.

HERTZ, ROBERT. 1960. *Death and the right hand,* trans. Claudia and Rodney Needham. Glencoe, Ill.: The Free Press.

HOCART, A. M. 1937. Kinship systems. *Anthropos* 32:545–551.

HOLMBERG, ALLAN. 1960. *Nomads of the long bow: the Sirionó of Eastern Bolivia.* Chicago: University of Chicago Press.

INSTITUTO BRASILEIRO DE GEOGRAFIA E ESTATÍSTICA. 1958. *Enciclopédia dos municípios Brasileiros,* vol. 36. Goiás.

KEESING, ROGER. 1964. Mota kinship terminology and marriage: a reexamination. *Journal of the Polynesian Society* 73(3):294–301.

—— n.d. Eastern Timbira kinship: a reassessment reassessed. Harvard University, Department of Anthropology.

KROEBER, ALFRED L. 1909. Classificatory systems of relationship. *Journal of the Royal Anthropological Institute* 39:77–84.

———— 1919. *Zuñi kin and clan.* Anthropological Papers of the American Museum of Natural History, vol. 18. New York.

LARAIA, ROQUE, and ROBERTO DA MATTA. 1967. *Índios e Castanheiros: a empresa extrativa e os índios do médio Tocantins.* São Paulo: Difusão Européia do Livro. 2nd ed.: Rio de Janeiro: Paz e Terra, 1979.

LAVE, JEAN CARTER. 1967. Social taxonomy among the Krĩkatí (Gê) of Central Brazil. Ph.D. diss., Harvard University.

———— 1979. Cycles and trends in Krĩkatí naming practices. In *Dialectical societies,* ed. David Maybury-Lewis. Cambridge, Mass.: Harvard University Press.

LEACH, E. R. 1958. Magical hair. *Journal of the Royal Anthropological Institute* 88:147–164.

———— 1961. *Rethinking anthropology.* London: Athlone Press.

LÉVI-STRAUSS, CLAUDE. 1960. On manipulated sociological models. *Bijdragen* 116.

———— 1963. *Structural anthropology.* New York: Basic Books.

———— 1966. *The savage mind.* Chicago: University of Chicago Press.

———— 1969. *The elementary structures of kinship.* London: Eyre & Spottiswoode.

LEWIS, I. M. 1963. Dualism in Somali notions of power. *Journal of the Royal Anthropological Institute* 93:109–116.

LOPES DA SILVA, MARIA ARACY DE PADUA. 1980. Nomes e amigos: da prática Xavante a uma reflexão sobre os Jê. Ph.D. diss., University of São Paulo.

LOUNSBURY, FLOYD. 1964. A formal account of Crow and Omaha-type kinship terminologies. In *Explorations in cultural anthropology,* ed. Ward Goodenough. New York: McGraw-Hill.

LOUNSBURY, FLOYD, and HAROLD SCHEFFLER. 1971. *A study in structural semantics: the Sirionó kinship system.* Englewood Cliffs, N.J.: Prentice-Hall.

LOWIE, ROBERT H. 1935. *The Crow Indians.* New York.

———— 1940. American cultural history. *American Anthropologist* 42:409–428.

———— 1943. A note on the social life of the Northern Kayapó. *American Anthropologist* 45:633–635.

———— 1959. *Robert H. Lowie: a personal record.* Berkeley and Los Angeles: University of California Press.

LYNCH, KEVIN. 1960. *The image of the city.* Cambridge, Mass.: MIT Press.

MAUSS, MARCEL. 1960. *The gift.* Glencoe, Illinois: The Free Press.

MAYBURY-LEWIS, DAVID. 1960a. The analysis of dual organizations: a methodological critique. *Bijdragen* 116.

———— 1960b. Parallel descent and the Apinayé anomaly. *Southwestern Journal of Anthropology* 16:191–216.

———— 1965. Durkheim on the relationship systems. *Journal for the Scientific Study of Religion* 4(2).

———— 1967. *Akwẽ-Shavante society.* Oxford: Clarendon Press.

———— 1969. Descent, residence and ideology in Jê kinship. Wenner-Gren Foundation for Anthropological Research.

————, ed. 1979. *Dialectical societies: the Gê and Bororo of Central Brazil.* Cambridge, Mass.: Harvard University Press.

MELATTI, JÚLIO CEZAR. 1967. *Índios e criadores: a situação dos Krahó na área pastoril do Tocantins.* Rio de Janeiro: Mobografias do Instituto de Ciências Sociais da Universidade Federal do Rio de Janeiro.

—— 1970. O sistema social Krahó. Ph.D. diss., University of São Paulo.

—— 1978. *Ritos de uma tribo Timbira.* São Paulo: Ática.

—— 1979. The relationship system of the Krahó. In *Dialectical societies,* ed. David Maybury-Lewis. Cambridge, Mass.: Harvard University Press.

MOOG, VIANNA. 1956. *Bandeirantes & pioneiros: paralelo entre duas culturas.* Porto Alegre and São Paulo: Editora Globo.

MOREIRA NETO, CARLOS ARAÚJO. 1959. Relatórios sobre a situação atual dos Kayapó. *Revista de Antropologia* (São Paulo) 8(1, 2).

MURDOCK, GEORGE PETER. 1949. *Social structure.* New York: Macmillan.

NEEDHAM, RODNEY. 1960. Lineal equations in a two-section system: a problem in the social structure of Mota (Banks Island). *Journal of the Polynesian Society* 69:23–30.

—— 1962. *Structure and sentiment.* Chicago: University of Chicago Press.

—— 1963. Introduction to Durkheim and Mauss. In *Primitive classification.* Chicago: University of Chicago Press.

—— 1964. The Mota problem and its lessons. *Journal of the Polynesian Society* 73:302–314.

NICHOLS, RALPH. 1965. Factions: a comparative analysis. In *Political systems and the distribution of power.* ASA Monographs, 2. London: Tavistock Publications.

NIMUENDAJÚ, CURT. 1939. *The Apinayé.* Washington, D.C.: Catholic University of America Anthropological Series, no. 8.

—— 1946. *The Eastern Timbira.* University of California Publications in American Archaeology and Ethnology, vol. 41. Berkeley: University of California Press.

—— 1956. *Os Apinagés.* Boletim do Museu Paraense Emilio Goeldi, vol. 12. Belém do Pará, Brazil.

—— n.d. Field-notes on the Apinayé. Department of Anthropology, Museu Nacional, Rio de Janeiro.

NIMUENDAJÚ, CURT, and ROBERT LOWIE. 1937. The dual organization of the Ramkókamekra (Canella) of Northern Brazil. *American Anthropologist* 39:565–582.

—— 1939. The associations of the Sherente. *American Anthropologist* 41:408–415.

PAINE, R. 1967. What is gossip about: an alternative hypothesis. *Man* n.s. 2:278–285.

RADCLIFFE-BROWN, A. R. and DARRYL FORDE, eds. 1950. *African systems of kinship and marriage.* New York and Toronto: International African Institute.

—— 1952. *Structure and function in primitive society.* Glencoe, Illinois: The Free Press.

RIBEIRO, DARCY. 1957. Línguas e culturas indígenas do Brasil. *Educação e Ciências Sociais,* no. 6. Rio de Janeiro: Centro Brasileiro de Pesquisas Educacionais.

RIVERS, W. H. R. 1968. *Kinship and social organization.* London: Athlone Press.

RUNCIMAN, STEVEN. 1960. *The medieval Manichee: a study of the Christian dualist heresy.* Cambridge: Cambridge University Press.

SCHNEIDER, DAVID M. 1969. *American kinship: a cultural account.* Englewood Cliffs, N.J.: Prentice-Hall.

SCHNEIDER, DAVID M., and JOHN M. ROBERTS. 1956. Zuni kin terms. Notebook No. 3, Laboratory of Anthropology, University of Nebraska.

SEEGER, ANTHONY. 1981. *Nature and society in Central Brazil: The Suya Indians of Mato Grosso.* Cambridge, Mass.: Harvard University Press.

―――― 1980. *Os índios e nós.* Rio de Janeiro: Editora Campus.

TAX, SOL. 1937. Some problems of social organization. In *Social anthropology of North American tribes: essays in social organization, law, and religion,* ed. Fred Eggan. Chicago: University of Chicago Press.

TURNER, TERENCE S. 1966. Social structure and political organization among the Northern Cayapó. Ph.D. diss., Harvard University.

―――― 1979. The Gê and Bororo societies as dialectical systems: a general model. In *Dialectical societies,* ed. David Maybury-Lewis. Cambridge, Mass.: Harvard University Press.

TURNER, VICTOR. 1967. *The forest of symbols: aspects of Ndemby ritual.* Ithaca: Cornell University Press.

―――― 1968. Mukanda: the politics of a non-political ritual. In *Local-level politics: social and cultural perspectives,* ed. Marc J. Swartz. Chicago: Aldine.

―――― 1969. *The ritual process: structure and anti-structure.* Chicago: Aldine.

TYLOR, E. B. 1889. On a method of investigating the development of institutions applied to laws of marriage and descent. *Journal of the Royal Anthropological Institute* 18:245–272.

URBAN, GREGORY. 1978. A model of Shokleng social reality. Ph.D. diss., University of Chicago.

VALVERDE, ORLANDO. 1957. Geografia econômica e social do Babaçú no Meio Norte. *Revista Brasileira de Geografia* (Rio de Janeiro) 19(4).

VELHO, OTÁVIO GUILHERME. 1967. Análise preliminar de uma frente de expansão da sociedade Brasileira. *Revista do Instituto de Ciências Sociais* 4(1):27–39.

―――― 1972. *Frentes de expansão e estrutura agrária.* Rio de Janeiro: Zahar Editores.

VIDAL, LUX. 1977. *Vida e morte de uma sociedade indígena Brasileira.* São Paulo: HUCITEC-EDUSP.

WEBER, MAX. 1947. *The theory of social and economic organization.* Glencoe, Ill.: The Free Press.

―――― 1963. *The sociology of religion.* Boston: Beacon Press.

ZUIDEMA, R. T. 1969. Hierarchy in symmetric alliance systems. *Bijdragen* 125:134–139.

Index